EARTHSHOCK

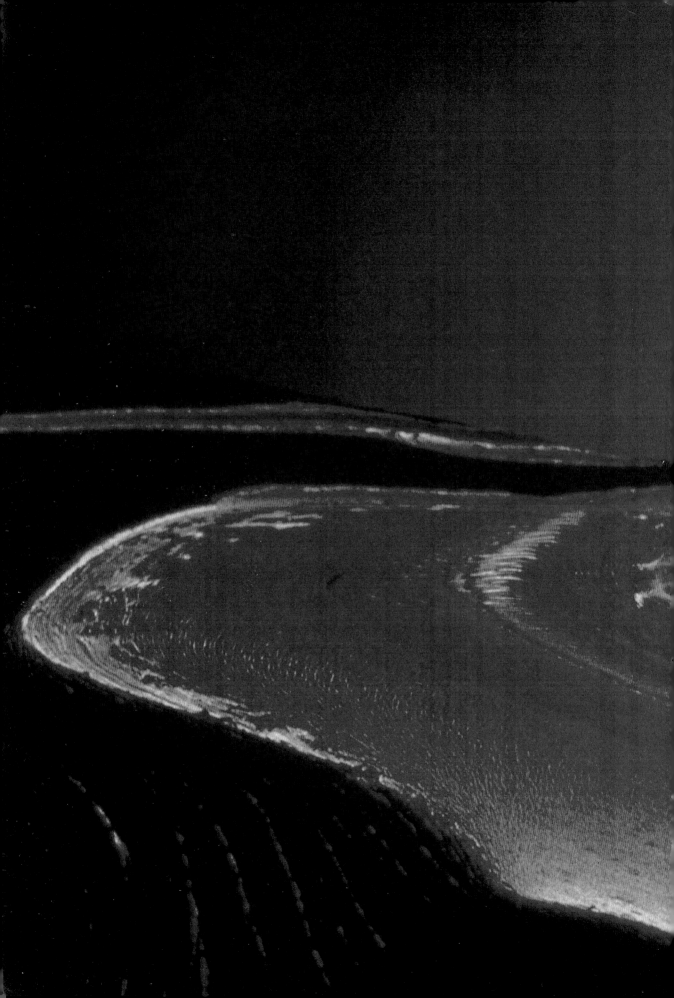

EARTH SHOCK

HURRICANES, VOLCANOES, EARTHQUAKES, TORNADOES AND OTHER FORCES OF NATURE

ANDREW ROBINSON

With 275 illustrations, 135 in color

THAMES AND HUDSON

Author's note

I dedicate this book to my father, with vivid memories of weekends spent soldering in the cellar and holidays spent picking over disused mine-tips (not to mention tears of frustration over recalcitrant maths homework).

Krishna was a willing non-scientific guinea-pig.

I am grateful to several scientists – duly credited in the appropriate places – who supplied photographs taken in the course of their work; to Dr Thomas Heaton for a summary of the latest thinking on earthquake prediction; and to Professor Geoff Brown, who died in a volcanic eruption during the book's writing, for information on the latest outpouring of lava from Mount Etna.

* * *

A mixture of imperial and metric units has been maintained throughout the book. Normally, the imperial unit is given first, with the metric conversion following in parentheses. However, miles have not been converted into kilometres, nor acres into hectares, on the grounds that these two imperial units are commonly employed in both ordinary and scientific usage when writing about the forces of Nature, especially in the older scientific literature. (The conversion is in fact 1 mile=1.6 kilometres; 1 acre=0.4 hectare.) On the other hand, the Celsius scale has been given before the Fahrenheit scale, since Celsius units are now widespread both in non-scientific writing – e.g. weather forecasts – and of course in scientific writing. All references to dollars mean US dollars.

'Man' and 'man-made' have been used in preference to more cumbersome (if all-embracing) alternatives; no other significance attaches to this choice – or to the fact that Nature has been rendered Motherless.

Half-title page: Volcanic eruption cloud.

Title page: Lava flow from Kilauea's east rift eruption, 1989.

Picture research by Georgina Bruckner

© 1993 Thames and Hudson Ltd, London

First published in the United States of America in 1993 by Thames and Hudson Inc., 500 Fifth Avenue, New York, New York 10110

Library of Congress Catalog Card Number 93–60201

Printed and bound in Singapore

CONTENTS

CHAPTER

—1—

MAN AND NATURE

Men argue; Nature acts.
Voltaire

The most incomprehensible fact about Nature is that it is comprehensible.
Einstein

JUST before lunchtime on 1 September 1923, as charcoal braziers were cooking the midday meal in a million wooden houses, Japan was struck by its worst ever earthquake. Tokyo, Yokohama and surrounding areas were subjected to almost a full five minutes' shaking, followed shortly after by a tsunami – a seismic sea wave – 36 feet (11 m) in height. Soon multiple small fires began and, feeding on the congested houses, merged to create a fire storm that burned through the night. By the morning of 3 September, at least 140,000 people were dead and two-thirds of Tokyo, four-fifths of Yokohama, were ashes. All that remained of Yokohama's Grand Hotel was rubble. Even now, in the small sepia-toned photograph printed in the official report on the disaster introduced by the emperor, the ruin is an arresting sight. The caption says simply: 'No human work can withstand the violence of Nature.'

Since the tragedy, the Japanese have studied earthquakes – their patterns of occurrence, their mechanism and underlying causes, and methods to limit their damage to life and property – more intensively than any other people. The scientific instruments monitoring earthquakes in and around Japan are the most sophisticated available; the skyscrapers of Tokyo are the most quake-proof in the world – safer in an earthquake, according to official guidance, than the streets outside. Yet in 1988, a Japanese government report predicted between 80,000 and 150,000 deaths and the destruction of millions of buildings by fire, were the Tokyo metropolitan area to experience a shock of the magnitude of the one

Man against Nature. The Eiffel Tower, illuminated by floodlights, is struck by lightning during a violent thunderstorm on 7/8 June 1992. The 984-foot (300-m) tower is securely protected by eight lightning rods, connected to iron conduits that run down into the bed of the River Seine. According to electronic detectors, France experiences some 800,000 lightning bolts per year. Their currents can be as high as several hundred thousand amperes, and they heat the air to more than 30,000 degrees C (55,000°F) – four or five times the temperature of the Sun.

in 1923; all of which would be followed, said a second report (from a Japanese bank), by calamitous economic repercussions throughout the world, especially in the United States, as Japan pulled back billions of dollars in overseas investments to reconstruct its capital. When might this happen? No seismologist can predict to within a few years, but most are agreed that a major shock is highly probable within decades.

In the past 100 years worldwide, some 1 million people have died in earthquakes, another million in hurricanes, typhoons and tropical cyclones, and as many as 9 million in floods: figures that do not include millions of deaths from disease and famine directly caused by these catastrophes. In the 1970s and 1980s alone, almost 3 million lives were lost in natural disasters, and over 800 million people were adversely affected. The early 1990s have proved no exception to these grim statistics. They have seen the worst floods in China this century when a river ruptured its dike; the largest volcanic eruption this century, in the Philippines, when ash permanently closed a nearby US airbase and severely disrupted Manila airport 60 miles distant; a cyclone in Bangladesh followed by a tidal wave that claimed at least 150,000 lives; an earthquake in Cairo that extensively damaged the city and its monuments and claimed several hundred lives, despite being of minor magnitude; and a hurricane in Florida that, while it did not cause many deaths, was nevertheless the most costly natural disaster in the history of the USA.

These are the most dramatic forces of Nature, the ones that hit the headlines. They are discussed in Chapters 3 to 6 of this book. But there are other forces, no less powerful (if less conspicuous because they act over a longer time scale), that have gripped large parts of the planet during recent decades. Drought is the most serious of them; it currently afflicts portions of Africa and Australia where farming was formerly possible, as well as much of the American West, not excepting California. This is not to mention chronic water shortages in many areas of the world where drought is not a familiar word, including some European countries. The global spread of drought may be part of a general global climatic change, which is now widely thought to be influenced by human activities. These longer-term forces of Nature are the subject of Chapters 7 to 9.

It is difficult to attribute exact figures to each kind of natural disaster. Still, the number of victims and the amount of damage resulting from the forces of Nature is generally reckoned to be increasing. But while the increase in deaths is in the less developed countries, which suffer over 90 per cent of the total fatalities, the main increase in costs is in the more developed countries, which sustain about three-quarters of the total damage though having only one-quarter to one-third of the total population.

Why this increase, one may ask, given the extraordinary strides made by science and technology this century, particularly in the past few decades? The most obvious reason is the rise in population, which is concentrated in the less developed countries. There are simply more and more people potentially at risk from the forces of Nature. Moreover, many of them live in places of high risk that were earlier regarded as unsuitable for habitation; they include the wealthy who choose to live in the landslide-prone canyons above Los Angeles, as well as the poor living on the slopes of volcanoes and in the slums of seismically-active areas. And the more capital people invest in houses in these regions, the more they stand to lose in a disaster, especially if, as is often still the case, a building is not designed to withstand extreme natural forces. A further factor is the mixed blessing conferred by technology such as weather satellites and giant dams: the more sophisticated it is, the more we come to rely on it – and the more helpless we then are when it is misapplied or malfunctions. Finally, there is our much enhanced mutual dependence. Economies have become linked, tied together by financial, transportation, and communication systems. 'Thus, disasters today are shared events, with repercussions far outside the immediately stricken area' in the words of the president of the US National Academy of Sciences, launching the United Nations' International Decade for Natural Disaster Reduction, in 1990.

That said, a Californian, for instance, has only a 1 in 600,000 chance of dying in an earthquake during any given year, as compared with a 1 in 20,000 probability of dying in an automobile accident and a 1 in 5000 likelihood of dying from influenza. Natural disasters therefore tend still to be categorized as 'acts of God' (less often 'divine chastisement for our sins', as Mahatma Gandhi called a devastating north Indian earthquake in 1934 – prompting Jawaharlal Nehru, the future prime minister of India and a worshipper of science, to protest: 'Anything more opposed to the scientific outlook it would be difficult to imagine.') Nevertheless, though our capacity to forecast natural disasters continues to be less precise than expected, the predominant goal of governments remains the one defined by Sigmund Freud in 1930 in *Civilization and Its Discontents*: to 'combine the human community and take up the attack on Nature, thus forcing it to obey human will, under the guidance of science.'

So, exactly how much of these shattering, awe-inspiring events is deeply understood by scientists – in the way that, say, the structure of the atom or the motion of heavenly bodies is mathematically analyzable, thereby making possible extremely precise predictions? Although many pieces of the jigsaw puzzle are in place, as yet we can only dimly perceive the overall picture. Since the late 1960s we have known that earthquakes, for example, generally coincide with the edges of known 'tectonic plates' that have been moving slowly within the Earth's crust for millions of years; we can monitor the ground stress produced to an impressive degree of accuracy and interpret the complex pattern of vibrational waves generated by an actual earthquake, which enable us to calculate its epicentre and magnitude as well as details of the Earth's structure; but scientists are currently locked in debate about the force that drives the plates and why massive earthquakes sometimes occur far from plate boundaries. We know too what conditions of ocean temperature, atmospheric humidity and wind movement are conducive to hurricane formation; we can track a hurricane once it forms with satellites in a way inconceivable only three or four decades ago; but we have yet to discover why it does or does not form, and why it frequently 'chooses' a complicated track, on occasions even reversing its direction. Even lightning – though controlled by Benjamin Franklin's rod over two centuries ago – is surprisingly enigmatic. We know that it originates in electrostatically charged thunderclouds and propagates initially from the cloud to the ground in a 'stepped leader' visible only to special cameras; we can measure the current that flows and the time of the flash; but we can only partially explain how the charge builds up, why it adopts more than one basic distribution pattern within a cloud (a point first noted by Franklin), why the bolt chooses a spectacular zig-zag to the ground, and why it strikes the particular point it does.

An earthquake, a hurricane or a lightning bolt, unlike a heavenly body, is not a system at equilibrium. Its course, unlike Earth's orbit around the Sun, is not reversible. Its future and its past are not interchangeable; time has an 'arrow' in the development of such an event (just as it does in the events of our lives). This difference is fundamental. Newton, and after him Einstein, built physics upon there being some underlying simplicity in Nature. If one could discover its laws, which must operate objectively, independent of Man, they believed one could determine Nature's behaviour for all time – past and future. They paid homage to Kepler, who had discovered that the planets had orbits that were ellipses (themselves a discovery of the ancient Greek geometers) even though he had no idea why this should be so and, by his own account, 'went nearly mad' searching for a reason. Einstein wrote of Kepler's feat: 'Our admiration for Kepler is transcended only by our admiration and reverence for the mysterious harmony of Nature in which we find ourselves.'

The longing to find order and simplicity in the universe is today as strong as it ever was, but the successors of Newton and Einstein, faced by their small comprehension of the most ordinary physical phenomena – such as turbulence in rivers or the formation of clouds or even, famously, the stability of a bicycle – have increasingly turned from the triumphant study of reversible, equilibrium processes on the atomic/subatomic/cosmic scale, to focus on human-scale and irreversible macroscopic processes, hoping eventually to illuminate global processes, global catastrophes. For Einstein, Ilya Prigogine has remarked, 'time was an imperfection, and science, a way to get away . . . from the turmoil, from the wars. He wanted to find some kind of safe harbour in eternity'. Prigogine's own search, in thermodynamics (for which he received a Nobel prize in 1977), is for order in time as well as in space: 'non-equilibrium as a source of order' (Prigogine's *Order Out of Chaos*). Could the fluttering of a butterfly in due course start a hurricane – the so-called butterfly effect? Or to put the point differently:

> For want of a nail, the shoe was lost;
> For want of a shoe, the horse was lost;
> For want of a horse, the rider was lost;
> For want of a rider, the battle was lost;
> For want of a battle, the kingdom was lost!

'No human work can withstand the violence of Nature.' The ruins of the Grand Hotel, Yokohama, after the Great Kanto earthquake of 1923.

Catastrophe is back in science, after well over a century's eclipse. Scientists are no longer preoccupied with the Flood, of course; they speak instead of diluvialism, the idea that great floods have shaped certain features of the Earth's surface. But now they combine this view with the younger idea of slow-acting, 'uniformitarian' forces that have built Earth's mountains and eroded its river valleys; the view first introduced in the 1790s by James Hutton and subsequently developed by Charles Lyell, which greatly influenced Charles Darwin's theory of evolution and natural selection. Meteorites colliding with Earth – a possibility dismissed by serious scientists for decades – may have indeed caused such great floods and, as some scientists maintain, the disappearance of the dinosaurs some 66 million years ago. A recent study of the Earth's surface identified more than 120 impact craters; more than 1000 further craters are estimated to await discovery on land and on the ocean floor. Other scientists have found evidence for a different catastrophe – volcanism – as the culprit.

The explosion of data about every part of the Earth since the late 1950s, made feasible by new and ever more sensitive instrumentation (much of it carried by satellites and stored and manipulated by computer), has fired speculation about Earth's working at all levels. But much, much more data is required for theories to be proved. The image of the Earth from space, first observed in 1968, was the culmination of centuries of scientific research – but it was also the beginning of a new phase in science. Whole-Earth scientists are at the stage of their Victorian forebears – generalists like Darwin who went forth into jungles to collect plant, animal and rock specimens – according, that is, to one of their number, the unorthodox James Lovelock, environmental chemist, inventor, one-time adviser to NASA, Fellow of the Royal Society and self-proclaimed 'geophysiologist'. Instead of waiting for further data, he has leapt ahead and proposed the Gaia hypothesis, a scientific exposition of the ancient idea (Gaia was the Greeks' goddess of the Earth) that the Earth is alive, a superorganism of which Man is a part: a most important part, but not the boss. Other scientists have preceded him in this belief, beginning two centuries ago with James Hutton, who is sometimes called the father of geology.

The majority of scientists are unconvinced. The idea that the Earth is alive, seen from any one scientific speciality, is likely to seem fantastic, unscientific – a criticism of which Lovelock is keenly aware. 'To me, and to many engineers I suspect,' he wrote in the British science magazine *Nature* in late 1990, 'the term alive also includes the concept of a system switched on and working, something very different from the same system switched off. Gaia is alive in this sense but in no way has foresight or purpose.' In other words Gaia is not God, and is certainly not a benevolent force; with due objectivity it may shift its state and dispose of humankind if our activities disturb its systems excessively.

Gaia or no Gaia, there is a gathering consensus both within science and beyond science, that Man and Nature are becoming increasingly intertwined, willy-nilly. 'Humankind has become a more important agent of environmental change than Nature', the president of the US National Academy of Sciences told the Group of Seven in Paris in 1989. In late 1992, 1500 scientists from around the world, including 99 Nobel prize-winners, signed a statement that 'human beings and the natural world are on a collision course' which 'may so alter the living world that it will be unable to sustain life in the manner that we know.' Consider global warming, for instance: were it to happen on a significant scale, would it be a natural change or a man-made one? A force of Nature or of Man? And, crucially, how soon will we know for sure that we are responsible? The debate is already urgent in the case of the depletion of the ozone layer, of many floods such as those in China and Bangladesh thought to be enhanced by deforestation and over-population, of the sustained drought in Sahelian and southern Africa and in the American West, and of the mass extinction of animal and plant species (biodiversity) mainly in the tropical rain forests. None of these problems yields to simple modelling or exclusively local analysis – after all, just 15–20 years ago global *cooling*, a coming ice age, was the scientific consensus – and none can be properly comprehended without fuller data, such as was gathered in the 1987 airborne Antarctic experiments that clarified the chemical role of chlorofluorocarbons (CFCs) in creating the ozone hole.

How the human race should respond to what the data shows is an even more complicated problem. As the Oxford and Harvard University economist Amartya Sen (who grew up in India) noted in 1992, evolution, left to itself, will perhaps provide a solution to the depletion of the ozone layer, by evolving genes that are less vulnerable to ultraviolet radiation.

> But if we value our lives and condemn disease and extinction, we would wish to consider a course of action which would vigor-ously resist the unfavourable change in the environment. From the point of view of human beings, as we are constituted, genetic natural selection may be a chilling prospect rather than a heartwarming one.

The 1990s will be a decade of accelerating global data collection; it will also be a decade of difficult decisions. Most difficult of all will be the collective perception of a better balance between Man and Nature, so as to begin to reverse the destructive trends so apparent in both the scientific statistics and in societies the world over. 'We do need Darwin,' in the words of Sen, 'but only in moderation.'

Maybe we also need to enquire afresh into the paradox of Einstein quoted above: why did he find it so incomprehensible that his mind could comprehend Nature? Perhaps – contrary to what Einstein (and Voltaire) believed – Man and Nature are not as divorced as they seem. Now scientists (and the rest of us) must grope towards an understanding of this interdependency: a picture of Nature's laws that better describes the world we all experience. Without such enquiry, humanity – and that means the developed world as much as the developing world with its frightening population growth – will remain largely at the mercy of unpredictable, self-inflicted, and most likely increasingly ferocious and unmanageable disasters.

CHAPTER

—2—

EARTH, OCEAN, ATMOSPHERE AND LIFE

*At a specified time the Earth can have had just one configuration.
But the Earth supplies no direct information about this . . . It is
only by combining the information furnished by all the Earth
sciences that we can hope to determine 'truth' here, that is to say,
to find the picture that sets out all the known facts in the best
arrangement and that therefore has the highest degree of
probability. Further, we have to be prepared always for the
possibility that each new discovery, no matter which science
furnishes it, may modify the conclusions we draw.*
Alfred Wegener, 'The Origin of Continents and Oceans', 1929

IN the spring of 1982, a barely known volcano in Mexico called El
Chichón erupted for the first time in recorded history, claimed
up to 3500 lives and caused tens of thousands of people to flee their
homes. Not long afterwards, scientists detected swarms of earthquakes and large submarine lava flows in the equatorial portion of
the East Pacific Rise, the ridge that runs north along the Pacific
floor some 1000 miles west of the Galapagos Islands. At the same
time, in June, there was a sudden and dramatic drop in atmospheric
pressure farther south on the Rise at Easter Island, and also at
Tahiti, well over 2000 miles away to the west. About a month later,
weather stations on Fanning and Christmas Islands in the mid-
Pacific reported an unusual rise in sea level, of 6 to 10 inches (15 to
25 cm). Simultaneously, in the western Pacific at Palau and
Guadalcanal, the sea level dropped 4 to 6 inches (10 to 15 cm).
Then, gradually but persistently, Pacific sea surface temperatures at
the equator began to rise. Off the coast of Peru, the temperature
reached over 26.5 degrees C (80°F), nearly 7 degrees C above
normal. In the mid-Pacific, the temperature climbed as high as 30
degrees C (86°F), a level described by one scientist as 'about as hot
as the ocean can get'.

Peru's multimillion-dollar anchovy industry was devastated that year as the fish moved away; on Christmas Island, 17 million birds disappeared without a trace. During late summer, coastal areas of Ecuador and Peru began to suffer torrential rains, in some cases 300 times the normal annual rainfall. Continuing for eight months, the rains produced some of the worst floods this century. Avalanches and swollen rivers cut off scores of towns; several hundred people died. In the mid-Pacific there was an abrupt rise in typhoons: French Polynesia, which receives an average of one typhoon every 50 years, was battered by five in as many months.

Across the Pacific, in Indonesia and Australia, and across the Indian Ocean in southern Africa, there was unprecedented drought and famine, by contrast. In Australia, thousands of acres of farmland desiccated and turned to desert; some of the worst bush fires in the history of the world's most fire-prone country left 72 people dead, as many as 8000 people homeless, and destroyed property worth several thousand million dollars. In due course the drought spread – to India, Sri Lanka, the Philippines, Hawaii and Mexico.

In December it was the turn of the United States. A dozen people perished on the West Coast in storms and mudslides that smothered crops and ravaged much of California's magnificent coastal highway. In Los Angeles, a freak tornado tore through the downtown area. On the Gulf Coast, floods drove 60,000 people from their homes and killed 50. No weather like it had ever been seen before by US meteorologists.

But although they did not predict it, they were able to fit it into a certain pattern. For centuries, Peruvian fishermen have known that warm water from the Pacific periodically overlays the usual upwelling of cold plankton-rich water off Peru and deprives them of their catch, while on land floods deprive them of their homes. Since the upset generally comes towards the end of the year, near Christmas time, the fishermen have given Nature's unwelcome gift an ironic name, El Niño ('The Child'). Looking at the records of El Niño this century, scientists can see that it has tended to follow a volcanic eruption and submarine earthquake swarms. But in their current state of knowledge of the Earth, all they can do is speculate as to whether or not major volcanic eruptions, submarine earthquakes and worldwide meteorological mayhem are connected phenomena. As Earth scientists sometimes like to remark about themselves, they are like the six blind men of Indostan who, after examining an elephant – or rather six different parts of an elephant – 'disputed loud and long,/Each in his own opinion/Exceeding stiff and strong,/Though each was partly in the right,/And all were in the wrong!'

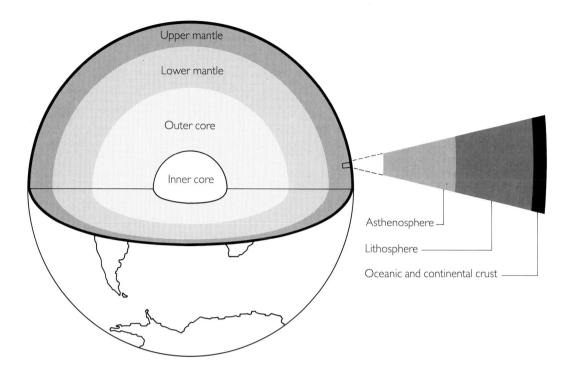

Upper mantle

Lower mantle

Outer core

Inner core

Asthenosphere

Lithosphere

Oceanic and continental crust

A number of deductions about the Earth are generally accepted by science, however. It is a near-sphere, with a diameter at the equator of 7926 miles and at the poles of 7900 miles. At some stage in its evolution it was a molten mass but after cooling it formed a solid skin with a series of concentric layers beneath. At its centre is a core made of iron with a smaller amount of nickel. The core's temperature is very high, in the thousands of degrees Celsius (the exact value is much disputed), but because the pressure at its centre is 3–4 million times greater than atmospheric pressure at sea level, the inner core cannot melt and is solid; the outer core, being under less pressure is like a very thick liquid. Around the core is the mantle, which is also iron-rich. Its upper part consists of two distinct layers: the asthenosphere (from the Greek *asthenos*, meaning 'weak') in which the rocks are close enough to their melting points to be malleable or partly molten, and above that the lithosphere, where the rock is more rigid. Above the lithosphere is the relatively thin skin of the Earth's crust, made of less dense rock; it is largely basalt below the oceans (where it averages about 3.7 miles thick) and granite below the continents (where the average thickness is about 20 miles). The boundary between the mantle and crust is known as the Mohorovičić discontinuity, or Moho, after the Yugoslav seismologist whose work helped to reveal it.

The age of the Earth is currently estimated at 4600 million years.

Inside the Earth. The Earth is a near-sphere, 7926 miles in diameter at the equator. The density, pressure and temperature increase with depth but the actual figures are controversial; current estimates of the inner core temperature lie between 3250 and 7800 degrees C (5900–14,100°F).

El Niño. Iguanas in the Galapagos Islands die during an El Niño event when increased sea temperatures reduce their supply of food, seaweed. Drought in southern Africa, fires in Australia, floods in Peru and storms on the US West Coast are other effects of El Niño. (*Far left*) Satellite images of the Pacific Ocean indicating, top, temperatures in January 1984, under normal conditions; middle, temperatures in January 1983, during an El Niño event; and, bottom, the difference in temperature between the two. Normally, the warmest water (red) is in the western equatorial Pacific (1), and there is a tongue of cooler water (blue/green) off the coast of Peru (2); during El Niño, however, the warm water spreads across the equatorial Pacific and the cooler water disappears. El Niño produces a pronounced warming of the eastern equatorial Pacific (3) and a corresponding cooling of the western equatorial Pacific (4).

Continental drift. Some 200 million years ago, the continents were conjoined as one land mass, Pangaea, surrounded by an ocean, Panthalassa. By the mechanism of plate tectonics, the continents then split into two land masses, Gondwanaland and Laurasia, separated by the Tethys Sea. The current configuration of the continents is shown at bottom.

This is calculated from the process of decay of its radioactive rocks, a method that continues to provoke argument; even so, most scientists accept the figure. (Until the early years of this century, when the radioactive dating method began to evolve, the Earth was thought to be a mere 20 million years old.) In order to impart some meaning to this unimaginable length of time, one may visualize the history of the Earth condensed into a period of 24 hours, from midnight to midnight. On this scale, accretion of the Earth ended shortly after 4 a.m., when the oldest rocks known to us were formed. By 6 a.m. there was life. Five hours after that, appreciable amounts of free oxygen had built up in the atmosphere. At about 5 p.m., cells containing nuclei (eukaryotic cells) made their entry; the first animals appeared at 8.20 p.m.; and at 9.10 p.m. the earliest organisms to leave well organized, calcified fossils came on the scene. Vascular plants colonized the continents at 9.50 p.m. The dinosaurs became extinct at about 11.20 p.m. At 10 minutes to midnight human beings arrived, and with only 3.7 thousandths of a second to go, the industrial revolution took place.

During the last hour of this history (i.e. within the last 200 million years) the continents came into being, created by the splitting of one congealed supercontinent. This idea is now widely accepted by scientists and non-scientists alike – but a mere 30 years ago (well within the careers of many scientists working today), moving continents were regarded as absurdly, even dangerously, unscientific. Since the late 19th century, the *vertical* movement of lighter crust as it floated buoyantly on the denser, less rigid mantle – thereby generating mountains and ocean basins – had been orthodox geology. But the horizontal displacement of the crust – and that over thousands of miles – was calculated to be physically impossible: where would the enormous force required come from? It was a simple matter for physicists to show that the gravitational force necessary to shift continents through the crust would be enough to stop the rotation of the Earth in less than a year.

But then how – without postulating physical links between the continents – to explain the discovery of unquestionably identical fossils of plants and animals on opposite sides of the Atlantic Ocean? The favoured explanation in the first part of this century was land bridges. The species in question had migrated over a bridge between, say, Brazil and Africa; subsequently the bridge had been buried as the Earth's crust collapsed inwards with the cooling and shrinking of the planet. (Before radioactivity was accepted as a source of heat within the Earth, the consensus was that the Earth was gradually cooling, losing its heat to space.)

In 1911, while pondering this unlikely theory of land bridges together with the striking apparent fit between the Atlantic coastlines of Africa and South America, a versatile German meteorologist and astronomer, Alfred Wegener, became convinced that continental drift had occurred. A megacontinent, which Wegener dubbed Pangaea ('all land'), had broken apart and after millions of years the bits had drifted into the present continental configuration. Announcing the idea in early 1912, Wegener eventually published it as a book in Germany in 1915. Nine years later, it appeared in English as *The Origin of Continents and Oceans*. Before Wegener's premature death in 1930, the book went through four editions and was translated into French, Swedish, Spanish and Russian.

Unfortunately for Wegener, although his basic idea – that continents move – was triumphantly correct, his proposed mechanism and his calculations of the rate of movement were flawed. Moving continents were therefore rejected by a large majority of scientists until the 1960s, when the mass of evidence in favour of the idea – emerging from an unimpeachable diversity of scientific studies – became so overwhelming that a revolution in the Earth sciences occurred. Out of the half-satisfactory notion of continental drift quickly evolved the more compelling and rigorous theory of plate tectonics.

The earliest – and probably the most striking – pieces of evidence came from the floor of the Atlantic Ocean. The existence of a mountain range beneath the mid-Atlantic had been suspected since the 1850s. In 1947, scientists from the Woods Hole Oceanographic Institution in Massachusetts began to plot the shape of this Mid-Atlantic Ridge using the most powerful depth sounder then

Alfred Wegener, in Greenland. From 1906, Wegener conducted three scientific expeditions to the Arctic and died there in 1930. His obituaries praised him lavishly as an explorer and meteorologist, but hardly mentioned his theory of continental drift.

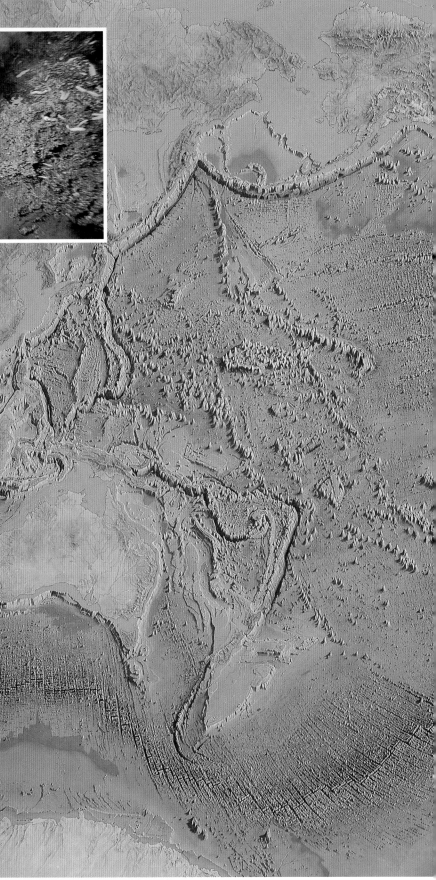

The floors of the oceans. In 1977, Marie Tharp and Bruce Heezen produced the first map to depict the entire mid-ocean ridge system, some 40,000 miles in length, part of which is shown here. (Compare it with the map of volcanoes, earthquakes and subduction zones on page 26.) (*Above*) Ocean ridges are the sites of volcanic activity. The water in miniature undersea volcanoes known as 'black smokers', such as this one on the East Pacific Rise, is superheated to nearly 400 degrees C (750°F) and is black with suspended minerals. The minerals precipitate and harden to form a rocky chimney. Volcanoes at oceanic ridges were predicted by scientists during the 1960s, but not observed until 1977.

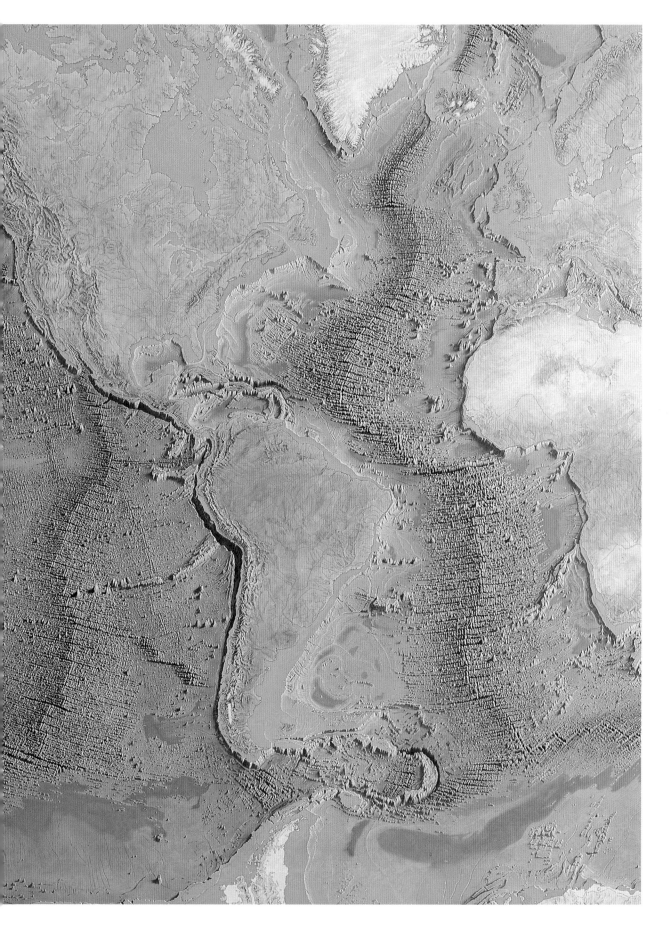

available. The Ridge was found to run down the centre of the Atlantic, roughly equidistant from the coasts on either side. It boasted peaks up to 10,000 feet (3050 m) high, a mile below the surface of the ocean. Dredge samples revealed that the rocks of the Ridge were of volcanic origin and much younger than expected; there was also far less sediment on the ocean floor than predicted on the basis of ocean floors having been formed early in the history of the Earth. Bruce Heezen, a geologist involved, became so fascinated that he and Marie Tharp, his drafting assistant, began to collect depth recordings from all over the world and from them to create the first profiles and three-dimensional maps of the ocean floors. It was one of these maps that led to a breakthrough. The Mid-Atlantic Ridge showed a deep V-shaped valley running along the centre of its entire length. When Heezen took this map and plotted on it the epicentres of Atlantic earthquakes then being studied by other scientists, he suddenly realized that the earthquakes were taking place in the rift valley of the Ridge. A parallel plot of breaks in transatlantic cables coincided with the earthquake data: the cables broke over the rift valley.

This was around 1956. Between then and 1960, US and British oceanographic expeditions trailed the world's oceans with depth recorders, tracing their ridge systems. (Nevertheless, even today less than 5 per cent of the ocean floors has been mapped.) These systems were found to run along the centre of the Indian Ocean as well as the centre of the Atlantic; to link together south of Africa; and to connect with a ridge midway between Australia and Antarctica that linked to a ridge that ran northwards through the eastern Pacific (the East Pacific Rise) until it reached California. A rift valley was not always found at the centre of a ridge; often whole ridge segments were offset from each other by as much as several hundred miles along tremendous fractures in the oceanic crust, which were sites of earthquakes. Measurements of heat flow along the crest of the Mid-Atlantic Ridge gave a figure up to eight times greater than elsewhere on the ocean floor. Clearly the surface of the Earth had once been – and probably was still being – torn apart on a grand scale.

In 1960, Harry Hess, a geologist at Princeton University, came up with a radical explanation of these observations couched in suitably cautious language. 'The birth of the oceans is a matter of conjecture, the subsequent history is obscure, and the present structure is just beginning to be understood,' he began. His paper on the subject, he warned readers, was 'an essay in geopoetry'. Rather than the drifting continents favoured by Wegener, Hess focused on the ocean floors. The floors behaved like twin conveyor belts carrying the continents, he suggested; new crust welled up at ridges/rifts and moved away from the ridge on either side in opposite directions, while old crust was simultaneously destroyed in the deep oceanic trenches that lie near the edges of the continents. This 'sea-floor spreading' (the name soon given to the theory by the geologist Robert Dietz) was calculated by Hess to proceed at the rate of about half an inch (1.25 cm) a year on each side of the ridge. At this pace the spreading should have created the ocean floors of the world in just 200 million years (rather than the one or two thousand million years formerly imagined) – an age that agreed with the measured age of the oldest rocks discovered there.

Not until the 1970s were scientists able to obtain eye-witness evidence of volcanic activity at oceanic rifts, when submersibles examined recent formations of lava at the Mid-Atlantic Ridge at close range. (They could however watch the fiery birth of Surtsey, a new volcanic island that in 1963 suddenly rose from the sea south of Iceland above the Ridge.) But in the meantime they conceived an ingenious new way of extracting from the Earth new evidence for the theory of sea-floor spreading. Samples of rock taken from ocean ridges showed a curious pattern of magnetism. Those from the East Pacific Rise south of Easter Island were particularly remarkable: the magnetism in the rocks, with an impressive symmetry about the axis of the ridge, switched back and forth in direction making a 'zebra' pattern: black stripes indicated magnetization in one direction, the intervening white gaps indicated magnetization in the reverse.

Two British oceanographers, Frederick Vine and Drummond Matthews, were the first to explain the phenomenon in a paper written in 1963. From other scientific studies they knew that the Earth's magnetic field had reversed direction frequently in its history – the north magnetic pole becoming the south magnetic pole and vice versa; the geological record said that the switch had occurred at least three or four times every million years during the past 70 million years. They therefore proposed that when molten rock extruded at an ocean ridge had cooled down, it retained its original direction of magnetism when the Earth's magnetic field subsequently reversed. New volcanic rock, by contrast, forcing apart the cooled volcanic rock, became magnetized in the reverse direction. The bands of magnetism stretching away symmetrically on either side of an ocean ridge were therefore a fossil record of the Earth's magnetism over the period that rock was extruded at the ridge. 'The crust can thus be viewed as a twin-headed tape recorder in which the reversal history of the Earth's magnetic field is registered', Vine wrote in 1990. And since the dating of the pole reversals was available independently, the rate of sea floor spreading too could be calculated from these measurements.

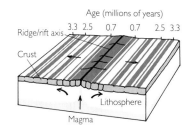

Sea floor spreading. As new rock has been formed over several million years on either side of an oceanic ridge/rift, its direction of magnetization has altered back and forth, mimicking the alterations in the Earth's magnetic field. The measurement of these magnetic 'zebra' patterns in ocean floor rocks was an important clue to the existence of plate tectonics.

(*Right*) **Subduction.** Oceanic crust is more dense than continental crust; it therefore subducts beneath the latter, forming trenches and volcanoes (see page 28).

(*Below*) **Earthquakes, volcanoes and plates.** The map shows recent earthquakes and volcanic eruptions, in relation to seven major tectonic plates and five minor ones (in brackets). Note the 'ring of fire' around the Pacific Ocean. Transform faults connect the offset portions of oceanic ridges: at these faults the direction of movement of the crust at the ridge is reversed ('transformed').

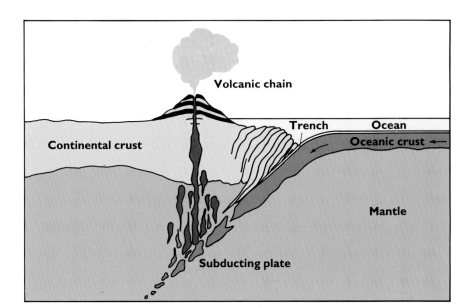

Volcanic chain

Trench   Ocean

Continental crust

Oceanic crust ←

Mantle

Subducting plate

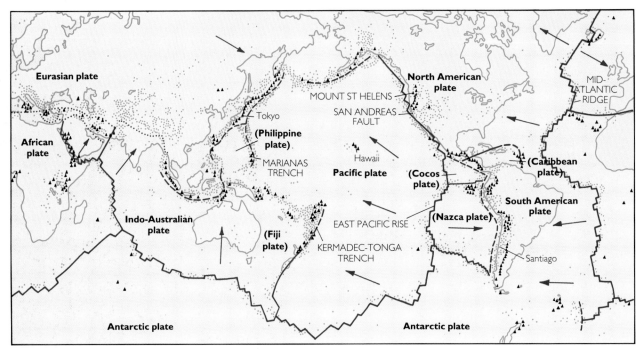

Eurasian plate

North American plate

MID-ATLANTIC RIDGE

MOUNT ST HELENS

SAN ANDREAS FAULT

Tokyo

(**Philippine plate**)

African plate

MARIANAS TRENCH

Hawaii

(**Cocos plate**)

(**Caribbean plate**)

Pacific plate

South American plate

Indo-Australian plate

(**Nazca plate**)

(**Fiji plate**)

EAST PACIFIC RISE

KERMADEC-TONGA TRENCH

Santiago

Antarctic plate

Antarctic plate

Plate boundaries:

▲▲▲▲▲▲ ▲▲▲   Volcanoes

⌐⌐⌐⌐   Spreading ridge offset by transform faults

.·.·.·.·.·.   Earthquake zone

– – – – –   Subduction zone

———▶   Motion of plate

....   Collision zone

(*Right*) **Where ocean currents meet.** Coral larvae, seen here in the Atlantic Ocean near Bermuda, are usually well-dispersed, but sometimes they form a distinct stripe across the sea surface, demarcating the meeting place of currents as they collide and sink.

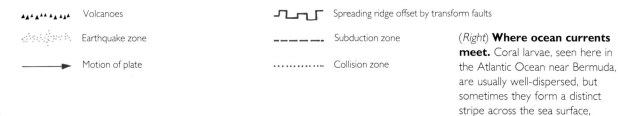

The scene was now set for the development of plate tectonics. In 1965, the Canadian geophysicist J. Tuzo Wilson suggested that, rather than rigid continents somehow drifting through a malleable crust, the Earth's crust was composed of 'several large rigid plates', which were growing at some edges and being destroyed at others, and which were also moving across the Earth. ('Tectonics' – from the Greek *tekton*, meaning 'builder' – was added three years later by others; the word had been used by geologists for more than a century to describe dynamic processes such as mountain building.) A plate, wrote Wilson, had three kinds of boundary with other plates: oceanic ridges/rifts, where two plates grew; oceanic trenches, where a plate was destroyed beneath a second plate; and what he termed 'transform faults', where plates were neither enlarged nor diminished. The San Andreas fault of California – the cause of numerous earthquakes – was a transform fault, he said.

Wilson's basic picture of the tectonic plates still stands. Today scientists count seven major plates and many minor ones, with an average plate thickness of 60 miles. Most of the world's earthquakes and volcanoes occur at plate boundaries. This is as we should expect; it is at the plate boundaries that friction and stress occur and rock is either extruded from the mantle in molten form (at ridges) or melted anew by being forced back into the mantle (at trenches) – a process of swallowing termed 'subduction'. As a plate dives into the depths, part of it, as it melts, is thought to find its way back to the surface in the form of volcanoes. (The details of the process are largely unknown.) Subduction is currently occurring beneath island arcs such as Japan and Tonga and beneath mountain ranges such as the Andes (which are growing in height as a consequence). It is also believed to be taking place on the northwest Pacific coast of the United States beyond the end of the San Andreas fault, where a subducted plate is thought to have disappeared beneath the North American plate in recent geological time, leaving the majestic volcanoes of the Cascades range as evidence of its past existence. (One of these volcanoes, Mount St Helens, erupted spectacularly in 1980.) In fact, subduction may occur at any plate boundary where two plates of sufficiently different density, such as an oceanic plate (more dense) and a continental plate (less dense), collide. In such cases, the more dense is subducted beneath the less dense plate. If, by contrast, the two colliding plates are of similar density, there will be no subduction; mountain ranges and earthquakes will still result, but generally no volcanoes. This is the case in the Himalayas, where the plate on which India rides is piling into the plate on which the rest of Asia rides. Here, there are frequent earthquakes (such as the major one near Tehri in late 1991), but no known volcanoes.

This so-called Indo-Australian plate that is butting into the Eurasian plate is an example of one of the many less convincing aspects of plate tectonic theory. In addition to earthquakes in the Himalayas – which are readily explained by the theory – there have been large earthquakes under the Indian Ocean, right in the *middle* of the Indo-Australian plate which, being supposedly rigid, should be incapable of deforming in the way said to cause earthquakes. In fact earthquakes occur quite often in a number of locations that lie far from the accepted plate boundaries – in the centre of the United States, for instance, and in parts of Western Europe. Some volcanoes, such as those in Hawaii, do not lie anywhere near a plate boundary. Attempts have been made to explain all these facts by postulating less rigid and uniform plates containing faults and 'hot spots' – but scientists recognize these exceptions as significant weaknesses in the present theory of crustal movement.

A second difficulty is: what causes the plates to move? Alfred Wegener suggested that the continents drifted under the centrifugal force generated by the spinning of the Earth and the gravitational attraction of the Sun and the Moon (the latter force being the cause of tides). He also admitted: 'It is probable that the complete solution of the problem of the driving forces will still be a long time coming.' He was right: the driving force – whether of drifting continents or of moving plates – has been continually debated without scientists coming to any consensus. They know too little about the inner workings of the Earth to make even an informed guess. In the development stages of plate tectonic theory (during the late 1960s) it was suggested that the buoyant force of molten rock deep down, known as magma, rising from the mantle would impact the underside of the plates and drive them along. But since this force should act on a plate roughly equally in all directions, there was no reason to expect the plate to move, at least not in a regular way. A second proposal, which is still popular, postulated convection cells within the mantle similar to the cells that form in a beaker of water heated over a flame: hot water rises in the middle of the beaker, cools at the surface, overturns on either side and falls at the sides of the beaker, thence to be heated again. Whether such a process happens in the Earth's mantle, and how far down the circulation of rock begins, is the subject of fierce argument. Assuming it does occur, how can it be reconciled with the plates' great variety of sizes and their odd, angular shapes that shift, grow and shrink in ways that do not resemble the behaviour of more familiar convecting fluids?

More than one leading scientist has suggested that living organisms may play a role in causing the plates to move. The sedimentation of limestone (the remains of sea creatures) on ocean floors at the margins of the continents may eventually have altered the chemistry and temperature of the crustal rocks and induced instability. 'Thus there is the interesting possibility that plate tectonics may exist on the Earth because limestone-generating life evolved here', the geologist Don Anderson (of the California Institute of Technology) wrote in the American journal *Science* in 1984.

'How inappropriate to call this planet Earth when clearly it is Ocean', Arthur C. Clarke has remarked. Oceans cover 71 per cent of the Earth's surface. With an average depth of 12,500 feet (3810 m) and a maximum depth of 36,198 feet (11,033 m) at the Marianas Trench in the western Pacific, the oceans provide 0.02 per cent of the Earth's total weight. The three-dimensional complexity of their ceaseless flow and mixing is hard to envision in the mind; it is 'like the circulatory system of an animal', in the words of James Lovelock. Storm winds whip the surface into transient waves of staggering power. Steadier, more constant winds, in conjunction with the spinning of the Earth, drive the currents – meandering rivers in the ocean that flow across its surface for thousands of miles in some cases, accelerating or slowing from season to season and year to year but never disappearing. Beneath the undulating surface unimaginable masses of water rise and sink, propelled by fluctuations in density and temperature. Mixing can take many hundreds of years. According to a series of studies conducted in the 1970s the deep waters of the Atlantic are about 300 years old on average; the bottom water of the eastern Pacific, which has circulated halfway around the globe and throughout the Pacific basin, last flowed at the surface some 2000 years ago.

The oceans store heat more effectively than the continents and the atmosphere. The difference in sea surface summer and winter

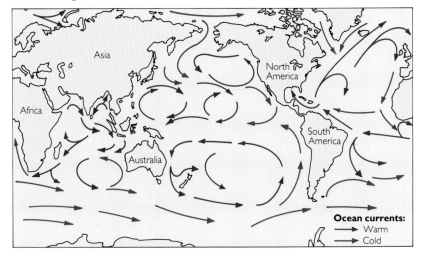

The Earth's principal ocean currents. Warm currents are shown in red, cold in blue.

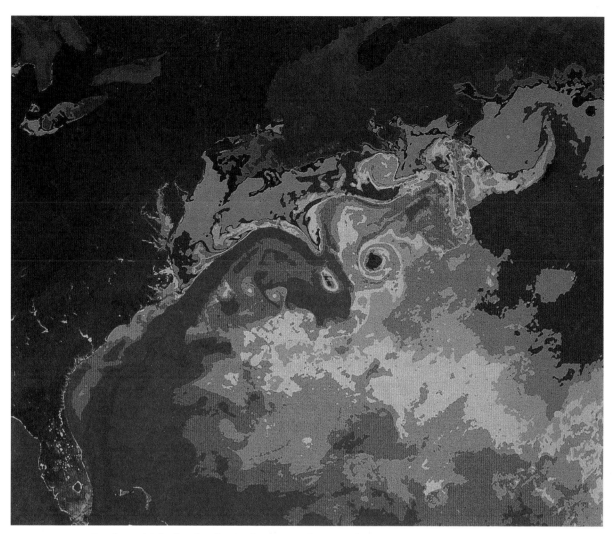

temperatures in the mid-latitudes is rarely more than 10 degrees C (18°F); in the middle of a large continent the difference can be as much as 80 degrees C (144°F). The top 10 feet (3 m) of the water stores as much energy as the entire atmosphere. Comparatively small changes in ocean temperatures can therefore have a dramatic effect on air temperatures, and hence on climate and weather: the Indian monsoon is one example of this link, El Niño is another.

The oceans also transport heat. Perhaps the best-known instance is the Gulf Stream which warms the northeast Atlantic Ocean, giving northwest Europe (notably the British Isles) a milder climate than expected for its latitude. First charted approximately by Benjamin Franklin in 1769 on the basis of sailors' reports, the Gulf Stream was extensively mapped by the US Navy hydrographer Matthew Fontaine Maury during the mid-19th century. He wrote vividly:

There is a river in the ocean: in the severest droughts it never fails, and in the mightiest floods, it never overflows; its banks

The Gulf Stream. This satellite image, covering 4.4 million square miles, shows the sea surface temperatures in the western part of the north Atlantic Ocean during early summer. Reds and oranges show the warmest waters (24.5–29°C/76–84°F); yellows, greens, blues and purples successively colder waters.

and its bottom are of cold water, while its current is of warm; the Gulf of Mexico is its fountain and its mouth is in the Arctic Seas. It is the Gulf Stream.

Science, regrettably for romantics, has proved this image largely erroneous. Detailed measurements of the Gulf Stream at various depths, combined with striking images of it made by satellite, show that it is no river. Not only do its boundaries continually change, its warmest water (at 29 degrees C, 84 degrees F) is scattered through the stream in bands, which alternate with ribbons of cool water. Its velocity varies similarly. It also commonly meanders on a giant scale, sometimes spawning large eddies which break off from the main stream, drift back through the Atlantic (tracked by scientific vessels and satellites) and then maybe return to the stream after several months. The structure of the stream in the region of this behaviour becomes so complex that oceanographers cannot clearly understand how any heat at all is carried northwards, as it undoubtedly is. Nor does most of the water in the Gulf Stream emanate from the Gulf of Mexico, despite its name; it comes instead from across the Atlantic, ferried in ocean currents. Overall, in fact, the track of the Gulf Stream is reminiscent of the equally baffling tracks of many hurricanes that originate off the west coast of Africa, cross the Atlantic, veer away from the US coast and finally disperse in the north Atlantic, often twisting, turning and even reversing in direction *en route*.

But at least the Gulf Stream always flows: Maury was right about that. El Niño, which has been closely studied for only a few decades, is both periodic and unpredictable. The British meteorologist Sir Gilbert Walker, searching for a method of forecasting monsoon rainfall in India in the 1920s, unwittingly provided the first clues to El Niño's origin. He observed a remarkable pattern of low-latitude atmospheric circulation that he called the Southern Oscillation. As he described it, 'When pressure is high (relative to the mean) in the Pacific Ocean it tends to be low in the Indian Ocean from Africa to Australia; these conditions are associated with low temperatures in both of these areas, and rainfall varies in the opposite direction to pressure.' But every few years, Walker found, pressures fell in the region of high-pressure over the southeast Pacific, and rose in the low-pressure region centred over Indonesia, which then experienced low rainfall. (In mid-1982 it happened again of course.)

In 1961, a California-based meteorologist, Jacob Bjerknes, recognized the link between the Southern Oscillation and El Niño and termed it a 'teleconnection'. He saw that reduced pressures in the eastern Pacific meant diminished winds off the Peruvian coast.

These winds, Bjerknes reckoned, were responsible for moving water to the west, drawing up to the ocean surface the cooler, deeper water desired by Peruvian fishermen. If the winds slackened, warm water would flow back and suppress the cold upwelling.

This system, now known as ENSO (El Niño/Southern Oscillation), is being extensively monitored by instruments in the ocean, on land and in the atmosphere. But while there has been a considerable advance in data collection since 1982 and some progress in modelling the system with computers – and hence in predicting the next El Niño and its effects – there are too many forces implicated in the event for scientists to have much confidence that they understand it. In the words of Vilhelm Bjerknes, son of Jacob, who also became a meteorologist in the US:

> We are in the position of the physicist watching a pot of water coming to a boil. He knows intimately all the processes of energy transfer, molecular kinetics and thermodynamics involved. He can describe them, put them in the form of formulas and tell you a great deal about how much heat will boil how much water.
>
> Now ask him to predict precisely where the next bubble will form.

The interaction of the atmosphere and the ocean is pivotal in Earth science. As far back as Aristotle, more than two millennia ago, it was understood that the Sun's heat falling on the Earth evaporated moisture from the oceans, which rose into the atmosphere until it cooled sufficiently and condensed once more into water; this water fell on the oceans and the Earth as rain. Storms have thus long been appreciated as heat exchangers that take heat from the hotter parts of the Earth and distribute it towards the cooler parts. But the precise conditions that produce a storm – why some storms grow to become hurricanes and typhoons and may spawn tornadoes while other, apparently similar storms do not, and the actual physical behaviour of water vapour, water, ice and wind within such storms (i.e. the variations in pressure, temperature, velocity and so on) – are still surprisingly ill understood. Scientists, even today's experts in chaos theory, still echo the lament of the great French mathematician Henri Poincaré, writing nearly a century ago in an essay entitled 'Chance': 'Why have the meteorologists such difficulty in predicting the weather? Why do the rains, the storms themselves seem to us to come by chance, so that many persons find it quite natural to pray for rain or shine, when they think it ridiculous to pray for an eclipse?' Even a phenomenon so apparently simple as a cloud – the reflecting and absorbing

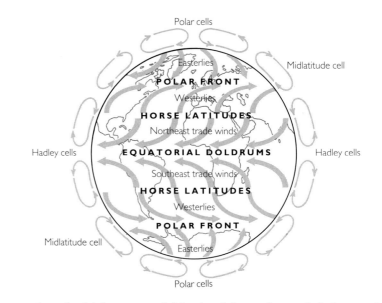

Earth's winds. Winds blow in complex ways but they are controlled by two basic facts: hot air rises at the equator, moves towards the poles, sinks as it cools, and then flows back towards the equator; and secondly, the spinning of the Earth bends the direction of winds away from the north–south axis (the Coriolis effect).

properties of which are crucial in the debate about global warming – is in many ways no more clearly understood by scientists than it was by Joni Mitchell in her well-known song: 'I've looked at clouds from both sides now/ From up and down and still somehow/ It's clouds' illusions I recall/ I really don't know clouds at all.'

Part of the problem of comprehension concerns the role of wind in making weather. Wind is even more ubiquitous than clouds. 'There are some whole countries where it never raines, or at least very seldome,' wrote Sir Francis Bacon in 1622, 'but there is no Countrey where the Winde doth not blow, and that frequently.' In northeastern Siberia, for example, the wind is known as 'the Chief' (a translation of a Yakut word); in southern California, it is the fire-raising Santa Ana; in Arabia, the *simoom* ('poison wind'); in Turkestan, the *tebbad* ('fever wind'); in the Sahara, the sirocco and the harmattan; in southern France, the *mistral*; and in Switzerland, it is the famous föhn.

The föhn (pronounced like 'fern' without the 'r') is a particularly intriguing wind. Hot and dry, it seems to defy Alpine logic by sweeping down from snow-clad summits. It often roars through Alpine valleys, especially in the late winter and autumn. For the Swiss it is both a blessing, since it ripens fruit and enables farmers to raise corn and grapes in the Rhine Valley, and a curse: the föhn snaps off trees, provokes landslides which block mountain torrents, and strips roofs off houses and barns. Scientifically speaking, it consists of Mediterranean air that cools and precipitates its moisture as it climbs the southern slopes of the Alps, then spills into the Swiss valleys and finally, as it descends, becomes compressed and heated at the rate of some 3 degrees C (5.5°F) every thousand feet (300 m). When it reaches the valley floor, the föhn is therefore some

15 degrees C (27°F) hotter than it was when it crossed the mountain top. The Swiss call its springtime manifestation 'the Snow-eater', because it can evaporate winter snow drifts in one day (often without bothering to form water).

A similar compression, but on a much greater scale, is believed to be the cause of the Earth's major deserts. These occur roughly at latitudes 30 degrees N and S, near the Tropics of Cancer and Capricorn. Here desiccated air presses down on the surface from a height of many thousand feet, having travelled there from the equatorial regions where it was propelled upwards by absorption of intense solar radiation, losing its humidity as it rose and cooled. Having reached the ground again, generating desert conditions, it flows back to the tropics as wind, gathering moisture on the way, and is once more lofted above. This convection cell of air and water vapour was first recognized by Edmond Halley (of comet fame) in 1686, during an astronomical expedition to the south Atlantic. Later it was modified by George Hadley, a London lawyer, whose name the cell now bears. Unlike Halley, Hadley was able to explain why the winds in the Atlantic did not blow directly from the north and from the south towards the equator as Halley's model predicted, but in fact blew from the northeast (in the northern hemisphere) and from the southeast (in the southern). (Christopher Columbus followed these northeasterly 'trade' winds in sailing to the New World.) The reason, Hadley told the Royal Society in London in 1735, was that the Earth was not stationary but rotating. The wind therefore 'lagged behind' the Earth's surface – the nearer to the equator it was (where the Earth spins fastest), the greater the lag – making its motion appear to have an easterly component.

A century later, the French scientist Gaspard Gustave de Coriolis put Hadley's explanation on a sound mathematical footing. The Coriolis effect, as it is known today, is best understood in terms of a merry-go-round. If a person sitting at the hub (a pole of the Earth, so to speak) throws a ball to a person sitting on the outside edge (the Earth's equator), the path of the ball will appear to both of them as if it is curved, and the person on the edge will have to stretch to catch the ball, either to the left or to the right depending on the direction of rotation of the merry-go-round. But to a person standing nearby, not on the merry-go-round, the ball will appear to travel in a straight line. Given the direction of rotation of the Earth, it turns out that a wind travelling from the north or south pole towards the equator appears to us (who are mostly near to or at the edge of the Earthly merry-go-round) to be bent as if coming from the east. (Seen from space, it would appear to travel in a straight line – that is if it were visible.)

The theory of Coriolis was applied in the 19th century to the first

Ocean–atmosphere interaction. In San Francisco Bay every summer, mist and fog roll in from the Pacific Ocean as warm, low-lying air chills rapidly over a current of cool water offshore. Here mist engulfs San Francisco and the Golden Gate Bridge.

compilations of worldwide wind data made by Maury in the United States, and it created a good basis for understanding the world's wind systems in different seasons. But until the early decades of this century there was not even a tentative theory to explain the way in which these winds interacted with water vapour and climates to produce the particular clouds, storms and rainfall patterns observed in different areas of the globe. Around 1903, a Norwegian scientist decided to tackle this problem. His name was Vilhelm Bjerknes and he is regarded now as the founding father of meteorology (besides being the actual father and grandfather of the two meteorologists we encountered earlier in the chapter). Having studied under Poincaré and the physicist Heinrich Hertz, Bjerknes hoped to apply the rigour of the laws of thermodynamics and hydrodynamics to the workings of the atmosphere so as to calculate, he hoped, the atmosphere's 'future state'.

At this time weather forecasters believed that storms resulted from 'cyclones', that was areas of low atmospheric pressure. (The

preferred term nowadays is 'depression' or 'low' for the middle and high latitudes; 'cyclone' is reserved for the tropics.) As a result of the Earth's spinning, cyclones were known to rotate anti-clockwise in the northern hemisphere, clockwise in the southern (anticyclones, areas of high pressure, rotated in the opposite direction in each case). By charting the movement of cyclones with barometric measurements, the idea went, one could predict the movement of storms. After an unhappy spell of war-related forecasting in Germany, Bjerknes – now assisted by his son Jacob – began in 1917 to measure precipitation patterns of storms in Norway and to compare these patterns with the storms' barometric pressure measurements. The two patterns did not coincide. This led him to a new and more complex conception of storms and weather. Instead of atmospheric pressure alone, temperature, humidity and velocity as well as cloud cover had all to be taken into account. Storms, said Bjerknes, were the result of the interaction of air *masses*, which had boundaries. Borrowing from the terminology of the war, he named

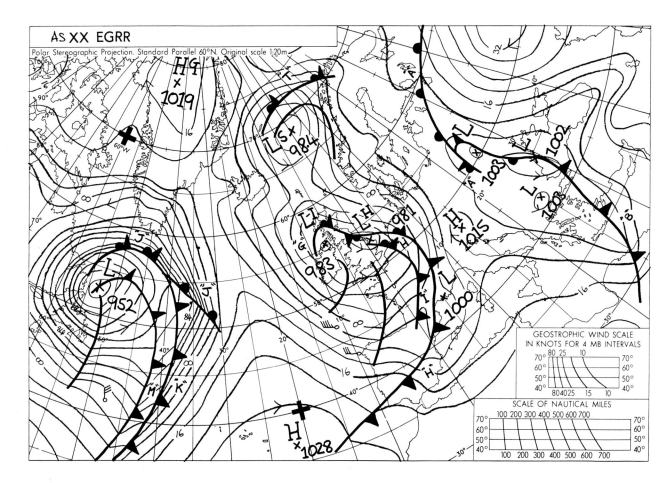

Weather map for 7 December 1992. The thinner contour lines are isobars, joining points of equal pressure measured in millibars (i.e. 983 indicates a pressure of 983 mb). The closer together the isobars, the more strongly the wind is blowing. It blows towards a low/depression (L) and away from a high (H). Thicker lines indicate fronts, that is boundaries between air masses. ▲ indicates a cold front; ● a warm front; and a mixture of both symbols an occluded front.

these boundaries 'fronts'. At a warm front, he suggested, a warm air mass would overtake a cold one and rise above it, producing various characteristic cloud patterns. At a cold front, on the other hand, a warm air mass would be forced to rise by an advancing undercutting wedge of cold air, and this would be accompanied by a sudden veering of the wind, a fall in temperature, and heavy rainfall. An occluded front was said to occur when a cold front overtook a warm front within a cyclone.

These concepts, though refined and added to by the later discovery of such phenomena as jet streams, still form the basis of weather forecasting today. But important as they are, they refer only to the lowest levels of the atmosphere and to relatively local disturbances. They tell us little about the structure of Earth's atmosphere as a whole. At the end of the last century, almost nothing was known about this beyond the fact that the chief constituents of the air were nitrogen, oxygen and carbon dioxide. The first scientific steps to investigate the atmosphere were taken around 1900 by the Frenchman Léon Philippe Teisserenc de Bort. He sent up kites and hydrogen-filled balloons that rose to a maximum height of 9 miles. The temperature dropped steadily with height, as had been expected by thinkers as far back as Aristotle, but at about 7 miles up, it was found to level off. Below this level, suggested Teisserenc de Bort, the atmosphere was turbulent, giving rise to all the phenomena of weather (clouds, wind, rainfall, storms and so forth); above it, he expected to find the gases in layers, the lighter above the heavier, undisturbed by wind and with the temperature static. He termed the atmosphere up to 7 miles high the troposphere (from the Greek root meaning 'to turn over'), and the supposedly stratified atmosphere above it, the stratosphere; the boundary between the two was the tropopause. (Today we know that the tropopause is higher at the equator, about 10 miles, and lower at the poles, about 5 miles; its height increases with increasing radiation at the Earth's surface.)

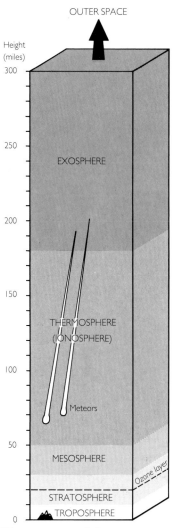

The structure of the atmosphere. The atmosphere becomes thinner with increasing height. The ozone layer is virtually coterminous with the stratosphere, but the highest concentration of ozone is in the middle of the layer.

Measuring the composition of the atmosphere. Some 12,000 feet (3650 m) above Paris, the physicist Joseph Louis Gay-Lussac collects an air sample while his colleague takes a temperature reading. This pioneering flight in 1804 showed that the air as high as 23,000 feet (7000 m) contained the same proportion of oxygen and nitrogen as the air at the Earth's surface.

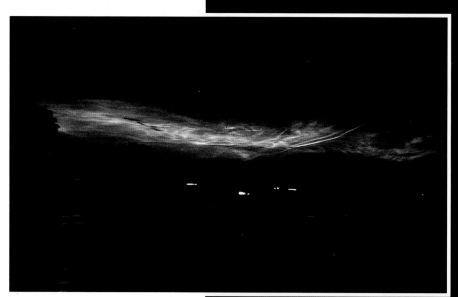

Mysteries of the upper atmosphere. (*Above*) Rare noctilucent clouds can be seen only at night. They form in the mesosphere at a height five times that of ordinary clouds in the troposphere. The bright spots beneath the clouds are surface lights. (*Right*) Aurora borealis, the 'northern lights'. Shimmering auroras in the high northern and southern latitudes are the result of solar winds striking gases in the ionosphere, making the gas molecules glow. The 'southern lights' are known as the aurora australis.

Experimental observation of meteor trails in the 1920s suggested, however, that the temperature about 30 miles up in the stratosphere was in fact about 21 degrees C (70°F) – far higher than the predicted minus 51 degrees C (−60°F). The explanation of this inversion came in the 1930s with the discovery of the ozone layer in the stratosphere. Ozone (a molecule consisting of three oxygen atoms) absorbs ultraviolet radiation from the Sun, becoming warm in the process and also protecting life on the surface of the Earth from harmful rays. The ozone layer turns out to be warmest where it is farthest from the Earth and therefore nearest to the Sun, even though the highest concentration of ozone is actually in the middle of the layer.

The stratopause – where the meteor trails were observed and where the ozone layer ends – is the boundary at which the atmospheric temperature at last starts to drop again. The mesosphere begins here and extends to a height of about 50 miles. In it puzzling noctilucent clouds are sometimes observed; lit by the Sun but visible at night, they hover at a height five times that of the highest clouds in the troposphere. In the ionosphere (sometimes called the thermosphere), which extends from about 50 to 180 miles up, there are wild fluctuations in temperature – reaching as high as 2000 degrees C (3600°F) – although temperature ceases to have its usual meaning when air becomes so rarefied. The aurora belongs to this region, and it is here that the electromagnetic layers lie, which are vital in radio communication. Beyond the ionosphere, the exosphere stretches towards interplanetary space; at an altitude of between 300 and 900 miles from the Earth, there are no longer any air molecules. Until the late 1950s, space was believed to be totally empty. In fact, as the early probes demonstrated, it is full of solar wind, which is responsible for the curved tails of comets and for auroras. The magnetic field of the Earth – a phenomenon yet to be satisfactorily explained – protects Earth from this wind.

Earth's atmosphere is quite different from the atmospheres of its two nearest neighbours in the solar system, Mars and Venus. It contains mainly nitrogen and oxygen, while those of Mars and Venus are almost all carbon dioxide. The average temperature at Earth's surface is 14 degrees C (57°F), suitable for life; Mars and Venus are respectively too cold and too hot for life to survive, so far as we know.

A second inexplicable fact has become known as 'the paradox of the faint young sun'. The Earth receives 99 per cent of its heat from the Sun (the rest comes from the radioactive decay of its core); and yet the Sun emits 25 per cent more heat now than it is estimated to have emitted at the beginning of the Earth, 4600 million years ago.

Planetary atmospheres

	Mars	Earth	Venus
Carbon dioxide	95%	0.03%	96.5%
Nitrogen	2.7%	78%	3.5%
Oxygen	0.13%	21%	trace
Methane	0.0	0.0000017%	0.0
Surface temperature (degrees C)	−53	+14	+459

If the Sun were to cool to its earlier state, the average temperature of the Earth, instead of being 14 degrees C, would fall to somewhere below freezing. Whereas if the Sun were to emit 25 per cent more heat than at present, Earth's average temperature would rise to an inhospitable 30 degrees C (86°F).

What has kept Earth habitable over time? Why has it not become a cold desert like Mars, or a furnace like Venus? This is one of the great riddles of science. Conventional wisdom, which views the Earth as an inert ball of hot rock spun from the debris of the Big Bang, subject only to the laws of physics and chemistry and forever circling the Sun with life clinging to its moist crust, has no convincing answer – just as it cannot shed much light on the origin of life. Scientists of the highest calibre from every major branch of science have examined the latter question. 'We know almost nothing about the origin of life', remarked the physicist Freeman Dyson in 1985. 'The question "What is life?" has many answers, none of which is ultimately satisfying', wrote the chemist Manfred Eigen in 1990. Obviously the composition of Earth's early atmosphere was vital to life, but whether it was a change in the atmosphere that permitted the first life (probably photosynthesizing, oxygen-generating cyanobacteria) to evolve, or the arrival of life that altered the atmosphere, or whether the two changes were symbiotic, is probably impossible to determine.

To define life here and now – in order to define exactly what it was that somehow appeared on Earth eons ago – is itself problematic. Some dictionaries of science avoid the difficulty altogether by omitting the word. 'If we ask a group of scientists, "What is life?", they will answer from the restricted viewpoint of their own particular disciplines', wrote James Lovelock in 1991. He went on to summarize the likely responses of three kinds of scientist:

A physicist will say that life is a peculiar state of matter that reduces its internal entropy* in a flux of free energy, and is characterized by an intricate capacity for self-organization. A neo-darwinist biologist will define a living organism as one able to reproduce and to correct the errors of reproduction through natural selection among its progeny. To a biochemist, a living organism is one that takes in free energy as sunlight, or chemical potential energy, such as food and oxygen, and uses the energy to grow according to the instructions coded in its genes.

*Entropy measures the degree of departure of a system from equilibrium. The *lower* the entropy, the further the system is from equilibrium, and the more ordered it is.

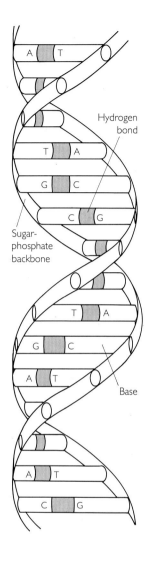

The double helix. DNA (deoxyribonucleic acid) is the basic genetic building block. The framework of the helix is composed of sugar-phosphate units; the rungs are formed by the four nitrogenous bases adenine (A), guanine (G), thymine (T) and cytosine (C). DNA's molecular structure was first proposed in 1953 by James D. Watson and Francis H. Crick. Since then, science has made giant strides in revealing the chemistry of life – but fundamental questions remain unanswered. 'Try defining the word "gene" – you will not find it easy', wrote Crick in 1992.

The origin of life? 'In some warm little pond', Charles Darwin suggested in a letter to Joseph Hooker, 'with all sorts of ammonia and phosphoric salts, light, heat, electricity, etc., present . . . a protein compound was chemically formed ready to undergo still more complex changes.' Early in the process of evolution came the first organisms with the ability to trap the energy of sunlight and use it to drive the chemical processes of life – the first simple, single-celled, photosynthesizing plants. These were the algae. Their modern descendants still flourish in shallow ponds along the world's shores.

Indeed, for the biochemist, life is peculiarly paradoxical. Genes are required to make proteins; proteins then act as catalysts (enzymes) to make all the other chemicals of life, including genes. Each is a prerequisite for the other – so, like the chicken and the egg, which came first? The gene or the protein?

We have no idea. It is barely 40 years since the 'double helix' of DNA (deoxyribonucleic acid), the basic genetic building block, was revealed. The mind-boggling diversity of life is only now dawning on scientists. In the past two and a half centuries, since Linnaeus began to classify species, about 1.5 million species have been recorded, of which only 4000 are mammalian. Many million more species almost certainly remain to be catalogued; some scientists reckon as many as 100 million species exist, which would be 65 times the number currently known to science. According to the theoretical physicist and zoologist Robert M. May, writing in *Scientific American* in 1992, scientists 'have as good a knowledge of the number of atoms in the universe – an unimaginable number – as they do of the number of species of plants and animals.'

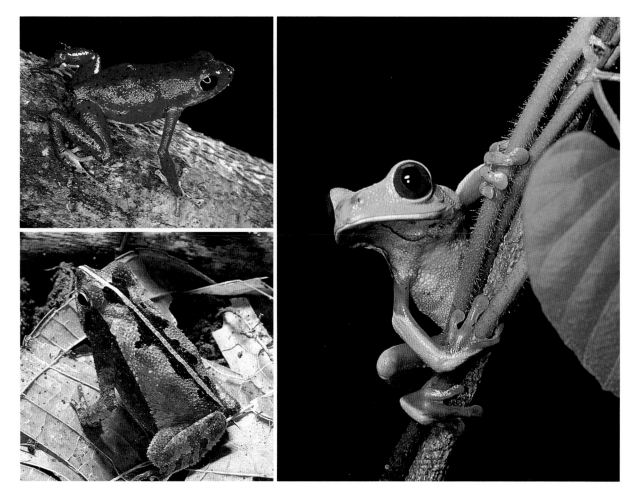

Some of these species are extraordinarily resilient. The diversity of life has largely returned, for instance, to the islands of the Krakatoa (Krakatau) archipelago between Java and Sumatra, a century or so after the devastating volcanic eruption of 1883 – I write 'largely', because we cannot exactly determine what species may have been lost forever, since there are no records of life on the islands prior to this particular big bang. Ordinary volcanic eruptions are not enough, then, to extinguish life at its source. And – another example of resilience – bacteria have regularly turned up buried in sediments more than 1000 feet (300 m) down; recently they were discovered at a depth of over 9000 feet in a borehole drilled by an oil company on the US mainland. Underground experiments with bacteria at shallower depths have proved that they are capable of breaking down organic molecules such as those found in crude oil and releasing acids that quite quickly erode minerals such as quartz. It appears that such deep-living bacteria may have been entombed when rock was first deposited tens or hundreds of millions of years ago and continued to flourish inside

The diversity of life. Frogs from the Panamanian rain forest include wonderfully camouflaged species and brightly coloured poison-arrow species that advertise their toxic nature to would-be predators. Many *millions* of unknown animal and plant species are thought to exist in the world's rain forests.

the Earth while attacking the rock. One of the scientists studying them commented in 1992 that 'things we once saw as abiotic, slow geologic processes may involve microbes.'

It is a significant observation, a small accretion to a gathering consensus that life and its environment are one, not inseparably divided. However, the fact that microbes have survived for millions of years does not mean that Man necessarily will. Scientists do not know why, but there have been at least five mass extinctions of life in Earth's history: the first one 440 million years ago, followed by four more, 365, 245, 210 and 66 million years ago. The last of these wiped out the dinosaurs, among other forms of life. In each case, of course, life recovered – although it seems to have taken at least 20 million years to do so, judging from the fossil record (and in one case it required perhaps 100 million years). The evidence of species extinction today – beginning with the inadequately explained disappearance of megafauna such as the woolly mammoth at the end of the last ice age – patchy as it is, strongly suggests that we are living in another period of mass annihilation. Reflecting on the past extinctions, Edward O. Wilson, a well-known biologist of Harvard University, wrote in 1992: 'These figures should give pause to anyone who believes that what *Homo sapiens* destroys, Nature will redeem. Maybe so, but not within any length of time that has meaning for contemporary humanity.'

CHAPTER

—3—

EARTHQUAKES

It is a bitter and humiliating thing to see works, which have cost men so much time and labour, overthrown in one minute; yet compassion for the inhabitants is almost instantly forgotten, from the interest excited in finding that state of things produced in a moment of time, which one is accustomed to attribute to a succession of ages.
Charles Darwin, March 1835
(reporting the ruin of Concepción in Chile, by an earthquake)

L IAONING province in Manchuria has a significance unique in the history of seismology. In 1975 it became the first place in which an earthquake was successfully predicted by scientific means.

No large earthquake had occurred there for over 100 years (and relatively few moderate ones) when, during early 1974, minor tremors began to increase. In the first five months of the year Chinese scientists measured five times the normal number. They discovered too that much of the region had been uplifted and tilted to the northwest; and that the strength of the Earth's magnetic field was increasing in the area. The State Seismological Bureau in Beijing issued a forecast: Liaoning should expect a moderate to strong earthquake within two years. On 22 December, there was another burst of tremors. The forecast became more focused: expect an earthquake of magnitude 5.5–6 somewhere in the region of Yingkou, a major industrial port, during the first six months of 1975.

All over the affected area, animals started to behave strangely. Snakes awoke from hibernation prematurely and lay frozen in the snow; rats appeared in groups so agitated that they did not fear human beings; small pigs chewed off their tails and ate them. In addition, wells began to bubble. A swarm of tremors – 500 were recorded in 72 hours – culminated in a magnitude-4.8 jolt on the morning of 4 February 1975. Then, quiet.

Animals and earthquake prediction. Reports of peculiar behaviour by animals prior to earthquakes have come from many parts of the world over the past two and a half millennia. Animal precursors are taken especially seriously in China, where they helped to predict a major quake in Liaoning province in 1975. Chinese government posters warn millions of villagers what to look out for.

At 2 p.m. the same day three million people were ordered to leave their homes and spend the night outdoors in straw shelters and tents. Without panic the citizens of southern Liaoning province obeyed. The outside temperature was already many degrees below freezing.

At 7.36 p.m. the earthquake struck – hard. Sheets of light flashed through the sky, the earth heaved; 15-foot (4.6-m) jets of water and sand shot into the air. Roads and bridges buckled; rural communes tumbled down. The majority of buildings in Yingkou and neighbouring Haicheng – the town of 90,000 people that would give its name to the earthquake – were wrecked. But instead of tens of thousands of deaths, there were only some 300.

Eighteen months later, at Tangshan (an industrial and mining centre with a population of a million, 100 miles east of Beijing), the people were much less fortunate. The earthquake, larger than that at Haicheng, struck at 3.43 a.m., unannounced by foreshocks. The few precursors that scientists had observed were either insufficient for a prediction or had been ignored by the authorities. Tangshan was asleep in bed. At least a quarter of a million people, maybe three-quarters of a million, were killed; the actual figure has been officially concealed. It was the worst earthquake toll this century.

The destructive power of earthquakes, coupled with the fires that follow them, is awesome. In China alone they have claimed 13 million lives since records began three millennia ago. Very likely it was an earthquake that destroyed Sodom and Gomorrah. Antioch, a trading and pleasure city on the shores of Asia Minor, was devastated three times by earthquakes, in A D 115, 458 and 526. In central America, Antigua, the capital of Guatemala, was ruined four times from 1586 in less than 300 years; Managua, the capital of Nicaragua, ten times in the past century and a half. In Japan, the 1923 Great Kanto earthquake (as we know) annihilated two-thirds of Tokyo and four-fifths of Yokohama; 7 square miles of Tokyo was left in ashes, as compared with almost 5 square miles in San Francisco after the famous 1906 earthquake. (Just two-thirds of a square mile went up in smoke in the Great Fire of London.)

Yet all these cities, excepting the biblical pair, were rebuilt and flourished on the same site. Within about six years, Tokyo was restored; today it is the world's wealthiest metropolis. How influential in history have earthquakes been, for all their horrors? Certainly less influential than Charles Darwin thought when, after looking at the effect of an earthquake in Chile and speculating on its potential impact on England, he wrote in his journal: 'Earthquakes alone are sufficient to destroy the prosperity of any country.' Tokyo, ironically (given its modern prosperity), is perhaps the one example that would support Darwin's contention, though only in the short term: its partial destruction in 1923 contributed to the making of an economic recession that took Japan down the path to world war in the 1930s.

Explanations of earthquakes until the 18th century were largely supernatural and religious, as might be expected; earthquakes were beyond even Aristotle's powers of analysis. The Greeks blamed Poseidon, god of the sea; Hindus imagined an elephant wearily shaking its head; the Tzotzil Indians of southern Mexico believed in a cosmic jaguar that scratched itself against the pillars of the world. In Japan, a hoary tradition associates earthquakes with the behaviour of the giant catfish, the *namazu*. This is said to live in the mud beneath the Earth's surface and to be restrained from pranks only by the watchful deity Kashima, who keeps a mighty rock on its head. When Kashima relaxes his guard, the *namazu* thrashes impudently about. Woodblock prints, known as *namazu-e*, depict the havoc thus wreaked and the attempts of the victims to revenge themselves on the *namazu* (all except the carpenters and other artisans, that is, who stand to benefit).

In Europe, earthquakes were God's punishment for sin – according to the Church at least. When a gigantic one laid waste Lisbon in November 1755, the Inquisition responded by roasting the survivors in the fires of the *auto-da-fé*; while the pessimist Voltaire published first a poem and then, in 1759, his famous story *Candide*. Both works attacked the Pope – for attributing the earthquake to Man's lack of faith in God – and also the German philosopher and mathematician Leibniz – who optimistically held that God must have sent the earthquake as part of His plan for the Earth. Why Lisbon? why not decadent London or Paris? questioned Voltaire in the poem: 'Lisbon lies in ruins, while in Paris they dance.' In *Candide* he satirized three typical reactions to the tragedy – that of the common man, the philosopher (Pangloss) and the innocent (Candide):

> The sailor said with a whistle and an oath: 'There'll be some rich pickings here.'
> 'What can be the sufficient reason for this phenomenon?' wondered Pangloss.
> 'The end of the world is come!' Candide shouted.

In London, Lisbon's shaking provoked perhaps the earliest recognizably modern thinking about earthquakes. Five years before, in 1750, Londoners had been disconcerted by several tremors. Observation of and reflection upon these and the Lisbon shock led John Michell, a clergyman lecturing at Cambridge University, to the idea that earthquakes were 'waves set up by

Earthquakes as acts of God. In Japanese tradition, a giant catfish (a *namazu*) was responsible for earthquakes. Its antics, depicted in popular wood-block prints, could be restrained only by the Kashima god who kept the head of the catfish pinned down with a keystone. Here, four penitent *namazu* – personifying past quakes – lamely explain that they were jealous because other fish were usurping their place in local cuisine.

shifting masses of rock miles below the surface': also, that there were two kinds of wave, one followed by the other; and that their speed and the centre of the earthquake could be determined by measuring the waves' arrival times at different locations. This principle is still used today to determine an earthquake's epicentre (surface location).

Michell's insights lay dormant in the world of science for almost a century. Meanwhile, in 1783, the world's first earthquake commission was appointed as a result of several disastrous quakes in Calabria in southern Italy, in which the Neapolitan secretary of war lost six members of his family. The Academy of Sciences and Fine Letters of the kingdom of Naples tabulated the effects of the earthquakes and produced a detailed report. It led to the creation of an intensity scale for earthquakes: the earliest, albeit crude, effort to quantify the phenomenon. Based on damage and loss of life, as today's scales are, it classified Italian earthquakes as either slight, moderate, strong, very strong or violent (those in Calabria).

The concept was further refined as a result of another shock in southern Italy in 1857. The report of it reaching London had immediately attracted a brilliant Irish engineer, Robert Mallet, to the kingdom of Naples. Assessing every crack of the damage with a trained eye, he compiled isoseismal maps: that is, maps with contours of equal earthquake damage/intensity (again a method employed today, with refinements, to map seismic hazard). Mallet's maps allowed him to estimate the centre of the shaking and the relative size of the earthquake. More important still, over 20 years Mallet assembled a catalogue of world seismicity. It contained 6831 listings, giving the date, location, number of shocks, probable direction and duration of the seismic waves, along with notes on related effects. The world map he created from this

Messina, Sicily, 1908. One of 120,000 victims of Italy's worst recorded earthquake, which registered a magnitude of 7.5.

(*Opposite*) **'Civilization exists by geological consent**, subject to change without notice', said the US writer Will Durant. On 23 November 1980, a 7.2-magnitude earthquake struck Lioni in Italy, 50 miles east of Naples. There were 3000 deaths; about 2000 people went missing and 300,000 people were made homeless. Here a young priest searches for a friend in the rubble. Shortly after the photograph was taken, the friend was found – dead.

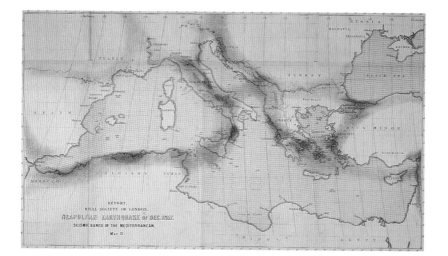

The first map of seismic zones. Still accurate today, the map was inspired by detailed observations of Italian earthquakes, and drawn in 1857 by the Irish engineer Robert Mallet on the basis of an enormous catalogue of historic earthquakes. Mallet could not explain the zones; now, plate tectonic theory provides some explanation, but by no means a complete one.

The earliest known seismometer (model). During an earthquake of sufficient intensity, a ball would drop from a dragon's mouth into a frog's. In AD 138, the seismometer was said to have enabled its inventor Chang Heng to announce the occurrence of a major earthquake 400 miles to the northwest of the Chinese capital Loyang – long before news of the devastation arrived by messengers on galloping horses.

information was the first indication that earthquakes cluster in certain belts around the Earth. An explanation of why this is so, involving plate tectonics, would wait another century, but in the meantime Mallet's map focused the attention of science on the problem.

Intensity of an earthquake is not to be confused with its *magnitude*, the figure generally reported in newspapers. Intensity measures the size of a quake, as does magnitude, but whereas magnitude is calculated from the vibration of a pendulum in a seismograph, intensity is based on visible damage to structures built by humans, on changes in the Earth's surface and on felt reports (e.g. the effects on a person driving a car at the time). Intensity measures what human beings see as a result of an earthquake; magnitude, what scientific instruments see.

The particular intensity scale normally used today – there are several others also in use – is a modified form of that created by the Italian seismologist Giuseppe Mercalli in 1902. It has major drawbacks. A glance will show the subjective nature of a measurement, and that it depends on building construction quality, which cannot easily be assessed: one house may remain standing in an earthquake, for instance, while another one next door fails. The scale is also 'culturally' dependent: an intensity indicator useful in one context may be useless in another. Damage to stone and reinforced concrete buildings is important in, say, San Francisco, but scarcely relevant in a Third World village. In fact, Californian earthquake scientists have suggested modifying Mercalli's scale for California so as to include the level of disturbance in grocery, liquor and furniture stores and even the motion induced in waterbeds! Finally, and least satisfactorily, the Mercalli scale takes no account at all of the observer's distance from the epicentre: a small quake close by him can register a higher intensity than a large quake far away from him.

Still, intensity scales are extremely useful. Many areas of the world lack seismographs capable of measuring the ground motion in strong earthquakes. Also, the seismic record before the 20th century consists only of intensity reports. Intensity is thus the only quantitative way to compare a pre-20th-century earthquake with a modern one.

The invention of the modern seismograph and the introduction of scientific rigour into earthquake measurement date from the 1890s and the work of an adventurous Englishman in Japan. John Milne became professor of geology and mining in 1876 at the new Imperial College of Engineering in Tokyo. His initial attempts to monitor earthquakes produced a flood of information, by the

simple means of sending out every week self-addressed question-
naire postcards to conscientious postmasters and middle-level
government officials within 100 miles of Tokyo, with the request
that they fill in details of all tremors. But by the late 1880s, Milne
had become dissatisfied with such imprecision and seismic paro-
chiality. He wanted an accurate instrument to measure earthquakes
all over the world.

Seismographs already had a long history. The earliest one in
existence (dated A D 132) was the work of the Chinese astronomer
and mathematician Chang Heng: it consisted of eight dragons
mounted around a base consisting of eight toads with open
mouths; even a slight tremor would shift a pendulum within the
base which activated lever devices that caused a bronze ball to drop
from a dragon's mouth into a toad's mouth with a resonant clang.
Later seismographs, although less fantastic and somewhat more
exact, continued to be cumbersome.

Milne's seismographs employed the pendulum principle too, as
indeed do all seismographs. The inertia of a large, freely suspended
weight makes it lag behind the movement of its frame: the
mechanism of the seismograph arranges for this relative motion to
be recorded. By using three pendulums that could bob up and
down and swing from side to side like a door on its hinges, both the

---

Modified Mercalli Intensity Scale (1931)

I Not felt except by a very few under especially favourable circumstances.

II Felt only by a few persons at rest, especially on upper floors of buildings. Delicately suspended objects may swing.

III Felt quite noticeably indoors, especially on upper floors of buildings, but many people do not recognize it as an earthquake. Standing motor cars may rock slightly. Vibration like passing of truck. Duration estimated.

IV During the day felt indoors by many, outdoors by few. At night some awakened. Dishes, windows, doors disturbed; walls make cracking sound. Sensation like heavy truck striking building. Standing motor cars rocked noticeably.

V Felt by nearly everyone, many awakened. Some dishes, windows, etc., broken; a few instances of cracked plaster; unstable objects overturned. Disturbances of trees, poles, and other tall objects sometimes noticed. Pendulum clocks may stop.

VI Felt by all, many frightened and run outdoors. Some heavy furniture moved; a few instances of fallen plaster or damaged chimneys. Damage slight.

VII Everybody runs outdoors. Damage negligible in buildings of good design and construction; slight to moderate in well-built ordinary structures; considerable in poorly built or badly designed structures; some chimneys broken. Noticed by persons driving motor cars.

VIII Damage slight in specially designed structures; considerable in ordinary substantial buildings, with partial collapse; great in poorly built structures. Panel walls thrown out of frame structures. Fall of chimneys, factory stacks, columns, monuments, walls. Heavy furniture overturned. Sand and mud ejected in small amounts. Changes in well water. Persons driving motor cars disturbed.

XI Damage considerable in specially designed structures; well-designed frame structures thrown out of plumb; great in substantial buildings, with partial collapse. Buildings shifted off foundations. Ground cracked conspicuously. Underground pipes broken.

X Some well-built wooden structures destroyed; most masonry and frame structures destroyed with foundations; ground badly cracked. Rails bent. Landslides considerable from river banks and steep slopes. Shifted sand and mud. Water splashed (slopped) over banks.

XI Few, if any (masonry) structures remain standing. Bridges destroyed. Broad fissures in ground. Underground pipelines completely out of service. Earth slumps and land slips in soft ground. Rails bent greatly.

XII Damage total. Practically all works of construction are damaged greatly or destroyed. Waves seen on ground surface. Lines of sight and level are distorted. Objects are thrown upwards into the air.

John Milne, the first modern seismologist. Though born in Britain, Milne did his most important work in Japan from the late 1870s, which included the designing of the first practical seismograph. In 1895, he retired with his Japanese wife to Britain, where his house became the headquarters of the world's first network for seismic monitoring. The montage is taken from the front page of Britain's *Daily Mirror*, which was entirely given over to Milne when he died in 1913.

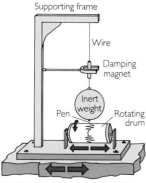

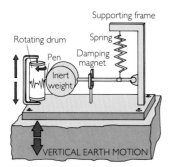

The essentials of the seismograph. The instrument at the top measures horizontal Earth motion, that at the bottom vertical Earth motion. In both cases, the supporting frame and rotating drum move during an earthquake while the inert weight does not: a pen attached to the weight therefore traces a line on the paper of the drum corresponding to the Earth's seismic movements.

vertical and the twin horizontal vibrations of an earthquake could be monitored.

The first version by Milne used a stylus attached to the weight that inscribed a trace on revolving smoked paper – a method sometimes still employed in the field for its reliability. Afterwards, in 1893, Milne adapted the instrument to record the trace on revolving photographic film. Nowadays, the relative motion is converted into an electrical signal, amplified electronically thousands or even hundreds of thousands of times, and recorded either by a stylus on paper or by magnetic tape. So-called 'strong-motion' seismographs positioned close to an epicentre record major ground movements that would overload normal instruments.

With enough knowledge and experience of an earthquake's region, and with the help of computers, a seismologist can derive much information from the tangled trace of a typical seismogram. The National Earthquake Information Service of the US Geological Survey (USGS) in Golden, Colorado analyses seismograms recorded at many hundreds of stations over the globe. It can determine the magnitude, duration and epicentre of an earthquake; its depth of origin below the surface (the focus or hypocentre); the direction and magnitude of movement of the geological fault that produced it; the orientation and extent of the fault; the physical properties of the material between the quake and the seismograph; and possibly details of the Earth's structure in the region.

There are two basic types of earthquake wave, as the clergyman John Michell had first perceived after the Lisbon earthquake: body waves, that propagate from the earthquake focus to the surface; and surface waves, that are produced by the transformation of some

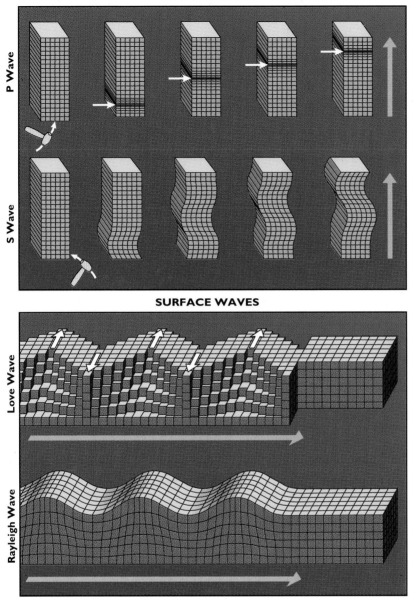

BODY WAVES

P Wave

S Wave

SURFACE WAVES

Love Wave

Rayleigh Wave

Waves in the ground. There are two basic types of earthquake wave: *body waves* (top), that are transmitted from the earthquake focus underground (the hypocentre) to the surface; and *surface waves* (bottom), that are produced in the ground by the transformation of some body waves once they reach the surface. The body waves consist of P (primary) waves, and S (secondary) waves. The two types of surface wave are named after the mathematician Love and the physicist Rayleigh who defined them. P waves travel fastest (up to four miles per second); the first movement felt in an earthquake is therefore caused by a P wave. It moves fastest because it is condensational, like a sound wave, compressing and expanding rock and liquid in the same direction in which it moves. On reaching the surface, it makes the ground – and the seismograph – move principally in the vertical axis. (It also compresses the air, sometimes creating the 'express-train' roar of a big earthquake.) The S wave, by contrast, is distortional: it moves with a side-to-side shearing motion, like a radio wave, and this makes it slower and unable to travel through liquids. It makes the ground move both vertically and horizontally. Since buildings can stand but little horizontal stress, S waves do far more damage than P waves.

body waves on reaching the surface. Both types may be monitored by a sensitive seismograph. A relatively simple calculation then permits the determination of the epicentre (see page 56).

After epicentre, the next most significant quantity connected with an earthquake is magnitude. Unlike intensity, magnitude is defined by science to be independent of the distance of the observer from the epicentre. It is, so to speak, the amount of explosive in a bomb, as opposed to the bomb's effects (the intensity of an explosion). An earthquake can have only one magnitude, fundamentally; but it will have many intensities.

Measuring an earthquake.

(*Below*) How to find an epicentre. A seismogram gives the distance of an earthquake's epicentre from the seismographic station. If three such distances are calculated from three different stations, the precise epicentre of the earthquake can be calculated using three intersecting circles. Here, the stations selected are Antofagasta (Chile), Honolulu (Hawaii) and Golden (Colorado); the epicentre is at Veracruz (Mexico). (*Below right*) This seismogram shows three traces made at Golden by a small earthquake at Veracruz on 11 March 1967. The top trace shows the *vertical* motion of the seismograph; the middle and bottom traces show the *horizontal* motions (at right angles to each other). The P waves arrive first, followed four seconds later by the S waves; then the Love and Rayleigh waves arrive. By combining the information from several seismograms of this earthquake obtained at various stations, scientists calculated the epicentre to lie at 19.10 N 95.80 W (in the sea just east of Veracruz); the focus to be 20.5 miles down; and the magnitude to be 5.5. There were three injuries and moderate property damage at Veracruz.

Scientists calculate magnitude from the shaking recorded on the seismogram and the distance of the seismograph from the epicentre. These calculations are quite tricky, and there are several scales currently in use. By far the best known is the Richter scale, originally devised in 1935 by Charles Richter to measure only local earthquake magnitudes in southern California, but later modified to apply globally. (Journalists generally report an earthquake's magnitude as having been measured on the 'Richter scale', whether or not it really has been – an imprecision that maddens seismologists.) Because the size of earthquakes varies enormously, the scale is not a linear but a logarithmic one. The effect is that an increase of 1 in magnitude corresponds to a *ten-fold* increase in amplitude of shaking. An earthquake of magnitude 8 shakes the ground 10 times more than one of magnitude 7, and 100 times more than one of magnitude 6. Nevertheless, a magnitude-6 earthquake may be *more* destructive than a magnitude-8 earthquake, if its epicentre happens to coincide with a heavily populated area.

The plotting of epicentres on a map of the world – first undertaken by Mallet – shows that 999 out of 1000 earthquakes, and an even larger fraction of those of high magnitude, occur in certain belts. A map of earthquake foci – the depth of the quake below the epicentre – is equally revealing. Together, these patterns provide powerful evidence for the existence of plate tectonics.

The foci of Californian earthquakes are all shallow, within the top 10 miles of the Earth's crust. The same is true of earthquakes near Pacific ocean trenches, such as the Tonga Trench and the Japan Trench. But as earthquakes move west towards Asia, away from the Japan Trench, their foci deepen dramatically: 50 to 150 miles deep below the Japanese islands, 300 miles under the Sea of Japan, and 400 miles beneath the coast of Manchuria.

The reason is the behaviour of the Pacific plate. For millions of

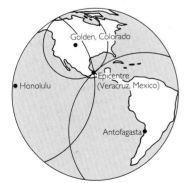

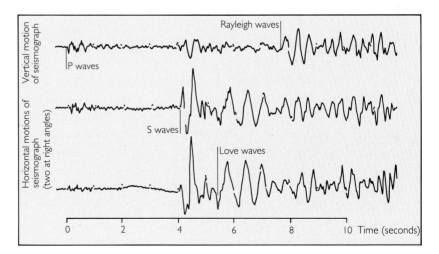

years it has been moving beneath the less dense plate on which Asia rides, dipping down into the Earth at an angle of 35 degrees and more. The 'subduction zone' thus created is where the earthquakes originate. By contrast, in California the Pacific plate is not being subducted beneath the North American plate – though there *was* subduction at an earlier geological time – but instead is grinding past it. Californian earthquakes originate at the shallow junction of the plates; the rock deep beneath California is comparatively undisturbed.

The explanations of earthquakes generated by plate tectonics have a 'seductive elegance', in the words of one geophysicist. But they can conceal some awkward facts, as we already know. Three violent earthquakes, among the greatest known in the United States, took place in 1811–12 in Missouri – far indeed from any plate boundary. There was another large one in Charleston, South Carolina, in 1886, again far from the usual earthquake zones. Nor are the more stolid parts of Europe entirely safe from earthquakes. In 1990, a magnitude-5.2 quake struck Britain – one of many recorded there since Roman times; it ruptured gas mains, cracked masonry and toppled chimneys. In 1992, a bigger and more

Nowhere in the world is entirely free from earthquakes, not even Britain. There have been more than 120 shocks each century in Britain, and one in 1990 registered a magnitude of 5.2. The worst British earthquake occurred on 22 April 1884. Felt within a radius of 150 miles, it shattered more than 1200 buildings and made virtually the entire population of a village in Essex homeless. In the Houses of Parliament in London, members were stopped in their tracks, jolted against walls, or had papers and briefcases jerked from their hands.

(*Opposite*) **The mighty forces of plate tectonics.** (*Above*) The southern section of the San Andreas fault exposed by a highway cut near Palmdale, some 45 miles north of Los Angeles, displays the inexorable power of shifting plates. It also shows the complexity of the fault – and hence the tremendous obstacles in the way of accurate earthquake prediction in California. (*Below*) In October 1989, the northern part of the fault moved abruptly and caused the collapse of a half-mile stretch of double-decker freeway on the east side of San Francisco Bay.

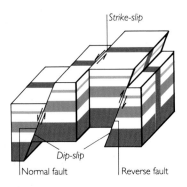

Types of geological fault (see page 60).

An earthquake that shouldn't have occurred. According to plate tectonic theory, Australia's Northern Territory should not experience earthquakes, being far from a plate boundary. But in 1988, a series of magnitude-6 quakes ruptured the surface there. At present, scientists have no satisfactory explanation for such 'stable-continent' quakes.

destructive earthquake struck the Dutch/Belgian/German border. Even the Lisbon earthquake of 1755, thought by Richter to be the world's greatest historic earthquake, is an odd one out of the pattern predicted by plate tectonics. As far as geophysicists know, there are no active plate boundaries in any of these areas of the US or Europe – at least none that fit into the existing map.

The great depth of many earthquakes is also a puzzle. The subduction theory seems to offer a reasonable explanation, until one learns of occasional earthquakes at depth in places where there is no apparent subduction. In 1977, for instance, Bucharest was shaken by an earthquake 100 miles down, and 1500 people died. This might be attributed to an old subduction zone obscured by later tectonic activity; not so the tremors recorded beneath Spain and north Africa. Rather more seriously, physics does not in fact expect *any* earthquakes below about 30 miles – some calculations indicate a much smaller figure – because rock in a laboratory squeezed at analogous temperatures and pressures becomes ductile, and flows rather than fractures. Indeed the fundamental concept of moving plates is predicated on the existence of such ductility at depth.

If these observations suggest that the theory of earthquakes rests on shakier ground than might be wished, that is undoubtedly the case.

'Earthquakes don't kill people; buildings do.' The earthquake in Armenia in 1988 reinforced this long-standing seismological truth. The magnitude of the first shock was 6.9 – the same as in San Francisco in 1989 – but it and the swarms of aftershocks levelled more than half the structures in the city of Leninakan, the result of both design deficiencies and faulty construction practices. Many churches, with their high unsupported roofs, collapsed, but some almost miraculously survived.

Let us have a look at how the mechanism is supposed to operate (though it is a model that has increasingly been challenged). It all starts with a fault, a joint between two rock planes. The joint is usually not exactly vertical and so one plane of the fault overhangs the other. If the overhanging plane moves downwards, the fault is *normal*; if it moves upwards, it is termed a *reverse* fault. Movement in the vertical axis is known as *dip-slip*; that in the horizontal axis as *strike-slip*. Of course, a real fault often shows both kinds of slip.

Friction between the two planes of the fault controls its movement or lack of movement. The lower the friction, the weaker the fault and the more easily it slips. If the friction is low enough, the fault may slip constantly and aseismically; this is known as fault creep. If it is of medium size, the fault may slip frequently, producing many small earthquakes. But if the friction is high, the fault may slip only occasionally, and there will be few, but large, earthquakes. Even then, the rupture may not be entirely visible at the surface. The 1906 San Francisco earthquake produced a huge surface rupture of 270 miles, while the 1988 earthquake in Armenia (somewhat less powerful but terribly destructive) produced a visible rupture of only 5–7½ miles out of a total of 30 miles of monitored movement; the rest remained underground.

The phrase 'elastic rebound' was coined by the seismologist H. F. Reid to describe the mechanism of rupture in the 1906 quake, and by extension in all earthquakes. He noticed how in the years before the earthquake, roads, fences, and streams crossing the fault area had been deformed, and how afterwards they were offset – by up to 21 feet (6.4 m). He proposed that friction between the sides of the fault – the plate boundary, as we now call it – had locked part of the fault together, deforming it as the plates moved past each other, until finally the fault snapped and the sides sprang away from each other and settled into less strained conformations.

The fault in question was, of course, the now famous San Andreas fault. The San Andreas fault system is undoubtedly 'the most well known plate-tectonic boundary in the world', in the words of the US Geological Survey's special report on it, published in 1990: a great scar running up most of California, geologically highly complex, where the Pacific plate edges northwest past the North American plate at the rate of 1–1½ inches (2½–4 cm) per year. Altogether, with its many adjacent faults, the system is 60 miles wide and 800 miles long.

Its origins were brilliantly suggested in 1965 by the pioneer of plate tectonics, J. Tuzo Wilson. He postulated that the San Andreas fault was a transform fault between two spreading oceanic ridges within the Pacific plate (see page 26). Later analysis by others elaborated his idea with calculations that took account of the forces acting globally on the Pacific plate, and confirmed the general picture of the Pacific plate slipping past – and sometimes sticking against – the North American plate, rather than being subducted as it is in the western Pacific.

The detailed picture is infinitely harder to unravel, alas, despite decades of labour and state-of-the-art instruments monitoring every conceivable aspect of the fault on and near its surface, if not as yet within its enigmatic depths. The motives behind such efforts are partly scientific and partly, of course, to anticipate and avoid disaster in San Francisco, Los Angeles, and the many other centres of population and industry in one of the world's wealthiest areas.

Attention is focused on two stretches of the fault: the northern section, 270 miles long, that ruptured in 1906; and, even more critically, the southern section, 185 miles long, that has not slipped since the equally powerful earthquake at Fort Tejon in 1857. At that time Los Angeles was only a small town, population 4000, located 40 miles from the fault. Some of its houses developed cracks but none was severely damaged. Two people in the entire region of

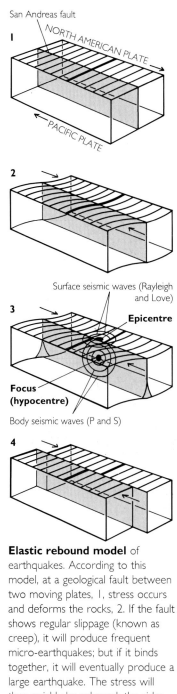

Elastic rebound model of earthquakes. According to this model, at a geological fault between two moving plates, 1, stress occurs and deforms the rocks, 2. If the fault shows regular slippage (known as creep), it will produce frequent micro-earthquakes; but if it binds together, it will eventually produce a large earthquake. The stress will then quickly be released; the sides of the fault will become offset, 3 (maybe producing a surface rupture); and the rocks will *rebound* to their initial state of stress, 4. Although in practice it has many difficulties, this model of earthquake mechanism remains the one most widely employed.

'*THE most well-known plate-tectonic boundary in the world'*, the US Geological Survey calls it, with justification. The fault runs up most of California. The photograph at left shows the fault at its most dramatic, as it bisects the Carrizo Plain some 100 miles north of Los Angeles. The slippage of the fault – creep – causes streams to be offset, drains to fracture and front doors to jam shut while house owners are away on holiday. It is the visible manifestation of the movement of two tectonic plates, the Pacific plate and the North American plate, grinding past each other. However, some sections of the fault do not slip regularly; they bind together, strain builds up, and eventually there is a rupture – a major earthquake.

In October 1989, such a quake struck south of San Francisco. A 30-foot (9-m) section of the Bay Bridge from Oakland to San Francisco collapsed, and cars had to be winched out of it (above). Altogether, 62 people perished, and the total repair bill was at least $6 thousand million. In mid-1992, an even more powerful (though infinitely less destructive) quake hit the desert area east of Los Angeles. A subsidiary fault, not the main fault, was responsible. Was the quake a precursor of the 'Big One' to come – or a welcome relief of strain? The debate among scientists is fierce.

The San Andreas fault

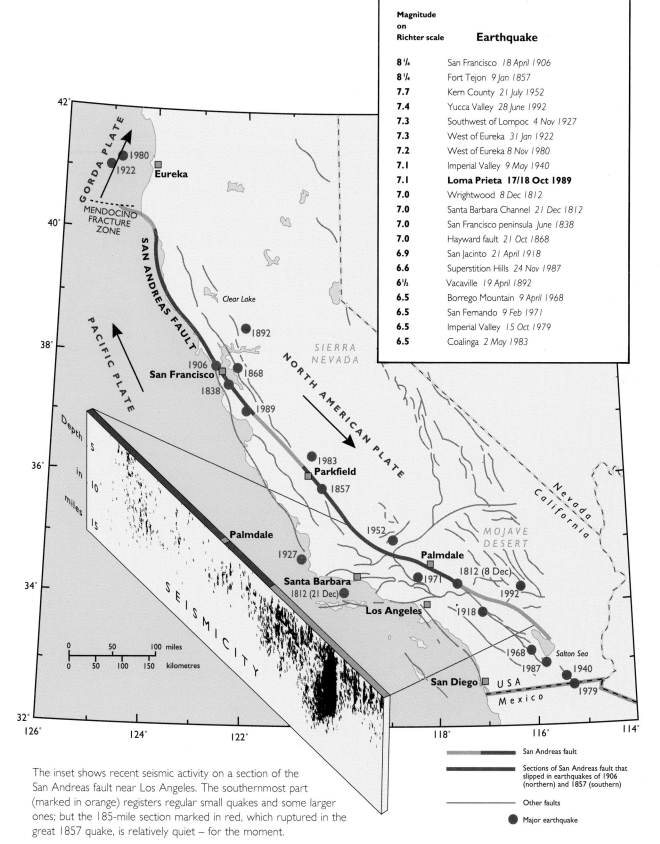

PRINCIPAL EARTHQUAKES OF THE SAN ANDREAS FAULT

Magnitude on Richter scale	Earthquake
8 1/4	San Francisco *18 April 1906*
8 1/4	Fort Tejon *9 Jan 1857*
7.7	Kern County *21 July 1952*
7.4	Yucca Valley *28 June 1992*
7.3	Southwest of Lompoc *4 Nov 1927*
7.3	West of Eureka *31 Jan 1922*
7.2	West of Eureka *8 Nov 1980*
7.1	Imperial Valley *9 May 1940*
7.1	**Loma Prieta 17/18 Oct 1989**
7.0	Wrightwood *8 Dec 1812*
7.0	Santa Barbara Channel *21 Dec 1812*
7.0	San Francisco peninsula *June 1838*
7.0	Hayward fault *21 Oct 1868*
6.9	San Jacinto *21 April 1918*
6.6	Superstition Hills *24 Nov 1987*
6 1/2	Vacaville *19 April 1892*
6.5	Borrego Mountain *9 April 1968*
6.5	San Fernando *9 Feb 1971*
6.5	Imperial Valley *15 Oct 1979*
6.5	Coalinga *2 May 1983*

The inset shows recent seismic activity on a section of the San Andreas fault near Los Angeles. The southernmost part (marked in orange) registers regular small quakes and some larger ones; but the 185-mile section marked in red, which ruptured in the great 1857 quake, is relatively quiet – for the moment.

San Andreas fault

Sections of San Andreas fault that slipped in earthquakes of 1906 (northern) and 1857 (southern)

Other faults

● Major earthquake

southern California were killed. And that, apart from bad damage to Fort Tejon, was about all.

Compare the effects of the recent major San Andreas earthquake – only magnitude 6.9 as compared to an estimated $8\frac{1}{4}$ in the 1857 and 1906 quakes – centred on Loma Prieta, south of San Francisco, in 1989. It happened when the southernmost 25 miles of the northern section of the San Andreas fault ruptured. There were 62 fatalities and nearly 4000 people were injured; about 1000 homes were destroyed and many more damaged; at least $6 thousand million of damage was done, mainly in San Francisco (especially its Marina area) – some reports said a great deal more.

A particular cause for alarm is the pattern of seismicity along the fault in recent decades. Tremors are frequent along a substantial part of its length (although not so much along the two sections that ruptured in 1857 and 1906). But the section closest to Los Angeles is eerily quiet, with barely the tiniest of tremors. When the fault finally ruptures again, this century or next, will there be pre-cursors: swarms of tremors as there were at Haicheng in 1975? Or just a sudden shocking wrench, like the one that levelled Tangshan the following year?

A series of moderate-sized quakes near (but not exactly on) the San Andreas south of Los Angeles, where the fault reaches the Salton Sea, began to worry scientists from the late 1980s. In 1992, the quakes culminated in a magnitude-6 quake at Joshua Tree, followed by a magnitude-7.4 quake at Landers. Were Californians witnessing a menacing build-up? No one has any clear idea: the recent series of quakes may have made a major quake more likely in the next few decades, but they could also, by releasing stress, have diminished the likelihood.

The principal difficulty in choosing an answer is that the fault does not properly obey the 'elastic rebound' model of how earthquakes are said to work. Take fault temperature, for instance. Leaving aside the bursts of heat produced by an actual rupture, one would naturally expect the temperature at the fault to be higher than it is away from it, since steady heat should be generated by friction as the two plates rub against each other (rather as heat is produced by rubbing one's hands together). 'However,' says the USGS report, 'the frictional heating predicted for the process has never been detected. Thus, in spite of its importance to an understanding of both plate motion and earthquakes, the size of this frictional stress is still uncertain, even in order of magnitude.'

The forces measured at the fault are in fact completely cock-eyed: in scientific terms, the stress is high-angle. Instead of being aligned along the fault, the stress acts principally at right angles to it, in a NE–SW orientation, instead of NW–SE, as expected.

Instead of acting to shear the fault, the stress seems to be trying to pull it apart. If this is correct, the San Andreas fault, far from being strong, is actually remarkably weak.

There is other evidence to support this surprising conclusion. Earthquakes do not produce the large drop in stress required by calculations based on the 'elastic rebound' model of a fault. If they did, even a small earthquake would cause the ground to move 100 yards (90 m) at 25 mph: not even insects would survive! Until recently, this was explained away by saying that much of the initial stress remained in a fault after a quake – hence the aftershocks. But studies of the San Andreas fault at the time of the Loma Prieta quake in 1989 have finally disproved this theory. A USGS team compared the direction of small shocks before and after the quake and found the aftershocks to be oriented 'every which way', not in the direction of the earlier shocks. In other words, the initial earthquake had dissipated virtually all the stress on the fault. They concluded that the initial stress on the fault must have been lower than that predicted by the model.

A further misfit between model and reality concerns the speed of rupture. Obviously scientists can rarely hope to observe a rupture as it occurs. But eye-witness accounts by others suggest that the process is much faster than 'elastic rebound' allows. The fault slips much more easily than expected. In a report of a 7.2-magnitude quake in Idaho in 1983, one side of a fault was seen to be shoved a yard into the air in just one second. If conventional friction had been restraining it, the slippage should have taken ten times as long.

'Weak Faults: Breaking Out All Over', headlined *Science* in a 1992 report on earthquake research. 'Earthquakes used to be simple', it warned at the outset, and promptly went on to quote a Stanford University geophysicist, Mark Zoback, with years of San Andreas experience: 'We fundamentally don't understand how earthquakes work. After all these years, we don't have a clue.' Not every earthquake scientist is as gloomy as this, but all admit the severe limitations of the existing model.

As an example of how far thinking about earthquakes has changed (leaving aside its validity, which is unproven), models of fault movement seriously proposed now include banana peels slipping slickly past each other; a melting ice cube that slides across a counter top when pushed from above rather than from the side (the direction of the force represents the high-angle stress in real faults such as the San Andreas); and a wrinkle passing rapidly through a rug instead of the entire rug being clumsily tugged (carpet fitters have long used this principle). This last model is akin to the movement of defects in metal crystal lattices during metal dislocation and deformation.

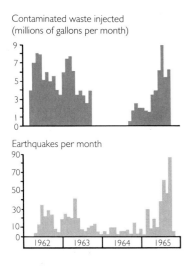

Contaminated waste injected
(millions of gallons per month)

Earthquakes per month

Lubricating an earthquake.
Fluids can help to trigger a quake:
this is evident from the comparison
of earthquake frequency between
1962 and 1965 near Denver,
Colorado and the frequency of
injection of fluid into a deep well
over the same period in the same
area. The fluid seems to reduce
friction in faults, rather as oil
reduces friction in a rusty hinge.

Despite their diversity, all the models are agreed on one point: something comes between the sides of the fault and lubricates it, making it weak. 'Upward migration of fluids may trigger the occurrence of earthquakes', wrote a USGS scientist, Thomas H. Heaton, in a significant survey of earthquake mechanisms. At the temperatures and pressures 3–10 miles down (where San Andreas earthquakes occur), the lubricant cannot be ground rock or clay, but it could be mineral fluids trapped in the fault when it was formed or alternatively pumped up from the more ductile region below the fault. It might also be water: there seems to be plenty of water deep in a fault, judging from the appearance of faults exhumed by erosion. In fact, evidence from areas other than the San Andreas fault substantially supports the idea that water can lubricate faults. In the early 1960s, for instance, a series of earthquakes occurred near Denver in Colorado, where hitherto the natural seismicity had always been low. Between April 1962 and September 1963 local seismographic stations registered more than 700 epicentres with magnitudes of up to 4.3. Then there was a sharp decline in seismicity during 1964, followed by another series of quakes during 1965. It turned out that the US army was injecting contaminated water from weapons production at its Rocky Mountain arsenal northeast of Denver into a deep well, bored to a depth of about 12,000 feet (3660 m). Injection of the water began in March 1962 and ceased in September 1963 for a year. It resumed in September 1964 and finally ceased in September 1965. Residents of Denver, alarmed at the earthquakes, succeeded in stopping the method of disposal.

With the knowledge of this chance experiment in mind, the USGS began a designed experiment in 1969 at an oil field in Rangely, western Colorado. Using existing oil wells, water was injected into a well or pumped out at will and the pore pressure of the crustal rock measured (that is, the pressure of fluid absorbed by the rock). At the same time an array of seismographs, specially installed in the area, monitored seismicity. There turned out to be an excellent correlation between higher fluid pore pressure and increase in seismicity. In both the Denver and Rangely cases, therefore, it appears that water entered faults underground and lubricated them, causing earthquakes. Conceivably the fact might be used to relieve stress selectively on a fault such as the San Andreas; if controlled small earthquakes could be triggered, large damaging ones might be prevented. The idea is potentially so hazardous, however, that it is unlikely to be applied until our grasp of earthquake mechanism improves dramatically. But it might be worth trying in order to relieve rock stress during the construction of a dam.

Dams provide incontrovertible evidence that water can lubricate rock movement – probably by infiltrating faults beneath the reservoir rather than by increasing the direct pressure on the rock (calculations show that this increase is fairly small, compared to normal rock pressures a few miles down). Not that the majority of large dams have demonstrated increased seismicity when filled, but there have been a number of significant exceptions, a few of them worrying. The first was at Lake Mead, behind the Hoover Dam in Nevada-Arizona: earthquakes reached a peak there in 1940, five years after impoundment (filling) of water began, and then decreased. When Lake Kariba in Zambia was being filled between 1958 and 1963, there were hundreds more earthquakes per year than usual; the biggest, in September 1963, had a magnitude of 5.8. After that, activity declined. And in Egypt, near the Aswan High Dam, an earthquake of magnitude 5.6 with aftershocks was reported in 1981. No significant earthquake had been measured in upper Egypt since global seismology began at the turn of the century, nor did the historical record going back 3000 years mention any large earthquake. The 1981 shock, with its epicentre below an extensive bay of Lake Nasser about 40 miles from the dam, was therefore probably an effect of the lake. It is likely that the very porous sandstones along the Nile have absorbed a huge volume of water, thereby creating large changes in pore pressure.

But the most serious case to date was at Koyna in India, in 1967. The area of the dam was one of low seismicity (unlike that of the dam planned in the Himalayas at Tehri, which was hit by a destructive magnitude-7.1 quake in late 1991). Reports of shaking in the Koyna region became common after 1962, when impoundment of the reservoir began, and seismographs showed the earthquake foci to be at shallow depths below the Shivajisagar Lake. During 1967 there were a number of sizeable quakes, climaxing in December with a shock that caused damage to buildings, killed over 200 people and injured many more. A strong-motion seismograph in the dam gallery registered a massive sideways acceleration of 0.63 times the acceleration due to gravity. The intensity of damage measured X on the Modified Mercalli scale (see page 53).

The fact that earthquake prediction as a science has had a chequered history is hardly to be wondered at. 'One may compare it to the situation of a man who is bending a board across his knee and attempts to determine in advance just where and when the cracks will appear', wrote Charles Richter in 1958. 'All claims to predict the future have a hold on the imagination; it is not surprising that even qualified seismologists have been led astray by the will-o'-the-wisp of prediction.'

Scientists' hopes for long-term prediction are pinned mainly on a cyclical concept arising from the 'elastic rebound' model: fault stress is thought to build at a constant rate and be dissipated abruptly in regularly occurring ruptures. We shall return to this idea. In the short term, everything depends on precursors and, by extension, the instrumentation, personnel and social organization necessary to observe and measure them. Possible precursors include foreshocks, changes in ground strain, tilt, elevation and resistivity, alterations in the local magnetic and gravitational fields, shifting of ground water levels, the emission of radon gas, deep sounds, flashes of light and the peculiar behaviour of animals. Some of these precursors appear months, or even years, ahead of a large earthquake; others only in the days and hours before it strikes.

Foreshocks are the most useful. Unfortunately, they frequently do not happen, at least not in the period immediately before the quake. There were none in Tokyo in 1923, none (or at least none recorded) in Tangshan in 1976, and none in a typical major Californian quake such as the one at San Fernando in 1971

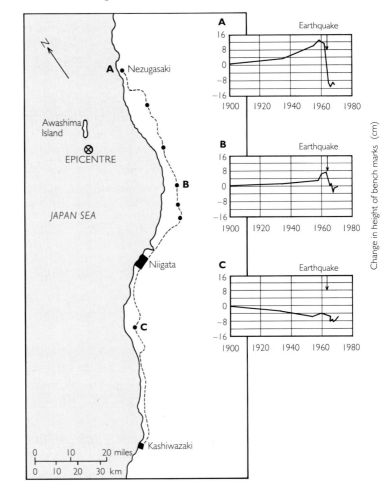

A method to predict earthquakes? In 1964, at Niigata on the west coast of Japan, there was a disastrous 7.5-magnitude earthquake. For about 10 years before that, there had been anomalous uplift of the land nearby, which was detected by plotting changes in the height of bench marks measured in repeated land surveys. The graphs at the right correspond to the lettered bench-mark sites (B. C) shown on the detailed map. There was also a drop in mean sea level observed by a tide-gauge station at Nezugasaki (A). If uplift in an area is monitored in sufficient detail over many decades, it may become a good precursor of earthquakes.

(magnitude 6.6). A later review of micro-earthquakes in the area during the 30 months leading up to the San Fernando quake showed, however, that a drop in speed of P (primary) waves by 10–15 per cent had taken place – followed by a return to normal speed just before the quake. A rather similar phenomenon had been observed by Soviet seismologists after detailed monitoring of small and large earthquakes in Tadzhikistan during the 1950s and 60s: they found that the ratio of P to S wave speed dropped for a variable period and then suddenly returned to normal just before a major quake. US monitoring, spurred on by the Soviet results, seemed to confirm this general picture, and for a while optimism about earthquake prediction reached a high. The *Scientific American*, introducing an article on the subject in 1975, went so far as to declare: 'Recent technical advances have brought this long-sought goal within reach. With adequate funding several countries, including the US, could achieve reliable long-term and short-term forecasts in a decade.' But subsequent extensive measurement of seismicity at the San Andreas fault revealed no such general predictable behaviour by P waves. If the method does prove useful in prediction, it will work (like so many other methods in seismology) only locally, within particular geological conditions that have been extensively studied over a sufficiently long period. It probably requires several generations.

This is certainly true of attempts to understand uplift and subsidence of the ground. On 16 June 1964 a major earthquake struck the coastal town of Niigata in western Japan, its epicentre just off the coast at Awashima Island. There was a sudden subsidence of the coastline by 6 to 8 inches (15–20 cm). This in itself was unremarkable, but when plotted on a graph of land elevation in relation to mean sea level since 1898, the sudden slump was shown to have followed a gradual rise in the land opposite

Monitoring Japanese seismicity. Japan receives nearly 10 per cent of the world's annual release of seismic energy; every year it has 1000 quakes strong enough to be felt. At the Earthquake Prediction Centre of the Japan Meteorological Agency in Tokyo (*above left*), computers keep constant watch, processing data from seismographs, strainmeters, tiltmeters, tide gauges, underground water monitors and other instruments. (*Above*) Measuring seismic intensity in Japan.

Awashima Island at the rate of nearly a tenth of an inch (2 mm) a year. The fact was of course noticed only after the earthquake. By keeping a constant watch on the elevation of likely troublespots, with the help of laser-ranging devices and the satellites of the Global Positioning System (since 1991), uplift may eventually turn into a useful indicator of a coming earthquake.

But even when uplift is successfully quantified in advance of a disaster, there remains the awkward question of interpretation. The most celebrated example is 'The Palmdale Bulge', the uplift of an area of southern California centred on Palmdale, some 45 miles north of Los Angeles, and extending 100 miles along the San Andreas fault. The uplift, measured from the 1960s, was said to amount to a striking $13\frac{3}{4}$ inches (35 cm), though subsequent studies suggested this might have been an overestimate. Both scientists and Californians in general have wondered whether an earthquake may be imminent in the area (which lies on the southern section of the fault, the 185 miles that have not slipped since 1857) without coming to any firm conclusion. There is nothing with which to compare the situation, and as yet neither enough data nor data spread over a long enough period.

If three Greek scientists – two solid-state physicists and an electronics engineer – are correct, studies of the electrical resistivity of the ground, hitherto neglected in seismology, might throw some light on phenomena like the Palmdale uplift and also provide the first real hope for reliable earthquake prediction. The VAN method, named after its inventors Varotsos, Alexopoulos and Nomikos, is based on a fact first reported by John Milne in an 1898 paper before Britain's Royal Society: ahead of a powerful earth-quake, the natural electrical currents that circulate and fluctuate in the ground (known as telluric currents) are disturbed, and hence the resistivity alters. Previous efforts to detect this so-called Seismic Electrical Signal (SES) and use it for prediction failed in many countries, and the approach was abandoned. But the Greek scientists took it up in the 1980s and achieved substantial results: during 1988 and 1989, they correctly predicted the location and magnitude of 17 earthquakes around Greece.

The VAN method has yet to be accepted widely, though it has influential scientific support all over the world. One difficulty, common to seismology as a whole, is that each area of the world presents unique problems of data interpretation. Another is the long time (decades) required to calibrate a network of VAN stations in areas where, unlike Greece, tremors are uncommon. A third difficulty is the lack of a satisfactory explanation of the Seismic Electrical Signal. But, as one of VAN's supporters, the French volcanologist Haroun Tazieff, pointedly notes: is there a fully satisfactory theory of the Earth's magnetic field and the fact that a compass needle points north?

Unlike resistivity, animal behaviour before earthquakes has yet to be subject to controlled experiment (at least partly because of the obvious difficulty). There is nevertheless ample evidence that animals may perceive an earthquake coming, as we saw at Haicheng in 1975. Reports exist from all over the world, and date back to the earliest times. Plutarch mentions a rabbit having had a premonition of an earthquake in Sparta in 469 B C, and Pliny the Elder describes something similar in his *Natural History*. Immanuel Kant noted of the Lisbon earthquake:

> The cause of earthquakes seems to spread its effect even into the surrounding air. An hour earlier, before the earth is being shaken, one may perceive a red sky and other signs of an altered composition of the air. Animals are taken with fright shortly before it. Birds flee into houses, rats and mice crawl out of their holes.

Before the 1923 earthquake in Tokyo, catfish (the mischievous *namazu* of tradition) were seen to jump agitatedly in ponds, and could be caught in bucketfuls. Before the Haicheng quake, rats came out of the ground and were easily captured. In fact in China the appearance of panicky rats is an officially designated earthquake precursor: in May 1974, according to a scientific report, it saved the lives of a family in Yunnan province. A housewife had found rats running about her house since 5 May. On the night of 10 May, they were so noisy she got up to hit them. Then she suddenly recalled a visit to an exhibition on earthquakes and evacuated the house. The following morning a magnitude-7.1 earthquake actually occurred, and the house collapsed.

Explanations of these and thousands of other reported instances may involve better-than-human sensitivity to vibrations and sounds, electrical and magnetic fields and the odour of leaking gases. An electrical explanation – perhaps exposure to charged clouds of particles emitted by the ground – seems the most likely. If the mechanism can be established, and an analogous, affordable detection instrument designed, then animals may no longer be required for prediction – just as canaries are no longer needed to detect gases in mineshafts.

Long-term earthquake forecasting is much less successful – and potentially a great deal more hazardous – than long-term weather forecasting. Geological processes are so slow that prediction, even on the basis of a century of data, is like trying to predict tomorrow's weather on the basis of one minute's observation.

Until the arrival of plate tectonic theory in the 1960s, about all that could confidently be said was that earthquakes mostly would occur where they had previously occurred. Today's theory focuses this statement a little by suggesting that the longer the period is since an earthquake has occurred, the more likely that place is to experience a quake. Many scientists also reckon that the size of the quake increases with increased time of quiescence.

At Pallett Creek, for instance, 34 miles northeast of Los Angeles, a geologist, Kerry Sieh, has dug a trench into the San Andreas fault and revealed well-differentiated strata of silt, sand and peat that appear to have been disturbed by a series of large earthquakes over the past 1400 years. Using carbon dating, he established the following dates for these earth movements, all but one of them approximate: 1857, 1745, 1470, 1245, 1190, 965, 860, 665, 545. The greatest interval is 275 years, the smallest 55 years, while the average is 160 years. Will southern California experience its next large earthquake – the Big One of Hollywood fame – this decade, next decade, some time next century? The recurrence interval is clearly too variable for any meaningful prediction.

Parkfield (population 39), situated on the San Andreas half-way between Los Angeles and San Francisco, is the self-styled 'Earthquake Capital of the World' where the Earth, allegedly, 'Moves For You'. It boasts the only officially endorsed earthquake prediction in the United States. The recurrence interval here is about 22 years: moderate-sized earthquakes were reported in 1857 and 1881 and were scientifically recorded in 1901, 1922, 1934 and 1966. In 1985, the USGS announced that there was a 95 per cent probability of a magnitude-6 earthquake occurring before the end of 1992.

Unfortunately, seven years and 18 million dollars later, the area has proved notable chiefly for its seismic *in*activity. The largest quake was one of magnitude 4.5 in October 1992. Promptly, the USGS issued a warning that the expected magnitude-6 quake might follow within 72 hours. The California Office of Emergency Services set up a mobile operations centre outside the Parkfield Café. In towns nearby, fire engines stood ready, and residents laid in extra supplies of water. Helicopters from four or five TV stations hovered overhead, and reporters from dozens of newspapers arrived on the scene. But there was no sign of the earthquake.

Though the Parkfield prediction may still come true, its failure to do so within the 1985–92 'window', combined with failures in other areas of prediction, has reinforced the scepticism of a majority of seismologists: few of them now share the confidence about earthquake prediction common in the 1970s. Consider a recent survey of predictions for Pacific ring earthquakes made by four geophysicists in 1979, for instance. They had defined segments of plate boundaries that had not experienced large earthquakes for 30 years as 'seismic gaps' having a high potential for a large earthquake. The survey of the 37 earthquakes with magnitude 7 that occurred in the north Pacific during the post-1979 decade showed that 4 quakes occurred in the postulated high-potential seismic gaps, 16 in zones predicted to have intermediate potential, and 17 in zones that should have low potential. The fit between fact and prediction would actually have been better had the zones been assigned their potentials randomly. Would it improve if only the largest earthquakes were considered, these being best explained by the 'elastic rebound' model? Apparently not: of the 9 earthquakes of magnitude 7.5 or greater, 1 was in the high-potential zone, 3 in the intermediate-potential zone, and 5 in the low-potential zone. 'The apparent failure of the gap model is surprising, given its intuitive good sense,' commented *Nature*. 'It may be that seismicity in some regions is quasiperiodic, whereas in others it clusters.'

The whole field of earthquake prediction is plainly wide-open for speculation. Many predictions are made by unscientific and pseudoscientific means, and most of these are ignored. But occasionally, for reasons that are not always clear, one of them catches on and causes panic. In winter 1989, a self-taught US climatologist predicted that a subtle bulging of the Earth caused by the gravitational pull of the Sun and Moon – calculated by astronomers to peak on 3 December 1990 – would trigger a catastrophic earthquake in the Mississippi Valley, comparable to the New Madrid, Missouri earthquakes of 1811–12. In addition to

Parkfield, California – site of the only officially endorsed earthquake prediction in the US. On the basis of a series of earthquakes in the area, spaced at roughly 22-year intervals, Parkfield (on the San Andreas fault) was predicted to experience a magnitude-6 quake before 1993. The reality, however, was not so obliging. The photograph shows one of an array of instruments around Parkfield: a laser ranging device capable of picking up fault movements of less than 1 millimetre (0.04 in) over a distance of 6 kilometres (3.7 miles).

having a PhD (in zoology) and the support of the director of Southeast Missouri State University's Earthquake Information Center, the predictor was said – by the *New York Times*, no less – to have forecast the October 1989 Loma Prieta (San Francisco) earthquake 'a week in advance'. The *San Francisco Chronicle* added, 'He missed by just 6 hours hitting the Oct. 17 San Francisco quake on the nose in a forecast published in 1985 and by only 5 minutes in an update a week before the disaster.' As the director of the Bay Area Regional Earthquake Preparedness Project later remarked, 'these things have a life of their own.'

The prediction caused frenzy for months in the Midwest which died down only when the Loma Prieta claim was shown from a videorecording and transcript to be baseless, and the Missouri seismologist publicly declared a belief in psychic phenomena. The scientific community could have scotched the story at the start, but failed to act in time – partly because it did not take the forecast seriously, and partly perhaps because of its general lack of confidence in the scientific approach to the subject.

Ten years previously, one of its own number – a bona-fide geologist studying quake-like rock bursts in mines, Brian Brady – had made a notorious prediction that a giant earthquake would strike Peru in June 1981. Examining rocks as they fractured in the laboratory had convinced him of the existence of a 'clock' in the fracture process: once started, it would inexorably run on and produce an earthquake, its ticks being bursts of moderate fore-shocks. Given the requisite historical and current seismicity data, Brady said he could tell exactly when the quake would occur.

Fellow geophysicists refused to accept the theory that the small-scale (microscopic) process of rock fracture and the large-scale (macroscopic) mechanism of earthquakes were basically the same, 'scale invariant' in scientific language; and they said so formally through the National Earthquake Evaluation Prediction Council. What they did not say, but certainly perceived, was that if the theory was right after all, it would mean wholesale realignment of earthquake research and funding towards laboratory work, away from field research.

The prediction had been news before; now it was headline news. But Brady refused to withdraw it and so it became thoroughly entangled in Peruvian–US politics. The Peruvian president, government and scientific community were taking it seriously, while in Washington DC, and at the US Geological Survey and the US Bureau of Mines, several different groups were vying to use the prediction for their own ends. The people of Peru, 66,000 of whom had died in an earthquake as recently as 1970, became more and more jittery as 28 June 1981 approached.

Nothing happened. But that does not devalue the thinking behind the prediction. The scientist concerned was not a crank; he simply pushed his model too far. In defending himself shortly before the date of the prediction, Brady wrote:

> Many within the seismological community are currently infatuated with simple fault models made more complex by the addition of asperities (hard zones along the fault surface) which tend to inhibit free body motion along the fault; an earthquake occurs once the asperities are broken . . . I believe we need to address the fundamental problem of *how* the fault gets there in the first place.

It was a prescient remark. Only now have seismologists begun to face this challenge head on. One of them recently compared himself with rueful candour to an 18th-century physician, 'who although lacking understanding of disease is compelled to do something and so prescribes bleeding.' The scientific problem, he remarked, is likely to get worse before it gets better: our expanding knowledge of the Earth, derived from the extraordinary sophistication of new instrumentation, has ironically 'served to magnify our lack of understanding.'

Cities at seismic risk. Hundreds of millions of city dwellers, particularly those in the Third World, are at risk from earthquakes, even comparatively minor ones. The Cairo earthquake of 1992 killed hundreds of people and caused considerable destruction in the older part of the city. Like the vast majority of threatened cities, Cairo had no earthquake contingency plan.

Disaster Day. In Tokyo, every year on 1 September – the day of the Great Kanto earthquake of 1923 – the city prepares for the next big quake. The photograph shows a shaking platform simulating a quake; other drills include target practice with buckets of water.

Aftermath of a Japanese earthquake. The Mino-Owari earthquake of 1891 was the greatest recorded inland earthquake to strike Japan. The seismologist John Milne, who took this photograph, reported 'the contortions produced along lines of railway, the fissuring of the ground, the destruction of hundreds of miles of high embankments which guard the plains from river floods, the utter ruin of structures of all descriptions, the sliding down of mountain sides and the toppling over of their peaks, the compression of valleys and other bewildering phenomena.'

While scientists from various specialities investigate and theorize about earthquakes, what can governments, organizations and individuals do to protect themselves from the menace? Nearly half the world's big cities now lie in areas of seismic risk. In Cairo, in 1992, a comparatively minor earthquake (magnitude 5.8–6.1), killed hundreds of Egyptians and seriously damaged buildings and ancient monuments. Although the city is historically no stranger to earthquakes, there was no plan to cope with them. Most of those who perished were the impoverished tenants of poorly constructed apartments or children crushed in the stampede to escape collapsing schoolrooms. At the same time large parts of the city were left untouched. As seismologists like to say: 'Earthquakes don't kill people; buildings do.' Around the globe, hundreds of millions of lives are now at permanent risk, along with countless thousands of millions of dollars worth of property; and the numbers and amounts are certain to increase.

The outstanding danger spot is Tokyo and its adjacent metropolitan area. Not only does Japan receive nearly 10 per cent of the world's annual release of seismic energy, but it has the dubious honour of being situated on the edge of three tectonic plates (as compared to two at the San Andreas fault). Earthquakes are a regular feature of Japanese life: there are 1000 every year strong enough to be felt. But Tokyo itself has not experienced a quake of magnitude greater than 4 since 1929, when the aftershocks of the Great Kanto earthquake at last died away. Three potential earthquakes are believed to be imminent. One of them, known as the Tokai earthquake after the region down the coast from Tokyo (around Shizuoka) it principally threatens, could be almost as

---

Some large cities at risk from earthquakes

Algiers	Chongqing	Kuala Lumpur	Naples	Taipei
Ankara	Davao	Kunming	Osaka	Tashkent
Athens	Dhaka (Dacca)	Lahore	Pyongyang	Teheran
Bangkok	Guatemala City	Lanzhou (Lanchow)	Rangoon	Tianjin (Tientsin)
Beijing (Peking)	Harbin	Lima	Rome	Tokyo
Bogota	Havana	Lisbon	San Francisco	Tripoli
Bucharest	Hong Kong	Los Angeles	Santiago	Turin
Cairo/Alexandria	Istanbul	Managua	Seoul	Wuhan
Calcutta	Jakarta	Manila	Shanghai	Xi'an (Sian)
Canton	Kabul	Mexico City	Shenyang (Mukden)	Yangon (Rangoon)
Caracas	Kanpur	Milan	Singapore	Yokohama
Casablanca	Kobe	Nanjing (Nanking)	Surabaya	

地震 火を消せ!!

powerful as the Great Kanto earthquake; 30 times the energy of the Loma Prieta quake. Another, known as a *chokka-gata* ('directly-below-type') quake, could be more damaging to Tokyo itself, by striking directly beneath it. (One of this type struck in 1988, but being 55 miles down, surface damage was nil.) The third threatens Kanagawa, the region immediately south of the capital. Japanese seismologists do not pretend to know just how soon any of these three shocks might occur, but they are of one mind in predicting a major earthquake in Tokyo within the foreseeable future.

In 1923, the devastation of two-thirds of Tokyo was of no great concern to the rest of the world, humanitarian concern apart. Three-quarters of a century on, however, Tokyo has the world's largest stock exchange and a gross national product larger than all but five nations; its production of goods and services exceeds that of Britain and its property value equalled, at the height of its boom, the entire real estate value of the United States. Even more importantly, it has huge sums invested abroad, in the United States, in Britain and in other countries. Great damage to the Tokyo area nowadays would seriously disrupt both the world's financial system and most national economies, assuming, as one must, that large-scale disinvestment would take place in order to rebuild the area. To sense the scale of the problem, one must agglomerate in one's imagination quake-threatened Los Angeles, New York, Chicago, Washington DC, Houston, New Orleans, Philadelphia, Detroit and the next 42 largest cities of the United States with all their resources. 'Put *that* on top of the San Andreas fault and watch the sparks fly', wrote Peter Hadfield, a former geologist and the author of a pioneering book on the 'coming Tokyo earthquake' published in 1991.

The disaster is, as we have just said, foreseeable, even if its timing is still desperately uncertain. What has been done by the Japanese to forestall it? A great deal, at first sight – undoubtedly more than in any other earthquake-prone nation. About 500 researchers are working on earthquake prediction, and a thousand million dollars have been spent on equipment alone. A barrage of instruments is in place to monitor aspects of the many faults that may affect the area; and these are connected to a high-tech control centre. Since 1977, an emergency committee of six scientists has been at permanent ready to respond to unexpected movements of the crust and advise the government whether to issue an alert. The government has designated evacuation areas and briefed the population through heavy publicity; every 1 September, the anniversary of the Great Kanto earthquake, there are city-wide earthquake drills. Most major buildings have been strengthened and new ones routinely constructed over many years to withstand the maximum possible shaking: Tokyo's skyscrapers and tower blocks are now the safest buildings in the city; indeed, people are advised to stay inside them in an earthquake, no longer to rush out and risk being cut by flying glass or killed by one of the shop signs that hang above the streets.

And yet a little probing of the reality shows how many loopholes remain, and, more seriously, how vastly more vulnerable a modern city is than the Tokyo of 1923. What about the bullet trains? What about the refinery and chemical complex built on soft reclaimed land beside the bay, the new tower blocks planned for that land against expert advice, and the nuclear power station at Shizuoka? What about rampant cost-cutting and corruption in the construction industry (a killer in Cairo in 1992)? What will happen to electricity cables, gas mains, water mains, telephone and computer lines, communications in general? And who will coordinate the rescue efforts and cut through the bureaucratic rivalries that bedevil the emergency planning? If the casual questioning of ordinary Japanese people means anything, most of those living in Tokyo do not truly believe such a disaster could happen. A young businessman with an international company told Hadfield:

I'm not so worried about it. I don't talk about it so much with my friends – only sometimes, when we're driving through a tunnel and I might make a joke about it. I don't know how many people will die. It depends on the severity of the earthquake. Maybe two million?

Across the globe on the other side of the Pacific, the dwellers on the San Andreas fault are equally fatalistic, perhaps more so. Not until 1990 did the state of California issue a detailed plan of what should happen in the event of an earthquake warning. In a land where the most trivial of things becomes a cult, earthquakes do not qualify. Parkfield is simply the exception that proves the rule: there is no real Californian earthquake culture.

The 1989 earthquake was the third major quake to strike San Francisco. The first was in 1868, nearly 40 years before the most

San Francisco's 'Big One'. The magnitude of this famous earthquake in 1906 is estimated to have been $8\frac{1}{4}$, as compared with 6.9 in 1989. Fires consumed almost 5 square miles of the city's heart (including Market Street, shown here). What would happen today, if a similar giant earthquake struck a megalopolis such as Los Angeles or Tokyo? The likely impact is alarmingly resistant to calculation.

famous one in 1906. It caused heavy damage in the city, and stimulated open discussion of the dangers of building on land reclaimed from the bay. Notwithstanding, in 1989 some of the most serious earthquake damage was in the city's Marina area. Two years later, the *Bulletin of the Seismological Society of America* came out with a special issue: 800 or so pages of densely written technical description and analysis of the earthquake. In their Introduction, the editors felt constrained to warn:

> Certainly, the Loma Prieta earthquake is a reminder that earthquakes do not have to occur where we want them to occur or forecast them to occur and that our understanding of how and why earthquakes occur and recur, even along the best studied active crustal fault in the world, is rudimentary and incomplete... The effects of earthquake strong ground motion on unreinforced masonry, soft first stories, decayed timbers, bad foundations, hydraulic fill and young Bay mud hardly qualify as news, especially in San Francisco where these 'lessons' had all been learned in 1906 if not before . . . Until there is a permanent, national consciousness that the hazards from earthquakes are very real and the potential losses very great, it seems inevitable that we shall learn the lessons of 1906 and 1989 yet again.

CHAPTER

—4—

VOLCANOES

*Under us, and stretching away before us, was a heaving sea of
molten fire of seemingly limitless extent. . . At unequal distances
all around the shores of the lake were nearly white-hot chimneys
or hollow drums of lava, four or five feet high, and up through
them were bursting gorgeous sprays of lava-gouts and gem
spangles, some white, some red and some golden – a ceaseless
bombardment, and one that fascinated the eye with its
unapproachable splendor. The more distant jets, sparkling up
through an intervening gossamer veil of vapor, seemed miles
away; and the further the curving ranks of fiery mountains
receded, the more fairy-like and beautiful they appeared.*
Mark Twain, Hawaii, 1866

THE volcanoes of the Hawaiian Islands are probably the most
intensively studied volcanoes in the world. Kilauea ('Ke-low-
way-ah'), which entranced Mark Twain in the last century, is the
most vigorous of them. Its eruptions have been watched for many
centuries by the Polynesians, who gave Kilauea its name, meaning
'rising smoke cloud'. The latest one began in January 1983; ten
years later, the lava was still pouring out of the volcano's rifts and
craters. The new flows have covered more than 35 square miles
(roughly the area of Manhattan), added almost half a square mile of
new land to Hawaii's Big Island, and flattened more than 180
homes, displacing hundreds of people.

For the scientists of the US Geological Survey, and volcanologists from every part of the world, Kilauea offers a peep at the inner
workings of the Earth. It is the nearest they can get under relatively
controlled conditions to examining the structure of the Earth's
crust and mantle at first hand. The deepest drills stop not much
more than 6 miles down; Kilauea's lava emanates from tens of miles
down – maybe even deeper. Its fantastic fire fountains that reach
1500 feet (over 450 m) in the air and a similar number of degrees
Celsius are startling evidence of the immense pressure and heat in

Lava

*T*HE lava fountains of Kilauea on Hawaii (right) are perhaps the most famous in the world. Volcanic activity began at Kilauea in 1790 and has continued ever since. The photograph shows a fissure in the east rift zone erupting in 1977. (Below right) Halemaumau – 'house of the everlasting fire'. The lava lakes of Kilauea periodically shift their position; this one was formed in 1924. When Mark Twain visited Kilauea's lava lake in 1866, he commented: 'The smell of sulphur is strong, but not unpleasant to a sinner.' (Below left) Lava tree moulds form when fluid lava surrounds the trunk of a tree and cools, creating a cylinder of solidified lava around the tree. When the tide of lava retreats, the mushroom-shaped cap of the tree mould is left standing up to 10 feet (3 m) above the lava flow. These moulds are from Kilauea.

(*Right*) **These spatter cones** were photographed on Kilauea in 1983, at the beginning of an eruption that was still continuing ten years later.

(*Opposite*) **Red rock river.** Hawaii's Mauna Loa is the tallest historically active volcano in the world. In 40 known eruptions since the 18th century, lava has flowed from its summit and rift zones. The photograph shows a braided lava channel flowing from the main vent.

the molten fathoms. Equally compelling are the lava lakes, the incandescent lava rivers that gradually darken as they cool – some becoming smooth and ropy, others jagged and clinkery – and the lava tunnels, contorted tubes of cold lava sometimes left behind when a river moves onwards.

To the native Hawaiians, Kilauea was the home of Pele, the volcanic goddess, and today it is still common, especially during major lava flows, to see gifts placed at the edge of craters: flowers (loose or in a vase), tobacco, food and, most of all, gin. Priests once stood on Uwekahuna ('bluff of the wailing priests'), the 330-foot (100-m) cliff where the Hawaiian Volcano Observatory has stood since 1912, and watched the antics of Pele in the great lava lake Halemaumau ('house of the everlasting fire'). Often, they noticed, the level of liquid lava dropped abruptly, simultaneously with the appearance of a red glow from an eruption on a flank of Kilauea. Pele, they said, must have moved along a subterranean passage from the lake to the flank.

Pompeii. The twin cities of Pompeii and Herculaneum near Naples, buried by an eruption of Mount Vesuvius in AD 79, were forgotten until the 18th century. At least 2000 people died in Pompeii, possibly many more; most of the residents of Herculaneum probably escaped. The victims have been delineated in death by pouring liquid plaster of Paris into the holes left by their bodies in the ash and pumice.

Volcanologists suspect that everything they see does indeed connect inside Kilauea. But the processes and plumbing involved are baffling. From 1983 until mid-1986, Kilauea spouted fountains spasmodically along its east rift zone. A spurt generally lasted less than a day and was followed by a month of quiescence. Then, several new fissures opened, the lava fountains fizzled out, and molten material started to flow into a large lava lake. This continued until the lake drained through lava tubes on to the surrounding landscape; and then a new lake formed a mile or two closer to the volcano's central crater.

Gentle stuff, one might reasonably think; almost magical, and fascinating to study. But what about a real volcano? What about the most famous volcano of all, Mount Vesuvius?

Vesuvius is a small mountain, only 4200 feet (1280 m), rising above the Bay of Naples in southern Italy. It is also young, scarcely 17,000 years old. It last erupted in 1944, before that it in 1906, and during the past 2000 years it has erupted more than 50 times: once every 40 years or so on average. But the actual intervals between eruptions – the repose time, in scientific parlance – bear little resemblance to the average. There was an eruption in 1037, after which the volcano slept for 600 years. When it finally awoke, in 1631, in three days it killed more than 4000 people living in villages on its slopes, interring them in mud, ashes and lava. Naples itself, some 10 miles distant, was knee-deep in ash. At Portici, a town on the coast just south of Naples at the very foot of the destroyer that had been completely ruined, the viceroy had a memorial tablet prepared and erected. It read, in part:

Children and children's children. Hear! . . . Sooner or later this mountain takes fire. But before this happens there are mutterings and roarings and earthquakes. Smoke and flames and lightning are spewed forth, the air trembles and rumbles and howls. Flee so long as you can. . . If you despise it, if goods and chattels are dearer to you than life, it will punish your recklessness and greed. Do not trouble about your hearth and home, but flee without hesitation.

By a twist of fate, it was this eruption of 1631, now almost forgotten, that made Vesuvius a household name. Portici had to be rebuilt, and in due course, wells were sunk. Ancient Herculaneum was discovered beneath; Portici had been built on top of the ancient city's port. The discovery of Pompeii, several miles further down the coast (and also at the foot of the volcano), soon followed. Both cities had been smothered by an eruption of Vesuvius in AD 79 and all but lost to memory. Were it not for a contemporary letter written by Pliny the Younger, describing Pliny the Elder's death in

Display on Mount Vesuvius.
Vesuvius has erupted more than 50 times in the past 2000 years, most recently in 1944. In an illustration by Pietro Fabris, a party of royal guests is shown an eruption in 1771 by Sir William Hamilton, Britain's envoy to the court at Naples. Hamilton's descriptions of Vesuvius formed the first work of modern volcanology.

Eruption of Etna. In January 1992, Sicily's Mount Etna began its largest eruption this century. Etna has been active since it came into existence half a million years ago, with eruptions that are characteristically non-explosive, lengthy and productive of lava. One eruption in 1614 did not stop until 1624; another, in 1669, engulfed much of Catania, the port 10 miles away. The eruption that began in 1992 attracted worldwide attention when a lava flow (*opposite*) threatened Zafferana, a town of 7000 people half a mile away. In 1792, lava pushed straight through the town; 200 years later, it destroyed only one house (*inset*) before being diverted with explosives into an artificial channel.

the eruption, the 18th-century excavators of Herculaneum and Pompeii would have known nothing about the cities.

Among those attracted to Vesuvius was Sir William Hamilton, Britain's envoy to Naples from 1764 to 1800 (and the husband of Emma, the mistress of Admiral Nelson). Vesuvius erupted violently nine times during Hamilton's stay; he made more than 200 sorties up its flanks, and became one of the pioneers of volcanology. It was he who began to compile a list of the dates of eruptions, by collecting the dates on which the priests in Naples and the villages and towns around the volcano had displayed their sacred images. He was intrigued by the stolid philosophy of the peasants that had both endured and magnified so many disasters such as that of 1631. He remarked:

> Each peasant flatters himself that an eruption will not happen in his time, or, if it should, that his tutelar saint will turn away the destructive lava from his ground; and, indeed, the great fertility of soil in the neighbourhoods of volcanoes tempts people to inhabit them.

Hamilton's letters to the president of the Royal Society in London, published in 1772, became the first modern work of volcanology. His scientific successors, volcanologists and archaeologists working together, have now reached a consensus about the events of 24 and 25 August A D 79. *There was no lava.* Pompeii and Herculaneum were buried by mud, ashes and fragments of solid rock borne by steam and other gases: a phenomenon known to

volcanologists by the catch-all term 'pyroclastic flow' (pyroclastic means 'fire-broken'). Pumice began to fall on Pompeii at 1.30 p.m. on 24 August. At 11.30 p.m. that night a fiery cloud of superheated gas, pumice and rocks shot out of the summit of Vesuvius, separated into a fast-moving surge and a slower, ground-hugging avalanche or flow, and reached Herculaneum, killing all in its path. Then followed a second surge and flow at 12.30 a.m. on 25 August and a third surge at 5.30 a.m.: the third surge reached the north walls of Pompeii, the flow buried Herculaneum. There was a fourth surge at 6.30 a.m., asphyxiating Pompeii, followed by a flow; and a fifth surge and flow at 7 a.m. Finally, at 8.30 a.m. a sixth surge and flow buried Pompeii. This one made the sky so dark, wrote Pliny, who was watching nervously at Misenum, 20 miles away, that it was like being in a sealed room with no lamp.

Plainly, Italy's Vesuvius and Hawaii's Kilauea have barely more in common than the basic definition of a volcano: that is, a vent in the Earth through which molten rock reaches the surface. Quite apart from the differences in repose time, explosiveness and volcanic products, hardly anyone – perhaps no one – was aware in A D 79 and 1631 that Vesuvius *was* a volcano. It is both the glory and the nightmare of volcanology that each volcano requires distinct treatment. Volcanologists can, and do, define types of eruption; but no real eruption fits the types perfectly, indeed it may change type during the process of eruption. If we ask such questions as 'Why do volcanoes erupt? Why are some eruptions explosive, while others are quieter emissions of rivers of molten lava? Why does an eruption stop, and why is the time between eruptions so variable from one volcano to another?' – questions posed by Robert W. Decker (former scientist-in-charge of the Hawaiian Volcano Observatory) in his book *Mountains of Fire* – there are no definite answers, as yet. 'It is easier to describe the character of various types of volcanic eruptions than to answer these questions, but some possible solutions are emerging from the studies of active volcanoes by scientists in many countries.'

Even to say exactly what we mean by 'active', 'extinct', and 'dormant' is difficult. UNESCO has estimated that out of the 50 or so volcanoes that erupt every year, one supposedly 'extinct' volcano erupts every five years on average. The International Association of Volcanology defines an active volcano as one that has erupted in historic time. That means within the last 3000 years in the Mediterranean, but only 200 years in Hawaii; and on some uninhabited Aleutian islands in Alaska, there are no historic records at all. Furthermore, there is no eye-witness account of a volcanic eruption older than Pliny's, written less than 2000 years ago. To a geologist, 2000 years is a mere blink of the eye. The

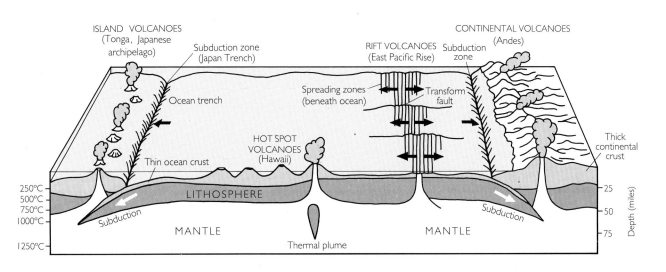

Island volcanoes labels: ISLAND VOLCANOES (Tonga, Japanese archipelago); Subduction zone (Japan Trench); Ocean trench; Thin ocean crust; HOT SPOT VOLCANOES (Hawaii); Spreading zones (beneath ocean); RIFT VOLCANOES (East Pacific Rise); Transform fault; Subduction zone; CONTINENTAL VOLCANOES (Andes); Thick continental crust; LITHOSPHERE; MANTLE; Subduction; Thermal plume; 250°C, 500°C, 750°C, 1000°C, 1250°C; Depth (miles) 25, 50, 75

Smithsonian Institution therefore settles for 10,000 years in its catalogue, *Volcanoes of the World*, and counts about 1350 potentially active volcanoes – as opposed to somewhere over 500, according to the 'historic time' criterion.

The location of most volcanoes is somewhat easier to categorize, thanks to the theory of plate tectonics. Broadly speaking, volcanoes and earthquakes occur in similar regions: first, at ridges/rifts – mainly oceanic rifts – where new rock is created; secondly, in subduction zones, where one plate is swallowed under another less dense plate. But unlike earthquakes, volcanoes do not occur where one plate butts into or grinds past another plate rather than diving under it: there are no known volcanoes in the Himalayas, and none at the San Andreas fault. (The Cascades volcanoes of northern California, Oregon and Washington result from the subduction of a plate that has now disappeared from view, as we know.)

Rift volcanoes on land belong chiefly to Iceland and East Africa, with 160 potentially active volcanoes combined; beneath the ocean there are perhaps 20 times as many – we cannot yet count them all, but we may be certain that 'hidden' volcanoes outnumber visible volcanoes very considerably. In subduction-related volcanoes the Pacific rim countries lead the world: Indonesia has 127, Japan 77, Chile 75, the United States (excluding Alaska) 69, the Aleutian Islands and Alaska 68, Kamchatka 65 (see map on page 26).

Unfortunately, plate tectonic theory breaks down in trying to explain the location of some other volcanoes, just as it does with 'mid-plate' earthquakes. It can give some account of the Italian volcanoes (13 potentially active), but it is totally stumped by the Hawaiian volcanoes (8) in the middle of the Pacific plate, 2500 miles from the nearest plate boundary and not at a rift. To account for these and other 'rogue' volcanoes, J. Tuzo Wilson, who

The erupting Earth. Volcanoes generally occur at oceanic ridges/rifts, where magma wells up; in subduction zones, where rock is melted as one plate dives beneath a second plate; and where a plate moves over a hot spot – a fixed plume of molten material rising from deep in the Earth.

conceived the transform fault, came up with the idea of the hot spot.

The Hawaiian Islands are believed to have been formed by a plume-shaped mass of molten material that rises from deep in the Earth and punches a hole in the Pacific plate as the plate moves northwest. (The location of the plume remains fixed.) If this is correct, the Hawaiian hot spot should have created a string of volcanoes trending to the northwest – like smoke signals floating away in a gentle breeze – each active for a while, and then becoming extinct as it moved away from the hot spot. The age of its rocks should become progressively older, the further away the extinct volcano is from the present site of the hot spot beneath the Big Island (page 92).

This is indeed the case. The rocks of the Hawaiian Islands do age towards the northwest, and there is a series of sunken, eroded, extinct volcanoes beneath the Pacific – the Hawaiian Ridge and the Emperor Seamounts – that trails off over 3500 miles of sea floor towards the Aleutian Islands. The rocks of extinct Kauai, the northernmost Hawaiian island some 300 miles northwest of the Big Island, are 5 million years older than those of the Big Island according to the radioactive dating of ancient lava flows. What is more, this age agrees with the age predicted by the speed at which the Pacific plate is believed to be moving. The Hawaiian hot spot has generated some 200 volcanoes over 75 million years.

Other hot spots – about 50 in all – may be responsible for the Galapagos and Society Islands, the Azores, and Yellowstone National Park in the western United States. Among the coral atolls of the Pacific, the hot spot clarifies an idea first suggested by the geologist Charles Lyell and investigated by Charles Darwin during his voyage on the *Beagle*. Lyell's proposal was that these puzzling islands in the middle of deep ocean – or at least some of them – were built on top of extinct volcanoes: as the volcano both sank under its weight and was eroded by the ocean, the dead skeleton of the atoll

A glimpse of the molten fathoms. In 1990–91, Mount Klyuchevsky on the Kamchatka Peninsula (in the former Soviet Union) erupted from both its crater and radial fissures at various altitudes on its slopes. Magma was located at a depth of 25 miles, filling an underground watercourse; the main core of magma was estimated to lie more than 100 miles down.

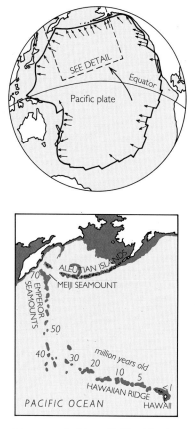

Hot spot in Hawaii. The islands of Hawaii, and the now-submerged islands of the Hawaiian Ridge and the Emperor Seamounts, are thought to have been formed by the volcanic action of a hot spot fixed in the Earth beneath the slow-moving Pacific plate. This accounts for the increasing age of the islands, the further away they are from Hawaii itself.

grew, so that the living coral remained in contact with the surface. Unexpected confirmation of the idea came in the 1950s when US scientists, drilling Eniwetok atoll before exploding a hydrogen bomb, came across the top of an old volcanic mountain about 2 miles above the sea floor, at a depth of 4000 feet (1220 m). According to the latest thinking, the dead volcano may also assist the atoll's growth. The geobiochemist Peter Westbroek describes it thus in his *Life as a Geological Force*:

> The gigantic calcium carbonate structure [the reef] may act like the wick of an oil lamp: evaporation at the atoll's surface may set in motion a current of water up through the volcanic cone, leaching the nutrients out of the basalt and bringing them to the covering film of biota [the coral polyps and algae]. One may compare an atoll with a beautiful oasis maintaining itself in a liquid desert.

Darwin, voyaging the world in the early 1830s, was among the world's first recognizably modern geologists. He fully embraced the idea of a dynamic Earth with a molten interior first introduced by James Hutton and elaborated by Lyell in his *Principles of Geology* (1830–33), which Darwin read as he travelled; an Earth that had evolved through the ages by the same processes visible to him in country after country: 'the present as the key to the past'. And, like Lyell, Darwin believed that these processes acted gradually and uniformly, not catastrophically. Volcanoes, to Darwin, were therefore products of grand Earth movements, uplift and subsidence. The creation of the Andes and the occurrence of volcanic eruptions and earthquakes in South America were side-effects, not causes, of these primary motions.

Earlier thinkers had treated volcanoes as even more peripheral. The seeming freakishness of volcanoes inhibited understanding. Philosophers and natural historians of ancient Greece and Rome, such as Pliny the Elder, guessed that volcanoes were responsible for many of the Earth's surface features. But their insight was lost until the 18th century, leaving only legends: volcanoes as chimneys of the forge of Hephaestus and Vulcan, for instance, where the shield of Achilles and the breastplate of Hercules were turned out; or Plato's story of Atlantis, which some think refers to the massive eruption of Thera in the Aegean Sea in about 1600 BC and the disappearance of the Minoan civilization. The scientists in Europe who thought about volcanoes were preoccupied by the Flood that had undoubtedly laid down the various layers of sediment visible at the surface of the Earth. Volcanoes were at best incidental to the great work of the waters. According to a French thinker writing in

1716, they were the result of the combustion of 'oil and fat of animals and fishes concentrated in certain places' during the Flood. While to an influential German scientist writing at the end of the 18th century, they were recent and superficial phenomena – merely the result of veins of coal catching fire underground and burning their way to the surface.

Considerable progress was made in France from the 1750s, where Jean-Etienne Guettard recognized the black stone used for construction in the Auvergne as being similar to rocks from Vesuvius and Etna. He discovered that it was quarried at Volvic, a village south of Vichy, and guessed that Volvic was a contraction of the Latin *volcani vicus*, 'volcanic village' – so it seemed that the Romans were aware of the connection too. On a visit to the quarry, Guettard climbed a hill behind it and realized to his excitement that before him stretched a series of old volcanic cones, now smoothed and vegetated. In 1752, he delivered a path-breaking paper to the French Academy of Sciences entitled 'Memoir on Certain Mountains in France That Have Once Been Volcanoes'. Over the next few decades he and others, notably Nicholas Desmarest, studied and mapped a chain of 50 volcanoes in the Auvergne, the most famous being the 4806-foot (1465-m) Puy de Dôme. Today we know that the last eruption in the Auvergne was about 6000 years ago, hence the solitary potentially active volcano listed under France in the catalogue of the Smithsonian.

Guettard, for all his flashes of insight, did not connect the black basalt of the Auvergne with basalt from other parts of Europe, where volcanism was much less obvious. Until the start of the 19th century, neptunists – believers in the Flood – continued to hold sway over vulcanists: basalt, and all other rocks, were of aqueous origin, they pronounced; even lava was aqueous rock melted by the burning of coal. Neptunism accounted for the awkward fact that basalt, and many other so-called volcanic rocks such as granite, were crystalline. If these rocks had once been molten, as was claimed by vulcanists, how could they show a crystal structure?

Laboratory experiments by Sir James Hall in the 1790s suggested an answer. He was an admirer of the 'uniformitarian' theories of fellow-Scotsman James Hutton. Ignoring Hutton's contempt for experiment as opposed to field observation, Hall took samples of whinstone – the name of basalt in his area near Edinburgh – and melted them in an iron foundry. He called the molten substance 'magma', a Latin term then used in chemistry to mean a pasty substance. When cooled quickly, the magma turned to glass. Cooled over a period of several hours, however, it reverted to crystalline rock very similar to whinstone. By varying the time of cooling, Hall was able to vary the size of crystals. In further work he showed how great pressure, as well as great temperature, could metamorphose rock. He placed ordinary chalk inside a gun barrel and sealed it with a plug. When 900 pounds of weight (some 400 kg) was applied to the plug and the apparatus heated to 1000 degrees C (1800°F), a chunk of marble was produced.

Scientists perform similar experiments today in order to simulate magma, lava domes, pyroclastic flows and so on; recent ones have used wax, clay, corn syrup and gelatin. And their relevance to processes inside the Earth remains controversial (remember Brady's failed prediction of an earthquake in Peru in 1981). In the 19th century, however, unlike today, no serious debate was possible: there was too little hard evidence concerning the Earth's deep structure.

What was available came mainly from eruptions. It was therefore patchy, unsystematic and hard to collect. The historic world's greatest volcanic eruption, on the island of Tambora south of Borneo in 1815, went largely unstudied until 1847, when a scientific expedition penetrated to the 3-mile-wide crater. Some geologists now estimate that more than 20 cubic miles of debris was blown into the sky. It hung in the upper atmosphere, cooling the planet by shading it from the sun's radiation. On the other side of the world there were strange and brilliant sunsets – thought by some to have influenced the murky light in the paintings of J. M. W. Turner – and record low temperatures in the extreme western parts of Europe and in a small part of northeastern America and Canada, including New England. Indeed, 1816 became known as the 'year without a summer'; a modern historian has called it and 1817, 'the last great subsistence crisis in the western world'. There was a typhus epidemic throughout Europe; food riots in France; famine in Switzerland, with the cantons refusing to export grain to each other; and crop failures in New England. Thomas Jefferson, farming his plantation 'Monticello' further south in Virginia, had to apply to his agent for a grant of $1000. The poet Byron and house guests, staying the summer at Lake Geneva, were kept indoors by the cold and rain, and wrote ghost stories to amuse themselves; it was there that Mary Shelley wrote *Frankenstein*.

No one at the time suspected Tambora to be the cause, even though Benjamin Franklin had speculated on a link between severe weather in 1783–84 and a major eruption of Laki in Iceland during 1783. Instead, a learned scholar at the Milan Observatory attributed the coldness to the introduction of Franklin's lightning rods! By 1883, however, the date of the century's second giant eruption, the connection between volcanoes and atmospheric effects was better appreciated. Of the 494 pages in the British Royal Society's report on Krakatoa (now more accurately known as Krakatau), 312 were devoted to 'the unusual optical phenomena of the atmosphere, 1883–86, including twilight effects, coronal appearances, sky haze, coloured suns and moons, etc.'

The volcano itself, located between Java and Sumatra – what was left of it, that is – was the subject of exhaustive study. Scientists landed on it less than two months after the end of the 100-day eruption and made repeated visits. They were particularly concerned to grasp the causes of three observations: the final titanic blast at about 10 a.m. on 27 August that destroyed the mountain and was heard as gunfire as far distant as 3000 miles; the large number of violent blasts that preceded it on 26 August; and the tsunami, the giant sea wave that reached 130 feet (40 m) in places and annihilated 36,000 people on the nearby coasts.

An important clue came from the ejecta, the material thrown out by the eruption and collected by the scientists. When this was analysed in a laboratory, it turned out to belong not to the rock of the old volcanic cone, but to be newly solidified magma from deep down. R. M. Verbeek, the Dutch mining engineer and geologist leading the expedition, decided that Krakatoa had ejected its magma chamber into the air, and the space had then been filled by the collapse of the cone, creating a caldera or giant crater. He further suggested that it was sea water penetrating the magma chamber that had provoked the megablast.

A century later, scientists generally agree with the first idea, but are doubtful about the second. The mixing of magma and sea water usually gives rise to 'a distinctive deposit of very fine-grained and widely-dispersed ash', one has written. No such deposits have been found at Krakatoa. Instead, they attribute the main blast to the violent mixing or 'convective overturn' of two magmas: a less dense basaltic magma injected beneath a more dense dacitic magma (see page 107). The first magma, being less dense, rose buoyantly and abruptly, and an explosion resulted. The presence in the ejecta of both types of magma in different proportions at different times during the eruption supports this theory.

Less certain at this remove from events are the causes of the other violent explosions and the tsunami. Some scientists have suggested a submarine explosion produced a tsunami. Verbeek favoured either the slumping of the cone into the caldera, or the sudden displacement of water by various surges of ejecta 'falling' into the sea: which is also a good explanation for the series of violent explosions. In other words, a pyroclastic flow. Such flows are a common and deadly feature of certain volcanoes – though only a twentieth of dated eruptions have included a pyroclastic flow – and they have been studied intensively as close-up as possible (quite often too close-up). But little is known about their effect on sea

Krakatoa (Krakatau). Though not the biggest volcanic eruption in history, Krakatoa's 1883 eruption is possibly the best known of all. About the same size as the eruption of Mount Pinatubo in the Philippines in 1991, it produced a tsunami – a seismic sea wave – that swept away 36,000 people. The sound of the eruption was heard as gunfire 3000 miles away. This illustration is taken from the report on the eruption by Britain's Royal Society.

water because few examples have been observed. We do not know, for instance, whether the flow displaces water and plunges to the sea floor, or whether it skims over the surface; probably it does both, in ways that depend on the exact nature of the flow.

Undoubtedly the most notorious of pyroclastic flows was the one from Mount Pelée in Martinique in 1902. In a few minutes just before 8 a.m. on 8 May, it slaughtered, almost silently, all but 2 of the 30,000 or so inhabitants of the charming port of St Pierre. There was no lava and comparatively little ash, just a boiling black cloud of superheated gas, at a temperature between 1300 and 1800 degrees C (2370–3270°F): hot enough to soften glass, but not to melt the copper in the ravaged buildings.

For obvious reasons there are no eyewitness accounts, but a description of a further outburst from Pelée two months later gives some sense of the monster. It was written by two British scientists from the Royal Society cruising past the ruins of St Pierre in a sailboat. In the dusk they saw a red glow suffuse the summit of Pelée. It became brighter and brighter, and soon the whole scene was lit up. The sailors cried in awe and terror, 'The mountain bursts!' Then an immense avalanche swept over Pelée's flanks and across the ruins of the ghostly city. 'It was dull red with a billowy surface. In it there were larger stones which stood out as streaks of bright red tumbling down and emitting showers of sparks.' Within about a minute it reached the sea. Here a second phenomenon was born, a cloud that formed precisely where the avalanche had been, sharing some of its momentum, as if lighter particles of volcanic ejecta had begun to rise slightly while the heavier ones settled to earth. Here the scientists' report takes on a new clarity and urgency:

> The cloud was globular, with a bulging surface covered with rounded protuberant masses which swelled and multiplied with terrible energy. It rushed forward over the waters, directly towards us, boiling and changing its form every instant. It did not spread out laterally; neither did it rise into the air but swept on over the sea in surging masses, coruscating with lightning.

About a mile from the transfixed observers, to their huge relief the cloud slowed. Its colour faded as ash began to settle onto the sea. A short distance away it rose from the surface of the water and passed right over their heads. First chestnut-sized stones, then pea-shaped pellets and finally ashes rained down. There was a faint smell of sulphuric acid in the air. Finally, moving out to sea beyond their boat, the cloud broadened and deepened until it covered the whole sky, but for the line of the horizon.

Alfred Lacroix of the French Academy of Sciences, author of the

The charnel house of St Pierre. On 8 May 1902, the eruption of Mount Pelée on the island of Martinique slaughtered some 30,000 people in the charming Caribbean port of St Pierre. There were only two survivors. The French volcanologist Alfred Lacroix gave the name *nuée ardente* – 'glowing cloud' – to the boiling mixture of gas, particles and rocks that swept over St Pierre.

landmark treatise on the 1902 eruptions of Pelée, termed the phenomenon a *nuée ardente*, 'glowing cloud'. For years volcanologists used this term to describe pyroclastic flows in other parts of the world. Now, as so often in volcanology, other terms have been coined, so as to describe different kinds of flow and the deposits they leave: terms like glowing avalanche, base surge, ash flow, pumice flow and ignimbrite. It is also clear that pyroclastic flows commonly behave like fluids, and are therefore known as 'fluidized'. An analogy may be drawn with the flow of fine powders like flour and cement. Dropped on the floor, a shovelful of cement lands with a *flumph*, and spreads out in all directions with 'rays' shooting off and 'smoke' rising. This happens because a small amount of air gets trapped beneath the main mass as it hits the ground. A pyroclastic flow may travel on a similar cushion of air, and on occasions this can leave the surfaces over which it travels, and even vegetation, unscathed. In the words of a pioneer US volcanologist:

the horizontal movement . . . is due to an avalanche of a dense mass of hot, highly-charged and constantly gas-emitting fragmental lava . . . extraordinarily mobile and practically frictionless because each particle is separated from its neighbor by a cushion of compressed gas. For this reason too its onward rush is almost noiseless.

Frank Perret, the writer, was better placed to know a *nuée ardente* than most scientists. In 1930, while watching Pelée from an observatory of his own construction, he had somehow lived through a *nuée*. By then he was 63 years old, had been the inventor Thomas Edison's personal assistant, had thrown up his own lucrative business career as an inventor after a serious nervous breakdown, had spent over a quarter of a century wandering the planet on the trail of major eruptions, and acquired a reputation even amongst volcanologists for being unusually obsessive.

Perret's first experience with a volcano was in 1904, working without pay for Raffaele Matteucci, the director of the observatory established on the northwest shoulder of Vesuvius in 1841. There is a story of Perret returning to the observatory in early 1906 to observe the major eruption. While panic gripped the Neapolitans, he and Matteucci worked steadily with instruments designed by Perret to record a series of fascinating phenomena, including the eruption's 'electrical wind' that made the metal on the caps of the Italian *carabinieri* 'hiss'. Then Vesuvius seemed to quieten down for a while. A little later in his stay Perret was lying asleep when he was awakened by a faint buzzing. He lifted his ear from the pillow and the buzzing stopped. He lay down again, and the buzzing resumed. Ever inventive, he got up and clenched an iron rod of the bedstead between his teeth. Now he could feel the tremor as well as hear it. The next morning he mentioned the experience to Matteucci, and remarked that Vesuvius was readying itself for a second explosion. The professor laughed, saying: 'You must have heard them grinding coffee for breakfast.' A few days later, the volcano erupted.

'The only way to know a crater is to live with it,' insisted Thomas A. Jaggar Jr, another veteran volcanologist with red rock fever, who founded the Hawaiian Volcano Observatory. He lived there for about 30 years until his retirement as director in 1940, studying the workings of ever-active Kilauea, often-active Mauna Loa, and potentially-active Mauna Kea – the highest mountain in the world (measured from the ocean floor).

It is Hawaiian lava that has given names to two basic types of lava found the world over. *Pahoehoe* ('pa-hoy-hoy') is the smooth kind

Frank Perret. Using a microphone of his own invention, this pioneering US volcanologist listens to the subterranean rumblings of a volcano near Pozzuoli in Italy, during the early 1900s. By detecting changes in the pitch of the sounds, Perret hoped to forecast eruptions.

Pyroclastic flow. What was once called a *nuée ardente* is now generally termed a pyroclastic ('fire-broken') flow: a boiling cloud of gases, particles and rocks. Although such flows are a common feature of certain volcanoes, only a twentieth of dated eruptions have included a pyroclastic flow. They are therefore difficult and potentially deadly phenomena to study. This one erupted from the Ngauruhoe volcano in New Zealand, in 1974.

that tends to form a ropy surface; *aa* is sharp, jumbled and twisted like clinker. One can walk easily on cooled *pahoehoe*; to walk across *aa* is very laborious, lacerating one's boots and hands too if one falls (the name is very expressive). Not surprisingly, native Hawaiians did not try to do so: trails in Hawaii – about 99 per cent of which are made of lava – often cross a *pahoehoe* flow, but hardly ever an *aa* flow.

Pahoehoe results from eruptions at high temperature (and hence low viscosity) with low-volume rates of emission. Low viscosity allows the lava to flow easily; and the low rate of flow allows a skin to form. The opposite conditions tend to produce *aa*. These conditions typically occur in high lava fountains: although the temperature of the jet of lava is high, the lava clots cool in the air and cannot form flows when they land – especially if they hit a steep slope, where gravity tends to break them up instead of allowing them to flow. Robert Decker, with years of experience watching Hawaiian lava, has compared it with fudge: 'If it is poured hot and allowed to cool into a smooth slab, it is like *pahoehoe*; if it is stirred too much and cools before pouring, it "sugars", or crystallizes into a rough broken slab that crumbles to pieces.'

The speed and dimensions of both kinds of flow are hard to distinguish, though *aa* tends to be the faster of the two. A *pahoehoe* flow mostly creeps ahead at roughly a yard or metre a minute or less. But with a steep slope and a high-volume rate of lava emission it can move at well over 400 yards per minute, nearly 14 mph – fast enough to outrun a person. Its thickness is typically 1 foot (30 cm). *Aa* flows are between $6\frac{1}{2}$ and $16\frac{1}{2}$ feet (2–5 m) thick, and often advance in surges. The flow front may move only a few yards in an hour, piling itself higher as it moves; but then it may surge forward more than 100 yards in a few minutes, subsiding as it does so to its original height by the time that the surge stops. Its width is typically more than 100 yards, fed by open channels of lava a tenth the width, moving at 6–12 mph and breaking up into many slower-moving channels that distribute the lava to the front.

These are the facts about lava flows. The impression of inexorability they create tends to make even the most dispassionate observer metaphorical. Here is Decker again:

> Watching a *pahoehoe* flow creep and sizzle across a lawn toward a doomed house is like watching a huge snake slowly and relentlessly approaching its prey. . . . The cooling skin on the top of the flow is stretched by the molten basaltic lava as it inflates the advancing lobe. The tough, glassy skin becomes thinner as it stretches, and orange blotches of more incandescent melt appear on the spreading surface.

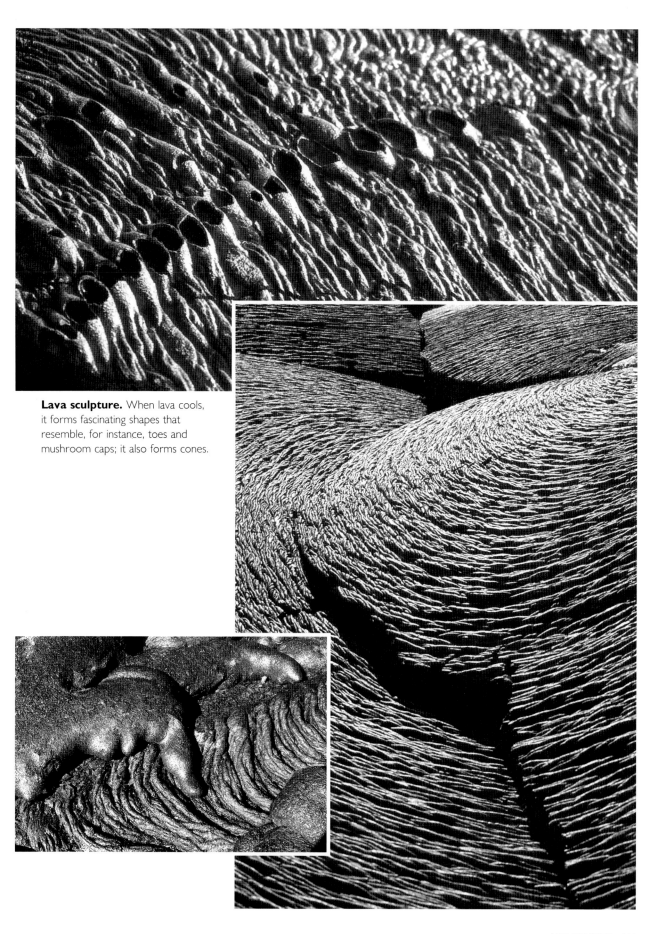

Lava sculpture. When lava cools, it forms fascinating shapes that resemble, for instance, toes and mushroom caps; it also forms cones.

Lava flows. The Hawaiian language has given names to two fundamental types of lava. *Aa* is sharp and clinkery; *pahoehoe* ('pa-hoy-hoy') is smooth and tends to form a ropy surface. (*Right*) An *aa* flow advances over an earlier *pahoehoe* flow in Hawaii. (*Below*) A *pahoehoe* flow emerges from the east rift zone of Kilauea in Hawaii in 1974. 'Watching a *pahoehoe* flow creep and sizzle [forwards] is like watching a huge snake slowly and relentlessly approaching its prey' (volcanologist Robert W. Decker). A *pahoehoe* flow moves at roughly a yard a minute or less. The fastest-moving lava tends to be basalt lava (*far right*). Basalt is relatively low in silica (quartz) and is therefore less viscous than many rocks when molten. It has spread out to form immense plateaus, such as the Deccan Traps in northwestern India.

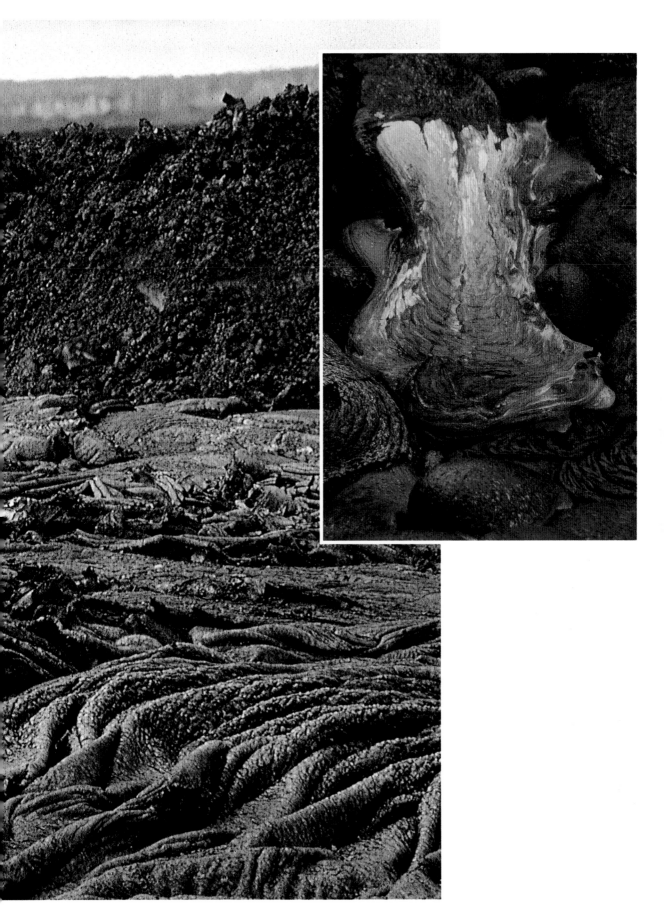

And this is Peter Francis, a British volcanologist, describing an *aa* flow:

> Every few minutes a large solid mass breaks off and topples forward in a cascade of loose, glowing material, and comes to rest a few feet from the main mass, leaving a fading, sullen red scar to mark the place on the flow where it came from. In this way, with one small rock fall following another, the flow continues to advance, very slowly, clinking and rattling forward like a shuffling slag heap.

The skin on *pahoehoe* to which Decker refers – or for that matter the lava tunnels that infiltrate Hawaii – suggests how lava is able to flow underwater at ocean ridges/rifts (contrary to one's expectation that the lava should immediately solidify). The skin turns out to be an excellent insulator. It forms, sack-like, on the molten lava at the ridge. These sacks inflate, burst, and molten lava flows from the tear; and then the process repeats itself. The accumulated layers look somewhat like a pile of pillows, and the name 'pillow lava' has stuck to them. There is a great deal of pillow lava on the sea floor. It has been observed since the 1970s by scientists in submersibles; but it is visible on the surface only when the sea floor is uplifted.

Tubes and bombs. A bomb (*above*) is by definition still molten when it is ejected from the volcano; a 'block', by contrast, is solid. Bombs are therefore fashioned by their passage through the air; on landing, they may gush red-hot lava. Lava also forms tubes – volcanic plumbing – such as the basalt tubes at Kilauea in Hawaii (*left*), left behind as lava drained away when the eruption stopped or changed course. Tubes may be several miles in length and are wide enough and high enough for a person to walk through them with ease. But to venture far into a lava tube can be an unnerving experience.

Assuming that submarine volcanoes produce only lava, then about half the material produced by the world's volcanoes is lava, and half is pyroclastic ejecta. If we consider only land volcanoes, however, lava accounts for a far smaller proportion of total emissions, about 20 per cent. The Hawaiian hot-spot volcanoes are most unusual in producing 99 per cent lava; rift volcanoes such as those in Iceland and east Africa produce 60 per cent lava; and subduction-related volcanoes – the dominant type of land volcano – produce just 10 per cent lava. So the common idea that lava is the main volcanic product is mistaken.

Erupting volcanoes chuck out material of all shapes and sizes, from fine ash to bombs weighing eight tons that travel more than half a mile. The collective term for all these pyroclastic fall deposits is 'tephra'. A widely used scale divides tephra smaller than 2 millimetres (nearly 0.1 inch) into ash; tephra less than 64 millimetres (2.5 inches) into lapilli ('little stones'); and anything larger into either blocks – rocks ejected solid – or bombs – those ejected plastic and therefore fashioned into different rounded shapes by passage through the air. Some bombs are still molten inside: on landing, they may explode and gush red-hot liquid. They are known to travel at least 3 miles, at initial speeds of up to 1250 mph.

Varieties of volcanic rock. The less silica (quartz) a rock contains, the less viscous (and more runny) it is when molten. Basalt (*right*) contains less silica than andesite (*opposite above*) which itself contains less silica than rhyolite (*opposite below*). Obsidian – volcanic glass – is formed by the fast cooling of high-silica molten rock (*below*).

The chemical composition of the rocks in a volcano and in the magma below it is as crucial to its eruptive behaviour as its location. Rock's silica content – silica being silicon dioxide, the formula of quartz or glass, and the most abundant of the Earth's minerals – varies from about 55 per cent in basalt to 73 per cent in rhyolite. Rhyolite has the same chemical composition as granite, but it is more finely crystallized because it has been erupted and cooled fast, rather than allowed slowly to cool within the Earth's crust like granite. If, as sometimes happens, it is cooled very rapidly, a volcanic glass known as obsidian forms instead of a crystalline structure. Obsidian was the steel of ancient civilizations, invaluable in making tools; it was also prized as a decoration, being used to make the sad, black eyes of Tutankhamen's funerary mask.

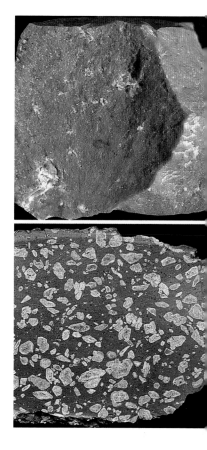

In between basalt and rhyolite come andesite and dacite, which are richer in silica and therefore more dense than basalt (recall how the injection of light basaltic magma into denser dacitic magma is thought to have triggered Krakatoa's eruption) but less rich in silica and therefore less dense than rhyolite. As magma, it is also more viscous than basalt and less viscous than rhyolite: the more silica there is, the thicker the magma. To borrow one scientist's analogy: the viscosity of Hawaiian basaltic magma is about that of honey at room temperature, while dacitic magma is more like tar.

Basalt therefore flows and forms sheets when molten, which more viscous rocks do not. These sheets may be quite small, as in the case of Hawaii, or of tremendous size, like the 88,000-square-mile Columbia River plateau in the northwestern United States or the 200,000-square-mile Deccan Traps in northwestern India. The Indian outpouring has now been dated to a period of 66 million years ago, give or take 2 million years – exactly the period of a mass extinction of life, including the dinosaurs. Some scientists have therefore proposed that volcanism on a grand scale wiped out the dinosaurs. (Others, notably Walter and Luis Alvarez, believe a meteorite collision was to blame; the debate is still wide open.)

The importance of silica content in magma, when considered in tandem with water content, suggests a possible model for the mechanism of volcanic eruptions. It is silica and other minerals in the magma that make up lava and ejecta, but it is superheated water and gases dissolved in magma at high pressure and temperature – somewhat like the bubbles of carbon dioxide in a warm fizzy drink – that can cause an eruption to go with a bang.

If the water content is low, and so is the silica content, the mixture yields a quiet eruption with runny lava. If, however, the water content is high, the steam will cause fire fountains. If, on the other hand, the water content remains low but the silica content is high, the volcano extrudes pasty lava and gradually builds a huge

Bubbles of water vapour

Silica crystals

Low water/Low silica

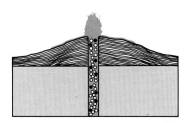

High water/Low silica

Low water/High silica

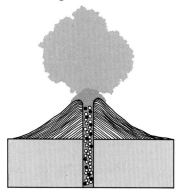

High water/High silica

Four types of volcanic eruption. Each has a different proportion of steam and silica in its magma, which reflects the explosiveness of the eruption and the lava it produces.

lava dome. But if *both* water and silica content are high, there is a build-up of trapped superheated water – i.e. water above its normal boiling point because of higher than atmospheric pressure – which flashes to steam in a geyser-like explosion.

What determines the behaviour of the plug of volcanic material that acts like the cork? Clearly the nature and strength of the rocks in the volcano itself – the so-called 'country rock' – must be involved, as well as the composition, pressure and temperature of the eruption mixture. More precise than this it is difficult to be at present, because we know so little about magma. The very word feels elusive, as vaporous as aether or phlogiston; but the substance it describes, when it churns out at the Earth's surface as lava, is abundantly, implacably real. 'The questions of where magma comes from and how it is generated are the most speculative in all of volcanology', a volcanologist wrote at the beginning of the 1980s. Despite much debate and many powerful techniques for looking inside the Earth, that statement still holds.

Take hot spots, for example. How far into the Earth does the hypothesized plume of magma that heats the crust under, say, Hawaii, actually begin? Is it from the Earth's core-mantle boundary, some 1800 miles down? Or from the discontinuity in the mantle about 400 miles down, below which earthquake foci cease? Some scientists insist it is the former and speak of 'plume tectonics'; they consider that hot-spot plumes cool the core, while plate tectonic activity cools the mantle. Others insist that there is no evidence for such deep plumes.

And what about the plates that are subducted and are believed to generate the volcanoes above subduction zones? How far into the mantle do they penetrate? Do they melt in the upper mantle, or do they dip down as far as the lower mantle, even to the core-mantle boundary? Those who favour deep plumes claim to have detected the subducting plates in the lower mantle; those who dismiss deep plumes disagree with such claims. Could the subducted oceanic sediments on the surface of the plates – limestone deposited over tens of millions of years – be responsible for the higher water/steam content and more explosive eruption mixtures of subduction-related volcanoes compared to rift and hot-spot volcanoes? Most scientists accept this as likely, but there is little agreement about the details beyond this general principle. Since no one can take a look, in the manner of Jules Verne's *Journey to the Centre of the Earth*, and no instrument will ever probe such depths directly, satisfying answers to our questions are likely to wait a long time.

Some idea of the scale and magnitude of the forces operating within the Earth is clear from the history of Man's attempts to control lava. Such endeavours have included walls, giant concrete blocks dropped into lava tubes, explosive charges and millions of gallons of water poured onto the lava. The earliest known attempt, at Etna in Sicily in 1669, used brute force.

On 11 March that year, following three days of earthquakes, Etna began the most violent eruption in its history. Two weeks later, a stream of lava poured down the southern slope of the mountain, heading straight for Sicily's second city – the ancient port of Catania – 17 miles below. It formed channels, as is usual with an *aa* flow, and ploughed through several villages on the slopes. Then a citizen of Catania, Diego de Pappalardo, with a cohort of perhaps 50 others, all clad in wetted cowhides against the heat, broke down one of the cooled levees at the side of the main lava channel using long iron bars. The molten flow divided as they hoped, and part of it poured through the breach. This, however, galvanized the citizens of Paterno, 11 miles northwest of Catania, whose village was now threatened. Some 500 of them, heavily armed and raucous with trumpets and drums, forced the Catanians to let the breach heal. The lava crept on and eventually, after halting at the city's walls for several days, engulfed the city. Some of Catania's streets are partly blocked by huge chunks of lava even today.

The aerial bombing of selected points in a lava flow was first tried in Hawaii in 1935 by the US Army Air Corps. Thomas Jaggar Jr, who directed it, was delighted and claimed some success in stopping the flow, which had been menacing Hilo, an important port. But subsequent detailed analysis has concluded that the bombs had no significant effect. There have been several more attempts to bomb lava, for example at Etna in 1992, but all have produced equivocal results at best.

The uncertainties in using explosives against lava are well illustrated by an attempt to blow up part of a flow moving due south from Etna in 1983, this time from beneath rather than from the air. Holes had to be drilled into the levee of the channel in tiers, so that charges could be laid. The levee was first artificially thinned with bulldozers, and then the holes were cooled – 80 degrees C (176°F) is the maximum acceptable temperature for explosives – by using water and packing them with dry ice. The cooling was insufficient, however, and had an unpredicted effect: it froze the lava on the interior channel wall, which, in turn, caused a reduction in the cross-sectional area of the channel. Since the river of lava continued to flow at the same rate, it now overflowed the bottleneck, burying the drill holes and forcing the crews to retreat.

In the end, about 900 pounds (some 400 kg) of explosive were injected into the remaining drill holes (which were by now

Humans against lava. There have been a number of attempts to stop lava flows using different techniques, most of them failures. In 1973 Icelanders appeared to achieve some success by hosing lava with vast quantities of sea water. But maybe the lava stopped for other reasons – who can be certain?

incandescent) via an ingenious air gun device, and immediately detonated. Again, the result was unpredicted. A small amount of lava poured out of the breach, but because the levee remnants were relatively cold, the breach quickly sealed itself. However, cooled chunks of debris from the levee, thrown up by the explosion, blocked the main lava channel downstream: much of the channel then roofed over as a lava tube, and about 500 yards (more than 450 m) downstream a major blockage diverted most of the flow to the southwest – exactly as intended.

Further use of explosive charges in 1992 worked more predictably, diverting Etna's biggest flow this century and saving the town of Zafferana in the nick of time. Italian volcanologists estimated that a third of the town would have been wrecked without the diversion; but there is no way for them to be certain. Indeed, this is the underlying question with all lava control experiments: what would the lava have done had it been left alone? To take a case in point, in Iceland, in 1973, scientists and citizens of the island of Heimaey hosed more than 5 million cubic yards (nearly 4 million cubic metres) of lava with 6 million tons of sea water for five months, in the hope of saving some of their homes and, most important, the best harbour on Iceland's south coast. To begin with, it was a national joke: '*pissa a hraunid*' ('a hraunid' means 'on the lava'). But when the eruption ceased in early June, the harbour had been saved, just: the lava had left an entrance 150 yards wide (which in fact improved the harbour). Who was responsible, Man or Nature? The Icelandic volcanologist in charge, Thorbjorn Sigurgeirsson, was unwilling to claim the credit.

Despite the astonishing technology of the late 20th century, volcanic eruption prediction, like earthquake prediction, remains a humbling science. Monitoring restless magma is one thing, forecasting when it will erupt quite another. The single most important aspect of monitoring is continuity. The history of a volcano, both its geology and its eruptions, if well enough known, is often a good guide to its future behaviour.

Among the indicators measured by scientists are seismicity, tumescence and tilt, chemical emissions, and gravitational, magnetic and electrical changes. Of these the first, seismicity, is the most important, because earthquakes almost invariably precede eruptions – as the story of Perret and the iron bedstead suggests. When magma forces its way to the surface, perhaps through cracks in the crust (scientists have little exact idea), it produces tremors, often in swarms. Sometimes there are major earthquakes: one such damaged Pompeii in A D 62, another damaged an important lighthouse near Krakatoa in 1880 (three years before the eruption); a magnitude-7.2 earthquake in Hawaii in 1975 was quickly followed by an eruption of Kilauea that changed the volcano's pattern of behaviour. But it may be a few hours, or it may be a year or more after earthquakes begin, before an eruption gets underway.

When the magma has risen very near the surface, it bloats the volcano and deforms its surface: a fact first observed in the early 1900s in Japan and Hawaii. Eruption may follow within minutes, or it may take days. Satellites of the Global Positioning System (GPS), which are beginning to be useful in earthquake prediction, are more helpful still in measuring the topography of volcanoes. Formerly, hundreds of reference points on the volcano's surface had to be fixed by standard land survey techniques. Now, receivers distributed across the volcano pick up radio transmissions from satellites and read out their relative positions to within a few centimetres. According to scientists monitoring Kilauea in the past few years, GPS has been used 'to great effect in following subtle changes in the volcano's shape, which in turn reveal the depth and volume of magma.'

The presence of magma and its movements produce very small changes in gravity at the surface of the volcano. A gravimeter can detect these, but it cannot distinguish between changes in density and mass: for unambiguous interpretation, it needs to be used in conjunction with measurements of ground deformation. 'Two types of change seem to signal danger: data that show deflation of the volcano at the same time as an increase in both mass and density below ground . . . and inflation with an increase in mass . . . Both could represent a rise of magma within the volcano', wrote a geophysicist expert in gravimetry.

Less useful – because less understood as yet – are magnetic and resistivity changes below ground. Basaltic magma contains no magnetic minerals, but basalt has a small proportion of magnetic iron oxide. Conversely, magma is a good electrical conductor, while basalt is not. Theoretically, it should be possible to track magma by measuring magnetic fields and taking electrical soundings within the volcano. (Recall the VAN method of earthquake prediction, which employs measurements of electrical resistivity.)

It was the onset of seismic activity at Mount St Helens in Washington state in mid-March 1980, following a long period of quiet, and the development of a pronounced bulge in the mountain during early May, that alerted scientists and millions of Americans to its imminent eruption. On 18 May it blew its top, leaving behind an ugly stump 1313 feet (400 m) lower than its earlier eminence and a grim amphitheatre with 2000-foot walls. Below it lay a blasted landscape of 232 square miles – a third the size of London – in which not one tree in this prime logging area had been left standing

A sleeping giant awakes. Mount St Helens, one of a chain of 'dormant' volcanoes in the northwestern corner of the United States, blew its top in 1980, less than two months after the top photograph was taken. The photograph of the eruption shows its first stage; eventually the summit was truncated by 1313 feet (400 m).

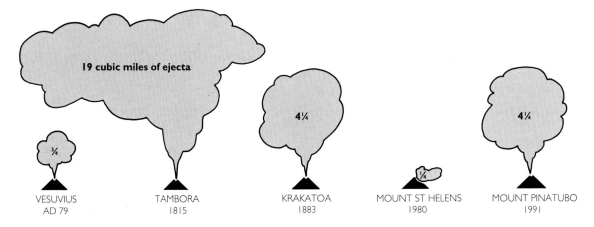

¾	19 cubic miles of ejecta	4¼	¼	4¼
VESUVIUS AD 79	TAMBORA 1815	KRAKATOA 1883	MOUNT ST HELENS 1980	MOUNT PINATUBO 1991

The eruption clouds of five famous volcanic eruptions.

by the pyroclastic flow. The trees were not the only casualty: 57 people were killed, including the volcanologist David Johnston, along with 5000 black-tailed deer, 200 black bears, 1500 elk and countless birds. Ash fell up to 3 inches (7.6 cm) deep over the northwestern United States and southern Canada, 600,000 tons of it alone on the small town of Yakima (population 51,000), 85 miles from the volcano. It took ten weeks to shift, and cost $2.2 million.

The aftermath of the eruption was expensive, but the US could afford it. The fatalities, though serious, could have been far worse had the authorities caved in to demands and allowed picnickers and campers into the restricted area. In most big eruptions the picture is very different. 'A brief profile of a volcanic hazard-prone country', writes the volcanologist R. J. Blong, 'suggests a relatively under-developed land, tropical, excolonial, with a relatively low gross national product, a poor communication network, limited infra-structure development, and a heavy reliance by the populace on subsistence agriculture.'

In other words a country such as Colombia. In November 1985, a minor eruption by the Nevado del Ruiz volcano melted part of its snowcap at high altitude and launched an avalanche of mud, rocks, uprooted trees and other debris that buried alive 22,000 people in the river valley town of Armero. Unlike Japan, where landslides are a constant threat too, Colombia has no simple warning devices, trip wires stretched across stream valleys and connected by radio to downstream police stations. The Colombian landslide took nearly two hours to reach Armero; if such devices had been in place, warnings would have been given in time to evacuate the town. In fact, Colombian scientists did issue a warning to evacuate Armero some eight hours before the disaster, based on a long series of tremors followed by small explosions from the crater, minor ash falls and a strong smell of sulphur. But they were ignored.

The volcano had a history of eruptions, notably in 1595 and early in the 19th century. In 1845 a volcanic eruption or earthquake sent mudflows pouring down the same route as in 1985. They killed about 1000 people. The increased death toll in 1985 is a reflection of a worldwide situation: as the world's population has increased, more people are living on the slopes of volcanoes, attracted by their soil fertility (volcanic ash renews soils leached of potassium and phosphorus, among other elements vital for plant growth) and therefore willing to take the risk of disaster. One million people are estimated to have died as a result of volcanic eruptions in the past 2000 years. Many of them starved to death. If one subtracts the deaths caused by starvation from the total number of deaths and calculates the rate of fatalities directly attributable to volcanic action, the fatality rate this century turns out to be more than $2\frac{1}{2}$ times that during the preceding three centuries. So it is the volcanoes, not human beings, that seem to be winning the battle of numbers.

The fact is, the acceptable level of risk from volcanoes varies wildly from one part of the world to another. Many underdeveloped countries prefer to let Nature have its way. Evacuations are immensely costly and disruptive, especially if a forecast turns out to be wrong. When, in 1976, the French government evacuated the entire population of Guadeloupe, fearing a major eruption of La Soufrière (and remembering, no doubt, the fate of nearby St Pierre in 1902), nothing happened – except a furious controversy about whether the evacuation had been necessary.

Two simultaneous eruptions in mid-1991 illustrated the dilemmas for both scientists and policy-makers well. Both were from subduction-related volcanoes on the Pacific rim: the most common and hazardous kind of land eruption. But whereas one, at Mount Unzen, was in Japan where the volcanoes are closely and sophisticatedly watched, the other, at Mount Pinatubo, was in the Philippines, where scientific resources are severely limited. Unzen, in the far southwest of Japan near Nagasaki, had not erupted since 1792, when 15,000 people were killed by mudslides (triggered by an earthquake associated with the volcanic activity). In late 1989, seismic activity began in the bay west of the peak and gradually migrated eastwards from July 1990. In early November, volcanic tremors were observed. The Coordinating Committee for Prediction of Volcanic Eruptions, based in Tokyo, asked the government for financial support to step up the seismic monitoring of Unzen by university groups, and this was immediately granted. The university team established a seismic network, with 21 sensors on the volcano, in cooperation with the Earthquake and Volcano Observatory of Kyushu University at Shimabara, the city at the east-northeast foot of the volcano. This in due course became the advance headquarters of the Committee.

Mount Pinatubo erupts. On 15 June 1991, Mount Pinatubo in the Philippines detonated. Pyroclastic flows advanced up to 9½ miles down the flanks of the volcano. This photograph was taken from Clark airbase, 15 miles east of the volcano, and shows the initial (smaller) eruption, on 12 June. The airbase was immediately evacuated, and later had to be abandoned.

Clouds that kill. Not all eruptions produce the swift, deadly clouds of gas, particles and rocks, known as pyroclastic flows. But when Japan's Mount Unzen erupted in 1991 after two centuries of quiet, it did. The flow seen here on 8 June was similar to one on 3 June that killed 42 people, mostly from the press and television but including scientists too.

On 13 May 1991, extremely shallow earthquakes just beneath the volcano's crater began to occur. The Committee expected lava to appear and issued a formal statement. Flows of debris started on 15 May, and the local government now recommended certain people living in the threatened area to leave. The following day, lava was seen in the crater. The first pyroclastic flow appeared on 24 May; and two days later, a worker was slightly burnt by hot ash from a pyroclastic flow. Television showed the injury. The same day, the local government issued an evacuation order for the entire threatened area and clearly marked a restricted area. The Committee predicted further pyroclastic and debris flows. On 31 May it decided to move to its headquarters so as to be able to respond

quickly to the volcano; the first member arrived at Shimabara on 4 June. Meanwhile, experts had prepared a hazard map of pyroclastic and debris flows for the local government. Using this map, 12,000 people were evacuated from the exclusion zone by 10 June.

But the Committee was unable to predict the exact timings of Unzen's major eruptions, and a number of lives were lost. On 3 June, a groove more than 300 yards (300 m) long connected to the crater on the east slope, suddenly produced a pyroclastic flow. Lava domes then grew along the groove as well as on the crater. Further explosive eruptions on 8 and 11 June shot cinders up to 6 inches (15 cm) long across Shimabara and spread volcanic ash over a distance of more than 350 miles. The 3 June flow killed 42 people, most of them television and press staff trying to capture spectacular footage within the restricted area. Also among the dead were three scientists: the French 'dare-devils of volcanology', Maurice and Katia Krafft, whose photographs and footage of volcanic eruptions are among the best ever taken; and the US volcanologist Harry Glicken, formerly field assistant to David Johnston, the scientist who had himself perished on Mount St Helens in 1980.

Could scientists have anticipated the timing and path of this lethal cloud and thus saved lives? Not in the present state of understanding of pyroclastic flows. Some people felt that they might, however, have announced the dangers more clearly and earlier than they did, and placed more emphasis on the uncertainties of volcano forecasting. The chairman of the Coordinating Committee for Prediction of Volcanic Eruptions later wrote in *Nature* that 'the prediction of eruptions is extremely difficult . . . prediction of the date and time of initial outburst is still like a kind of betting.' In that case, said a scientific critic, 'Given the limitations of the science, should not the committee be renamed so as not to raise false expectations in the general public?'

When Mount Pinatubo erupted, some 750 Filipinos lost their lives. None of them was a scientist or a journalist; they were local farmers and workers living on the slopes of the volcano. About one third died as a direct consequence of the eruption; the rest fell victim to mudslides during the monsoon rains that picked up ash from the several eruptions, or to disease in refugee shelters. 650,000 people lost their livelihoods in a country already suffering from over 15 per cent unemployment; about half a million of them crowded into the capital, Manila, 60 miles distant.

The ash, which was similar in amount to that of Krakatoa's eruption in 1883 (but only a quarter of that produced by Mount Tambora in 1815), closed Manila international airport for several days. It buried the important Clark airbase 15 miles east of the volcano so deep that the US government later abandoned it

Ash not snow. Volcanic ash from the eruption of Mount Pinatubo fell on Manila, 60 miles from the volcano, temporarily closing its international airport. On the flanks of the volcano itself, it blanketed and obliterated houses and even whole towns (*top*): within about 2 miles of the rim of the main crater, ash fell up to 6½ feet (2 m) thick.

In late April 1991, some weeks before the eruption of Mount Pinatubo in mid-June, American and Filipino geologists examine ash deposits on the rim of a small crater that exploded on 2 April (*above*). Behind, gray vent emissions are visible, consisting of mainly steam with the odour of hydrogen sulphide.

altogether. It also buried 200,000 acres of farmland, at least two dozen towns and the homes of 1.2 million Filipinos. In the stratosphere it reached a height of 49,000 feet (15,000 m), and its cloud of sulphuric acid particles shortly began to affect the global climate (see Chapter 9).

These are striking, not to mention grim, statistics – but from the point of view of both scientists and politicians, they are not the whole story. The monitoring of the eruption and the public response to it was a considerable success, especially in comparison to other recent eruptions in the Third World. As soon as Pinatubo awoke in early April (after 600 years of quiet), the Philippine Institute of Volcanology and Seismology contacted friends at the US Geological Survey. An American team was soon on its way with equipment not available in the Philippines: seismometers, tiltmeters and personal computers that used a new program capable of plotting, locating and examining earthquakes around the volcano in real time – as the events unfolded: such analysis would previously have taken much longer. Filipino and US scientists could 'follow easily and rapidly the creaking and bulging of the mountain as fresh magma welled up within it', in the words of a *Science* report on the eruption.

In addition, they used a relatively new technique: sulphur dioxide detection. In mid-May, the volcano was emitting about 500 tons of sulphur dioxide daily. Two weeks later, the rate was ten times that. But then it dropped abruptly to only 280 tons daily. The monitoring team attributed this to a blockage, which pointed to a build-up of pressure underground. By then, the foci of earthquakes had closed in on the summit, which had begun to bulge. The main eruption began within a week on 12 June.

Throughout the two months leading up to the eruption, the scientists had been briefing the authorities. As a direct result of their advice, more than 80,000 people had been progressively evacuated. Most of the population near the volcano had listened to the warnings and cooperated. Unquestionably many lives had been saved. People still died unnecessarily, but there was no catastrophe like that in Colombia in 1985. Instead of a possible death toll in the tens of thousands, hundreds only perished. The eruption of Mount Pinatubo was the most energetic volcanic event of the 20th century, but, thanks to science, it did not set a record for human fatalities.

THUNDERSTORMS, HURRICANES, TORNADOES AND LIGHTNING

*An earthquake, a landslip, an avalanche, overtake a man
incidentally, as it were – without passion. A furious gale attacks
him like a personal enemy, tries to grasp his limbs, fastens upon
his mind, seeks to rout his very spirit out of him.*
Joseph Conrad, 'Typhoon', 1902

Tʜᴇʀᴇ are roughly 2000 thunderstorms in progress over the
Earth at any moment. Together, they generate a million
million watts of lightning power – more than the combined output
of all the electric power generators in the United States. One storm
alone can release 125 million gallons (well over 500 million litres) of
water and enough heat to power the US for 20 minutes. A full-
blown hurricane, 500 to 1000 miles or more across and with winds
of up to 200 mph, contains 12,000 times the water and heat: enough
power for half a year. The New England hurricane of 1938 altered
the shape of the US east coast. Tropical cyclones in Bangladesh
regularly refashion the Ganges delta (and kill hundreds of thousands of people). Storms can even affect the fate of nations. In 1588
the Spanish Armada was smashed by storms on the shores of the
British Isles; in 1281 a typhoon in Japan left the invading forces of
Kublai Khan, the Mongol emperor, at the mercy of samurai
warriors, who gave thanks to Kamikaze – the Divine Wind – for the
deliverance of their islands. (And, at a less dramatic level, the tardy
official response to 1992's hurricane Andrew, the most costly
natural disaster in US history, was said to have contributed to the
election defeat of the Republican government.)

Few people have entered the centre of a thunderstorm unpro-
tected, and lived to tell of it. One of them was a US pilot, William
H. Rankin, a decorated veteran of two wars. In July 1959, on a
routine flight over Virginia, he was forced to eject at 47,000 feet

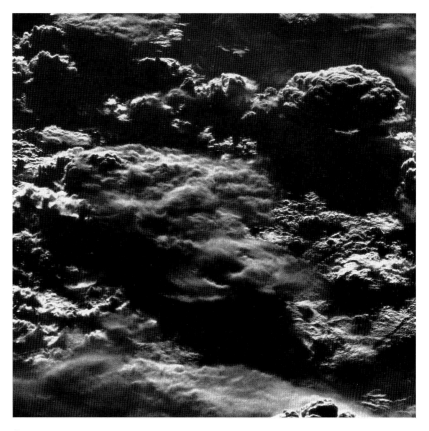

Storm centre. Storms are Earth's air-conditioners; they are also brimming sources of energy. Cloud formation and the working of thunderstorms are, however, surprisingly ill-understood. 'As one watches the shape of clouds they don't seem to change,' remarked the celebrated physicist Richard Feynman, 'but if you look back a minute later, it is all very different.'

(14,300 m), with the temperature at nearly minus 60 degrees C (−70°F), clad only in summer-weight flying gear. His parachute opened as he was about to enter the heart of the storm. 'A massive blast of air jarred me from head to toe,' he recalled.

I went soaring up and up and up. Falling again, I saw that I was in an angry ocean of boiling clouds – blacks and grays and whites, spilling over one another, into one another, digesting one another.

I became a molecule trapped in the thermal pattern of the heat engine, buffeted in all directions – up, down, sideways, clockwise, counterclockwise, over and over. I zoomed straight up, straight down, feeling all the weird sensations of G forces – positive, negative and zero. I was stretched, slammed and pounded. I was a bag of flesh and bones crashing into a concrete floor.

At one point, after I had been shot up like a shell leaving a cannon, I found myself looking down into a long, black tunnel. Sometimes, not wanting to see what was going on, I shut my eyes . . . All this time it had been raining so torrentially that I thought I would drown in mid-air. Several times I had held my breath, fearing to inhale quarts of water.

Storms are Earth's atmospheric air-conditioners. They inhale moist heated air that has built up in the tropics, release the heat into the atmosphere, and propel it towards the polar regions, thus restoring global thermal balance; storms therefore operate as the escape-valves in the mechanism of the Hadley cell (see Chapter 2). The heat released is the latent heat of condensation in water vapour as it turns into cloud droplets, followed by the latent heat of sublimation as those cloud droplets turn into ice particles. Much of the converted vapour then falls as rain, hail or snow.

Storms also move. The observation seems commonplace, but it was not made until 1743, a few years after Hadley had put forward his theory. The observer was Benjamin Franklin. He noticed that a storm had obscured an eclipse of the moon in Philadelphia, where he was, but not in Boston, 260 miles to the northeast. He observed too that the wind direction in Philadelphia had been *from* the northeast, opposite to the storm's direction of movement. This puzzled him, but he did not draw a conclusion. The fact that storms rotate – which we now know to occur anti-clockwise in the northern hemisphere and clockwise in the southern – awaited discovery for some three-quarters of a century. It came from another American, William Redfield, who in 1821 documented a hurricane in Connecticut in which trees 70 miles apart fell in opposite directions. Today's terminology to describe the motion, 'cyclonic', was coined in the 1840s by Henry Piddington, a British merchant captain stationed in Calcutta who had been collecting data on ships caught in storms south of the equator: one such ship, the *Charles Heddles*, had been whirled clockwise for nearly a week off the coast of Mauritius – to the bemusement of its captain, who imagined he had been blown hundreds of miles off course.

In the late 1850s, with the wide application of the electric telegraph, storm forecasting became a real possibility. Three countries – France, Britain and the United States – set up weather services. By 1860, there were 500 stations across the US telegraphing daily weather reports to the headquarters of the Smithsonian Institution in Washington DC. In 1870, Father Benito Viñes, a Spanish Jesuit priest and scientist, settled in Cuba (then a Spanish colony), and became the first scientific hurricane forecaster. Using telegraphic reports from other Caribbean islands, his own copious meteorological observations and an intuition that successful hurricane forecasters would continue to require, Viñes became famous. But he had no real comprehension (nor did he claim to) of the physical processes at work in the hurricane.

A hurricane is defined as a storm with winds of 74 mph or more, up to a maximum speed of about 200 mph. The name, which comes

Typhoon Tip, the most intense typhoon ever measured in the Pacific Ocean. In the first satellite image (*near right*), the typhoon is seen some 1200 miles south of Japan and 900 miles east of the Philippines. Six days later (*far right*) it has lost intensity and spread out to form a giant depression.

The Saffir-Simpson scale of storm intensity

Storm category	Maximum sustained wind speed (mph)
Tropical storm	31–73
Hurricane:	
Level 1 (Weak)	74–95
Level 2 (Moderate)	96–110
Level 3 (Strong)	111–130
Level 4 (Very strong)	131–155
Level 5 (Devastating)	156–

from the Carib Indian *urican*, meaning 'big wind', is restricted to storms in the Atlantic Ocean. In the Pacific, the same phenomenon is known as a typhoon (from the Chinese *taifeng*); in the Indian Ocean and around Australia, it is called a tropical cyclone. There are five levels of hurricane strength defined by the Saffir-Simpson scale. (Tornado, a term used worldwide, refers to a much smaller, shorter-lived and more intense storm than a hurricane; its wind speeds may easily exceed 300 mph.)

This century has brought scientists much closer to an understanding of hurricanes (using the term to cover typhoons and tropical cyclones too) than, say, Viñes possessed; but only of certain aspects of them. Many of the big questions remain largely unanswered. We still have relatively little idea, for instance, why some storms turn into hurricanes and others do not; why some hurricanes make landfall and others remain at sea; what causes a hurricane to wobble or even to reverse; or to what extent a hurricane can steer itself.

This should not surprise us, given the comparative rarity of hurricanes, their size and complexity, and, most of all, their awesome power. Until the arrival of satellites, hurricanes were

awkward phenomena to study, impossible to encompass in their entirety. Through the satellite eye, however, they become the ocean equivalents of the whirling galaxies in space seen by telescopes. Consider typhoon Tip, for instance, the most intense typhoon ever measured in the Pacific Ocean. The chief information Tip's satellite image gives us (which we could have obtained in no other way), concerns the high degree of concentricity of the typhoon, with its well-defined eye, and the spread of the great system of convection, which eventually extended over 1250 miles. The image also yields the temperature at the top of the clouds above the eye: minus 93 degrees C (−135°F), an extraordinarily low figure – showing how high up in the atmosphere the clouds were being expelled from the centre of the storm. But at the same time the image demonstrates some of the satellite's limitations. It shows only the top of the typhoon, the typhoon's exhaust: the infrared scanner on the satellite cannot see through clouds (unlike micro-wave scanners). We are seeing not what the typhoon looks like 'on the ground', but what it looks like high up in the troposphere. Consequently, the satellite cannot accurately determine crucial quantities such as the typhoon's atmospheric pressure at sea level, its wind speed at the sea surface and the orientation and altitude of its clouds. For these we need to turn to other more conventional technologies, in particular aircraft reconnaissance planes that are able to fly in and out of a typhoon. The sea level pressure in the eye of typhoon Tip on 12 October 1979, measured from a plane, was found to be 870 millibars – the lowest value on record.

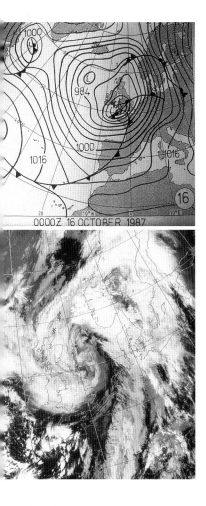

The Great Storm, Britain, 1987. Flattening at least 15 million trees in the southeast of the country, the storm was Britain's worst since 1703. The county of Kent was especially badly affected in its western part; the town of Sevenoaks became 'one oak' when six of its famous seven oaks were felled by the force of the wind. The weather map (*top left*) indicates the pressure above Britain at midnight on 15/16 October 1987; the satellite image (*above left*) shows the storm some hours later, further north above Dundee in Scotland; and the photograph (*above right*) shows Toys Hill near Westerham in Kent.

Clearly, the typhoon would have done enormous damage if it had made landfall. In fact, it vented most of its energy at sea; over the next six days the central pressure rose, the eye disappeared, and Tip expanded and eventually dissipated harmlessly.

A typhoon's behaviour at the surface cannot be forecast, nor even reliably ascertained simply by tracking it from space. South-east Britain discovered this the hard way during the 'hurricane' of 15–16 October 1987, the country's worst storm since 1703. Though it caused just 19 deaths, it flattened more than 15 million trees, cost well over £1 thousand million in damage, and changed the face of Sussex, Kent and Surrey (the counties south of London). There had been no warning from the forecasters. They knew about a large depression heading towards Britain from the Bay of Biscay, but on the basis of satellite information fed into their computer model of Britain's weather, they expected the centre of the depression to pass over London. Instead, the centre passed 80 miles to the west, and part of the 150-mile-wide band of winds swept across the eastern counties during the night. The error could probably have been avoided had the forecasters received surface data from the ocean southwest of Britain; but the weather ship there – at 'Point Romeo' – had recently been withdrawn from service, partly as an economy measure, but also in the (misguided) belief that satellites were superseding the job of weather ships.

The next day, the director-general of the Meteorological Office announced in defence of his organization that 'The Met Office said there would not be a hurricane, and there was no hurricane.' Since the highest wind speed had been 73 mph, and 74 mph is the minimum speed for a hurricane, the director-general was technically correct. But judged by its effects, both physical and psychological, a hurricane it certainly was.

Officially, however, it remains the Great Storm of 1987. Real hurricanes have proper names – at least they have had since 1953. (Before that only the most devastating acquired names, usually given after the event.) Today's practice was the invention of George R. Stewart, who published a novel *Storm* in 1941 in which the junior meteorologist at the San Francisco office of the US Weather Bureau justifies 'the sentimental vagary' by telling himself (privately) that each storm is 'really an individual'; that he could more easily say 'Antonia' than 'the low-pressure center which was yesterday in latitude one-seventy-five east, longitude forty-two north'. The idea caught on among American servicemen in the Pacific during the Second World War, where the pilot who first spotted a typhoon was allowed to name it. From 1953 until 1979, only women's names were used; then feminists persuaded the World Meteorological Organization to use men's names too. But Asian meteorologists, preferring to be more business-like, have tended to use numbers not names.

Yet it is true: these giant storms do act like individuals, quirky and unpredictable, as Joseph Conrad described in *Typhoon*, the story of Capt. MacWhirr's lone battle with a typhoon in the China seas. Two veteran hurricane scientists, Robert H. Simpson and Herbert Riehl, agreed, if more matter-of-factly, in their 1981 study *The Hurricane and its Impact*: 'there are no rules without exception in anything pertaining to hurricanes.'

From a glance at almost any hurricane track chart, prepared annually by the US National Hurricane Center, there appears to be almost no pattern. But when one looks at several decades of tracks worldwide, patterns emerge. Hurricanes, typhoons and tropical cyclones originate only in specific stretches of the west Atlantic, east Pacific, south Pacific, western north Pacific, and south and north Indian Oceans (puzzlingly, none ever occurs in the south Atlantic Ocean). They seldom move closer to the equator than latitude 4–5 degrees north or south, and they never cross the

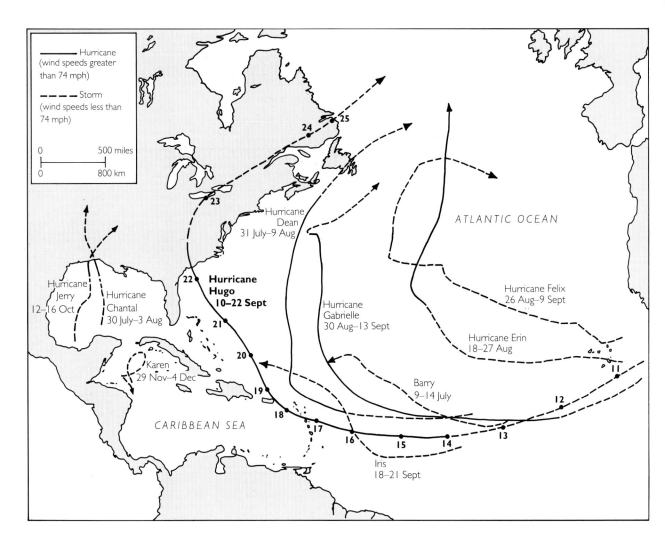

Hurricane track chart for 1989. Note the track of Hurricane Hugo, the year's most destructive hurricane. Like many hurricanes it began as a tropical depression off west Africa, intensified into a tropical storm, and eventually reached hurricane force (four days after becoming a tropical storm).

equator. They are much more common at certain times of year, which vary with the ocean in question. August and September is high season in the Atlantic, for instance.

The latitude condition is easily explained. Because of the Earth's rotation, air (and thus a storm) tends to rotate around depressions: the effect of the Coriolis force (see Chapter 2). The influence of the rotating Earth on wind flow increases with distance from the equator; at the equator it is nil. In order to start spinning – and then keep spinning – hurricanes need help from the Earth's rotation; the further away from the equator they stay, the more help they will get.

They also need heat from the ocean. And this now suggests the reason for the regions in which they are born: the ocean surface must be near enough to the equator to be warm, far enough away for rotation to be induced. The threshold temperature for hurricane formation is found to be 26 degrees C (79°F). If a map of the 26-degree-C isotherm is drawn during different seasons of the year, hurricanes are found to originate within it. At this temperature winds blowing over the ocean surface can collect sufficient heat both by direct contact with the surface and ocean spray, and by the evaporation of ocean water. The heat required to vaporize the water is sucked from the ocean reservoir, which therefore cools. As the warm moist air rises it forms clouds and, as the hurricane begins to form, the air shoots skywards to a great height, shedding the rest of its water and energizing the rotation of the storm. At the top (30,000 feet, 9150m, or more above the ocean) and watched by the satellite, cooled and dried air flies off under centrifugal force in outflow jets (and a little of it subsides into the eye of the hurricane). That hurricanes do cool the ocean is vividly shown in satellite images of the eastern seaboard of the US before and after the passing of a hurricane. Cooling of more than 3 degrees C (5.5°F), lasting more than two weeks, has been observed in the open ocean; and with colder oceans at higher latitudes or near a shore, the cooling can be even greater.

The dependence of hurricane formation on sea surface temperatures has led some scientists to predict more frequent and fierce hurricanes as a result of global warming (the greenhouse effect). The Great Storm of 1987 in Britain might have been the beginning, they say (and the same was said in late 1992 when unpredicted storms battered New York City, shutting down its subway system for the first time in its history). But the link is by no means an obvious one: indeed the opposite may be true. If the oceans do

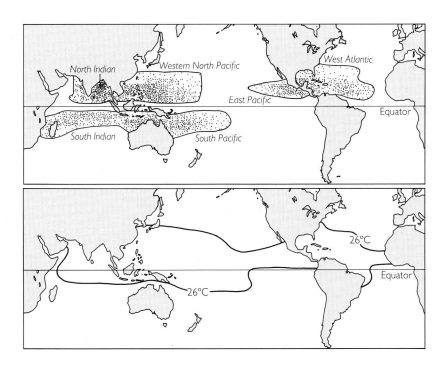

Storms and hurricanes. A 'tropical storm' is defined as a storm with wind speeds more than 39 mph (gale force) and less than 74 mph (hurricane force). On the top map, each dot shows the area of origin of a tropical storm during the period 1952–71. No tropical storm originated on the equator itself, or in the south Atlantic Ocean. Hurricanes require a sea surface temperature of 26 degrees C (79°F) or more. The bottom map shows the 26°C-isotherm for the period July to September: high season for hurricanes, typhoons and tropical cyclones in the northern hemisphere. Note the similar shape of this isotherm and the area of tropical storm origin, north of the equator. (A comparable fit exists south of the equator, using the 26°C-isotherm for January to March.)

Manhattan at a standstill. In December 1992, a giant storm battered New York City, flooding part of the subway system and closing it for the first time in its history. Cars were stranded on Manhattan's Upper East Side when the East River jumped its banks. Insurance companies blamed the storm – which was entirely unpredicted – on global warming.

warm, they are predicted to warm more in the high latitudes than in the tropical latitudes. There should therefore be less, not more, need for hurricanes to distribute heat from the equator to the poles. Furthermore, as well as the oceans, the atmosphere would warm – with unpredictable effects on hurricane formation.

So now we have at least two conditions necessary for hurricane formation: the latitude must be more than 4–5 degrees polewards of the equator, and the surface temperature must be at least 26 degrees C. What else is conducive to the production of a vortex? Here we reach uncertain territory.

Plainly wind shear – divergent winds of differing speeds – must be important. Humidity, helpful in forming clouds, is likely to be required too. Another theory, entirely unproven but described by experts as a 'reasonable suggestion', links high rainfall in sub-Saharan Africa with the high incidence of strong hurricanes in the west Atlantic. The two decades from 1970 were relatively free of fierce hurricanes, while in sub-Saharan Africa there was severe drought. Then, in 1988 and 1989, the African rains were near normal, and in 1989 hurricane Hugo slammed into South Carolina. Is there a real link? It is too early to say.

What may not be doubted is that a wavy jet of wind shot out from west Africa starts off many hurricanes. To begin with they are atmospheric disturbances, known as 'hurricane seedlings' (see page 133); around 70 per cent are known as 'Cape Verde types'. As they migrate west towards the Caribbean, they are tracked by satellites and aircraft to see if they metamorphose into 'tropical storms', that is storms with wind speeds between 39 mph (gale force) and 74 mph (hurricane force); and then maybe intensify further. An average of 100 seedlings cross the Atlantic each year. Of these, 9 or 10, on average, reach tropical storm force; and 5 or 6 of these then become hurricanes. (The year 1990 produced 14 named tropical storms, 8 of them hurricanes; 1991 produced only 8 tropical storms, 4 of which were hurricanes.)

As the vortex of wind, water vapour and clouds increases its speed of rotation, a 'still centre' – the eye of the hurricane – may form. Beyond the eye wall, which in some hurricanes can be a double eye wall, lies the maelstrom. Within, all is calm: the sky is blue, sometimes free of clouds, and the sun shines; at night the stars are visible; and exhausted birds rest on the railings of ships. Eye diameters vary from 3 to 40 miles, and the calm varies from minutes to hours, depending on the size of the eye and the speed at which the hurricane is moving. Many people caught in hurricanes have mistaken the eye for the end of the hurricane and emerged from their shelters, only to be lashed again by winds from the opposite direction.

Under the right conditions an Atlantic hurricane may last for many days, even up to a month, and wander several thousand miles, typically at speeds of 15 to 30 mph, sometimes reaching 60 mph. Its track may be a simple one, straight into the Caribbean, or a parabolic veer away from the east coast of the US into the Atlantic; or it may oscillate, execute loops or reverse direction altogether. Approaching land, it may march on and peter out after wreaking havoc, or it may appear to hesitate and stay at sea, eventually slowing and expanding into a less vigorous, higher pressure 'extratropical depression'; if it crosses land, it may intensify again over water, in some cases more than once. Whatever its track, its decay finally occurs because it runs out of its fuel: warm water vapour. It may encounter a cold current at sea, or a cold air mass may invade it at surface level or higher up. Friction with the surface, both on land and over an agitated sea, also assists the decay of a hurricane, but is not its principal cause.

What guides a hurricane? Or can it somehow steer itself? The New England hurricane of 1938 apparently did the latter, instead of veering away into the Atlantic as expected. So, on a smaller scale, did the Great Storm of 1987 in Britain. But after each event it was possible to rationalize the storm's behaviour by reference to surrounding pressure systems. (In 1938, the Bermuda High was not where it usually was in mid-September.) In fact, meteorologists used to imagine that hurricane steering currents were those of known wind systems in the Atlantic. They went on to calculate parabolic paths that hurricanes were expected to follow in different seasons. Needless to say, the hurricanes did not obey.

A convective system as vast and powerful as a hurricane must influence its atmospheric environment, and hence, in a sense, steer itself – especially if other steering influences are weak. For instance,

Hurricane over New England. The 1938 hurricane in New England has never been forgotten, partly because it was so destructive of life and property, and partly because it was so unexpected. Gusts of 90 mph toppled this 165-foot (50-m) church steeple onto the main street of Danielson, Connecticut. Two men had to hold the photographer upright as he captured the moment of fall.

The most lethal hurricane in US history. The storm that hit Galveston, Texas, in 1900 took 6000 lives (more than a seventh of Galveston's population) and destroyed half the town. The photograph shows the shell of Galveston's Sacred Heart Church, a haven for 400 refugees on the night of the hurricane.

in the absence of strong wind shear whisking away the exhaust air of a hurricane from its outflow jets, an accumulation of air builds up and tends to push the hurricane to the left of its existing track (in the northern hemisphere) or to the right (in the southern hemisphere).

That at any rate is the favoured explanation for the behaviour of hurricane Gilbert in 1988. By 15 September it had crossed Yucatán and was heading for . . . Texas? or would it land further west, in northeast Mexico? A private weather forecasting service in Pennsylvania announced a landing somewhere between Galveston and Corpus Christi, both in Texas; the National Hurricane Center (NHC) said no, it would be Mexico. Galveston sits on a low-lying island where 6000 people died and half the town was destroyed by a hurricane in 1900; in 1988, city officials advised evacuation. But surrounding areas decided to follow NHC advice, and stay put. The result was mass confusion. In fact the hurricane missed Texas and hit Mexico late on 16 September, close to the point predicted by the NHC.

When a hurricane makes landfall, it can kill people and destroy property in four principal ways: wind, tornadoes, rainfall and storm surge. Wind speeds are regularly over 100 mph, and may be as much as twice this. Few buildings remain undamaged; many are stripped of their roofs. A quarter of hurricanes spawn tornadoes, 10 each on average per hurricane, 141 during hurricane Beulah in 1967. Rainfall can reach astronomical proportions: one day's rainfall from a moderate hurricane equals the average *annual* discharge of the Colorado River at its point of largest flow. But it is the storm surge that is most lethal, causing over 90 per cent of hurricane deaths.

'I thought it was a thick and high bank of fog rolling in fast from the ocean,' said a survivor of the 1938 hurricane who had watched the storm surge from Long Island. The bank was 40 feet (12 m) high, and loomed above the houses. 'When it came closer,' the man recalled, 'we saw that it wasn't fog. It was water.' Storm surge is caused by the drop in atmospheric pressure at sea level inside the hurricane, which sucks up the sea; at the same time winds ahead of the hurricane pile up water against coastlines. The first effects of the latter can be felt nearly a week in advance of the hurricane, when the weather is often otherwise fine: the 'calm before the storm'. When the hurricane arrives, the surge is estimated to diminish in depth by 1–2 feet (30–60 cm) for every mile it moves inland. Its size has been calculated for much of the US coastline, using a computer model programme called SPLASH (Special Program to List Amplitudes of Surge from Hurricanes). For a level-5 hurricane, a storm

surge of 32 feet (nearly 10 m) has been calculated for Cedar Key on the upper west coast of Florida; the coast south of Miami should receive surges of up to 15 feet. A surge of 5 feet there would be enough to cause major damage and probably loss of life. Alas for the model – if happily for the battered Floridians living south of Miami – the surge expected during 1992's hurricane Andrew, did not materialize.

But during hurricane Camille, a level-5 hurricane in 1969, it most certainly did. Camille was the most lethal storm to hit the US mainland on record. The hurricane reached the Mississippi coast on 17 August 1969. At 9 p.m. the National Hurricane Center issued the following bulletin:

CAMILLE . . . EXTREMELY DANGEROUS . . . CENTER HAS PASSED MOUTH OF THE MISSISSIPPI RIVER . . . CONTINUES TOWARD THE MISSISSIPPI ALABAMA COAST . . .
THE FOLLOWING TIDES ARE EXPECTED TONIGHT AS CAMILLE MOVES INLAND . . . MISSISSIPPI COAST GULFPORT TO PASCAGOULA 15 TO 20 FEET . . . PASCAGOULA TO MOBILE 10 TO 15 FEET . . . EAST OF MOBILE TO PENSACOLA 6 TO 10 FEET. ELSEWHERE IN THE AREA OF HURRICANE WARNING EAST OF THE MISSISSIPPI RIVER 5 TO 8 FEET. IMMEDIATE EVACUATION OF AREAS THAT WILL BE AFFECTED BY THESE HIGH TIDES IS URGENTLY ADVISED.

Storm surge. High winds combine with low pressure in the eye of a hurricane to suck up the sea; the effect, as a hurricane makes landfall, is a wall of water known as storm surge. The wall can reach heights of 40 feet (12 m) and more, which diminish as the hurricane smashes its way inland. Surge accounts for over 90 per cent of hurricane deaths and is highly destructive.

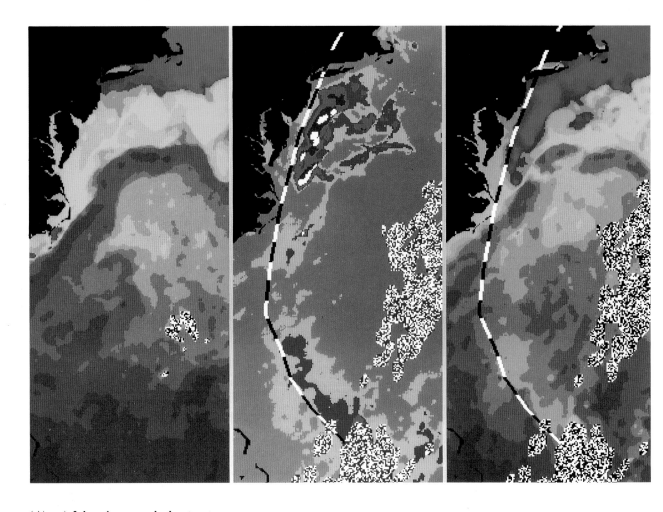

(Above) **A hurricane sucks heat** from the ocean and funnels it into the atmosphere. The temperature of the ocean therefore drops, as these three images of sea surface temperature make clear. The left-hand image is a composite of temperatures over 19–23 September 1985, just *before* the arrival of hurricane Gloria off the east coast of the United States; the right-hand image shows sea surface temperatures just *after* the passing of the hurricane, on 27–28 September. (The hurricane's track is dotted.) The centre image is the difference between the left and right images: yellow indicates a temperature drop of 1 degree C, white a drop of 5 degrees C. The greatest cooling evidently occurred to the right of the storm's track.

(Right) **How a hurricane works.**

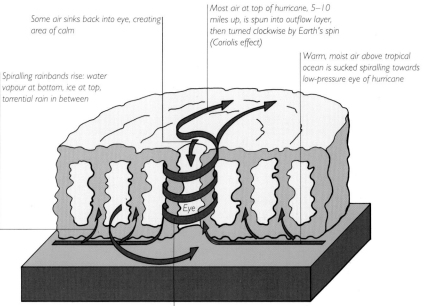

Some air sinks back into eye, creating area of calm

Spiralling rainbands rise: water vapour at bottom, ice at top, torrential rain in between

Most air at top of hurricane, 5–10 miles up, is spun into outflow layer, then turned clockwise by Earth's spin (Coriolis effect)

Warm, moist air above tropical ocean is sucked spiralling towards low-pressure eye of hurricane

Eye

Eye wall: region of highest velocity winds, spinning and soaring

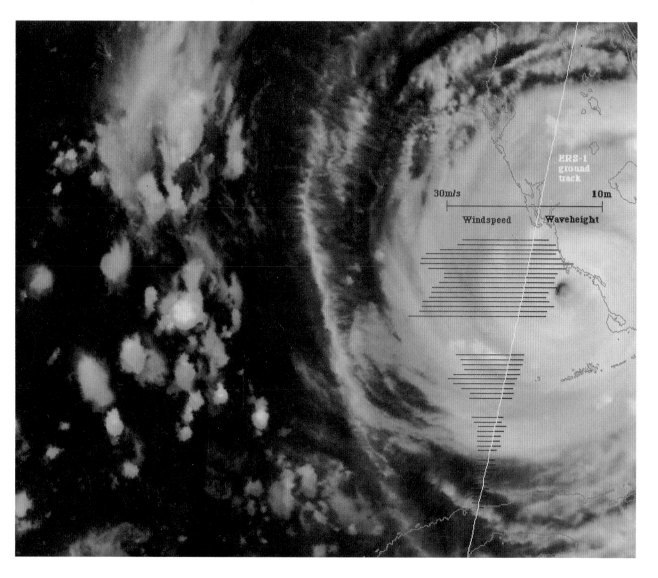

Tracking hurricanes

*R*ELATIVELY *little accurate sampling of the conditions inside a hurricane exists. By sheer luck, a satellite passed over the area of hurricane Andrew in 1992 a few hours after its centre made landfall near Miami (the satellite's track is indicated in the image above by the diagonal line). Radar enabled wind speed and wave height to be measured. The horizontal bars are 7 kilometres (4.3 miles) apart: those to the left of the track indicate wind speed, those to the right wave height. Hurricane Andrew was the most costly natural disaster in US history. It wrecked parts of south Miami with winds of up to 160 mph, maybe more; the photograph (right) shows the remains of a trailer park in Homestead, Florida. But casualties were low because of good advance warning.*

Some 139 people died in Mississippi and southeast Louisiana, including 12 people on the third floor of an apartment complex who had ignored the warnings and arranged a party to celebrate the coming of Camille. They and 11 other people still in the complex were swept away when water flattened it to the ground. But the hurricane had not yet spent itself. Two days later, passing over central Virginia, it dumped 30 inches (76 cm) of rain in six hours at night, mainly on Nelson County. Mudslides buried homes and left 109 people dead as they slept.

But the memory of Camille saved lives ten and more years later. When hurricane Frederic struck Mississippi/Alabama in 1979, half a million people fled. The towns on the Gulf were practically ghost towns during the hurricane. Although Frederic was a level-4 hurricane and the damage was still immense, just 5 people died. In 1992, during hurricane Andrew, about a million people were evacuated, and the casualties were similar.

The burden of responsibility on forecasters is obviously daunting. In the US, it falls chiefly on the National Hurricane Center at Coral Gables in Florida (which in 1992 found itself smack in the path of hurricane Andrew and was put out of action). The NHC watches cyclones as they develop in the Gulf of Mexico, the Caribbean and the Atlantic Ocean, as well as in the eastern Pacific off the coast of Mexico. Central Pacific hurricane forecasts are issued from Honolulu in Hawaii. The bulletins are of two basic kinds: a Hurricane Watch or a Hurricane Warning. A Watch is an advice to a specified part of the coast that within 36 hours there is a 50 per cent probability of a strike by a hurricane. It alerts residents to the possible need for evacuation, so that they can plan. A Warning means that the specified part of the coast is in imminent danger and action must be taken to protect life and property.

The scientists behind hurricane forecasting are only too aware that the US public has come to expect a higher level of accuracy from their forecasts than they can deliver as a rule. Although gross errors of 200 to 300 miles, normal in the 1950s, are a thing of the past, the typical accuracy is still not better than 100 miles. In 1990, the official track forecast error averaged over all tropical storms and hurricanes in the Atlantic basin – that is the difference between a hurricane's position forecast 24 hours ahead and its actual position determined by satellites, radar, aircraft and other means – was 119 miles. This was a 7 per cent improvement on the average for 1980–89. The fact is, noted *Science* in 1990, that 'after 30 years of advances in weather satellites, computer forecasting models, and basic research, forecasters have reduced errors in predicting the paths of hurricanes by just 14 percent.'

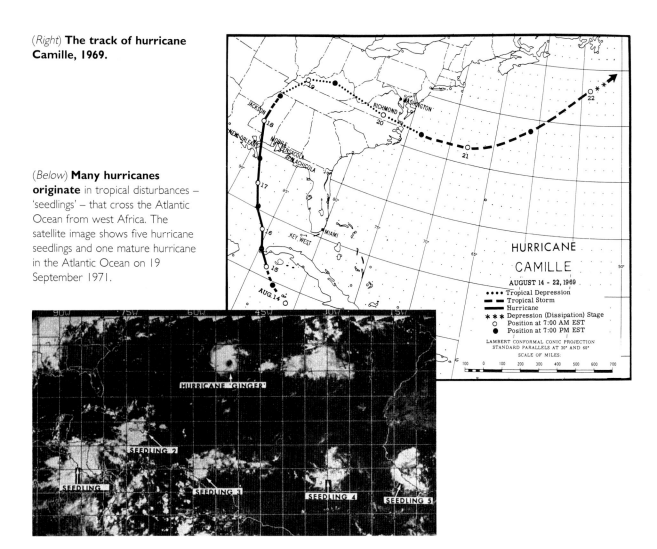

(*Right*) **The track of hurricane Camille, 1969.**

(*Below*) **Many hurricanes originate** in tropical disturbances – 'seedlings' – that cross the Atlantic Ocean from west Africa. The satellite image shows five hurricane seedlings and one mature hurricane in the Atlantic Ocean on 19 September 1971.

The models now being used – a great improvement on those of the 1960s and 1970s that invariably forecast raging storms – are probably not themselves the main source of weakness; it is the data fed into the models, i.e. their starting picture of the weather. The forecasters, according to Kerry Emanuel, a hurricane specialist at the Massachusetts Institute of Technology, 'are not going to make substantial progress until they sample the hurricane a lot better. The conditions over the ocean are so undersampled, even with weather satellites.'

Sampling hurricanes is of course neither easy nor cheap. The first flights into them, from 1943, were feats of derring-do; even today, most planes cannot cope with hurricane and thunderstorm conditions, especially hailstones. The flights soon revealed bands of heavy precipitation and turbulence like the arms of an octopus, and shafts of supercooled water that coated the wings of the plane with ice and threatened to stall it. One of the most dramatic sights was the eye and the eye wall, in its many permutations. This is what Robert Simpson saw in typhoon Marge in 1954:

> Marge's eye was a clear space 40 miles in diameter surrounded by a coliseum of clouds whose walls on one side rose vertically and on the other side were banked like galleries in a great opera house. The upper rim, about 35,000 feet high, was rounded off smoothly against a background of blue sky. Below us was a floor of smooth clouds rising to a dome 8000 feet above sea level in the center. There were breaks in it which gave us glimpses of the surface of the ocean. In the vortex around the eye the sea was a scene of unimaginably violent, churning water.

To reach an understanding of such a vast and veiled system – and hence to programme a computer model of it – requires observation at all levels. Which part of the hurricane, the sea surface interaction, the internal convection or the upper-level flux/exhaust, is most important in determining its behaviour? Inevitably, scientists disagree. And how does the whole system interact with the wider weather? Why, for instance, do Atlantic hurricanes arise chiefly from the waves of air emitted by a land mass, whereas Pacific typhoons grow quite differently?

With such questions unanswered, projects to 'seed' hurricanes with dispersive chemicals from aircraft, were bound to be controversial. How, since one could not predict the behaviour of an unseeded hurricane, could one know if seeding had been a success? The theory was that particles of the right kind (silver iodide was chosen) would act as nuclei and trigger the freezing of supercooled water within the hurricane, thus releasing latent heat which would generate turbulence and disrupt the vortex, causing the eye wall to expand. This would in turn slow the wind speed, like the expanding arms of an ice skater, and reduce the destructiveness of the storm. But as critics pointed out, the scientific logic was dubious: the released energy, instead of disrupting the pattern of air and water vapour in the vortex, might even cause the hurricane to intensify. Experiments carried out on four Atlantic hurricanes between 1961 and 1971 were inconclusive (and provoked charges, unfounded as it turned out, that the seeding had diverted a hurricane onto Florida). Trials in the Pacific were not even started, following objections from countries such as China and Japan (Japan obtains a quarter of its rainfall from typhoons). For the present the experiments have been abandoned.

The basic problem remains: hurricanes are hard to predict, because each one is so different, both in itself and in its steering environment. Even today, there is still much room for human judgment of the kind exercised by Father Viñes in the 1870s – or by

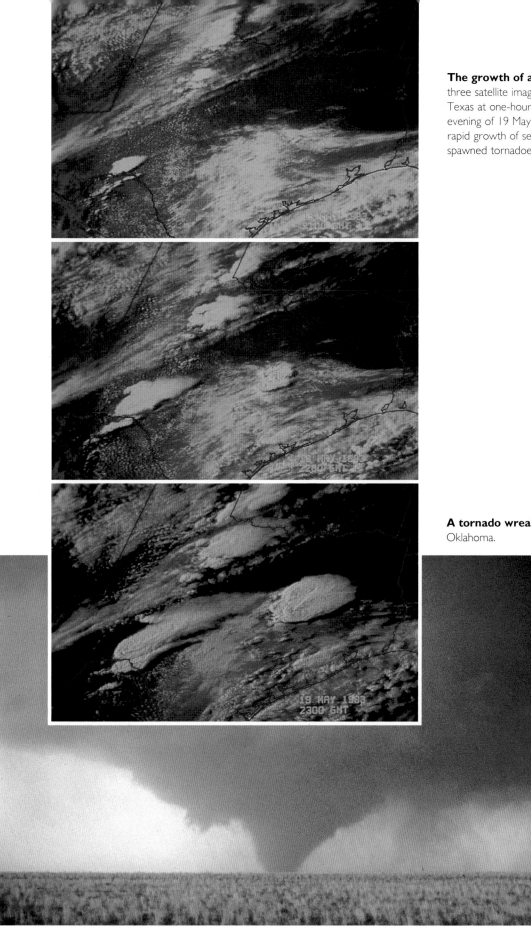

The growth of a tornado. These three satellite images, made above Texas at one-hour intervals on the evening of 19 May 1983, show the rapid growth of severe storms that spawned tornadoes. (See page 141.)

A tornado wreaks havoc in Oklahoma.

Grady Norton, this century's best known forecaster. From 1935 until 1954, when he died in harness, Norton was chief hurricane forecaster for the US Weather Bureau. In 1944, Robert Simpson, then part of the forecasting team, recalls Norton predicting that a storm apparently heading past Florida into the Gulf of Mexico would make a sudden turn northwards and hit Tampa Bay 48 hours later. To Simpson's amazement, it did just that. But when he tackled Norton for an explanation, his response was imprecise, to say the least. He turned towards a set of glass doors that led onto a 19th-floor penthouse deck outside his office and said, 'When I am not sure about the way things are going, I go out there, sit down, put my feet on the parapet and look out over the everglades. I watch the clouds and ask my question. Usually, the answer comes to me.'

Compared with tornadoes, hurricanes are quite predictable. Tornadoes are terrorists, hurricanes lumbering armies. 'Vicious', 'freakish', 'whimsical', are adjectives that tend to attach themselves to any account of tornadoes. Tornadoes combine terrifyingly powerful wind speeds – 300–350 mph, maybe even 500 mph: no one knows for sure – with vanishingly small lifetimes (often 10 minutes, maximum 2 hours), and absurdly localized tracks, as little as 50 yards (some 50 m) wide and a few miles in length: only 0.5 per cent travel more than 100 miles. In shape they can resemble a long, thin rope, an elephant's trunk, or a fat, inverted bell. They think nothing of collapsing a substantial house or even carrying it away whole, picking up a school bus and dumping it upside down inside a classroom, carrying a jar of pickles 25 miles unbroken, plucking the feathers off a chicken or opening the fibres of a telegraph pole and inserting a straw.

Tornadoes occur worldwide, though they are rare in Africa and seldom reported in India. They are quite common on the European continent, and more common still in the British Isles, where there are on average 30 tornadoes a year, nearly 10 per cent of which have winds exceeding 115 mph – enough to strip a roof. But it is the United States that has given tornadoes their reputation. About 1 per cent of all thunderstorms in the US gives birth to a tornado; there are between 700 and 1150 tornadoes a year; and the figure is rising. Approximately 79 per cent of them are weak, 20 per cent are strong and 1 per cent rank as violent. It is the violent ones that claim 70 per cent of lives lost to tornadoes. In the most deadly recorded case, 689 people died – 234 of them in one town – when a tornado touched down in three midwestern states in March 1925.

About a third of US tornadoes ravage just three states: Texas, Oklahoma and Kansas. Warm, moist air flowing up from the Gulf

Tornado Alley, the most aerodynamically wild patch of the American Midwest.

'Vicious' and 'freakish'. Tornado damage can be total in one street, almost nil in an adjacent street. Designing against tornadoes is all but impossible, so great are their wind speeds. Formerly, house owners were advised to open their windows if a tornado approached, so as to equalize the pressures inside and outside the house; nowadays, the advice is the opposite. But such precautions are seldom of much use in a direct hit.

of Mexico meets cool, dry air from Canada channelled east by the Rockies. This aerodynamically wild patch of the Midwest, 460 miles in length and 400 miles in width, is known as Tornado Alley. In 1991 it proved no exception to its name: of the 1125 tornadoes to sweep across the US, 378 hit Texas, Oklahoma and Kansas. These included all the most violent ones, and the year's most lethal at Andover, Kansas.

But before we come to that, here are some of the less noteworthy, not to say ordinary, tornadoes of 1991. They struck at all times of the day. On 15 January, at 3.15 p.m., a teacher at an elementary school in Miami was thrown to the ground and suffered

Tornadoes have many shapes and shades of colour. They may be as thin as a rope or as fat as a bell; as white as the whitest cloud or as black as soot (the black colour coming from the dirt they pick up). They may last as little as ten minutes or as long as two hours, and travel a mile or two or more than 100 miles. No one knows their maximum wind speeds, but they could be as high as 500 mph.

minor injuries. On 3 March, mid-morning, a tornado at George-town, Florida caused over $1 million damage. On 29 March, around daybreak, 5 people died and 13 were injured in Munford, Alabama. On 26 June, in the early morning hours, an 80-foot (24-m) windmill was toppled northeast of Warren, Minnesota. On 18 August, at 7 p.m., four weak tornadoes spawned by hurricane Bob on the coast of North Carolina travelled narrow paths less than 100 yards long, damaging property. On 29 November, around 6 p.m., a tornado killed a man near Springfield, Missouri, when it flipped a pick-up truck off a highway. The ensuing pile-up injured 10 more people.

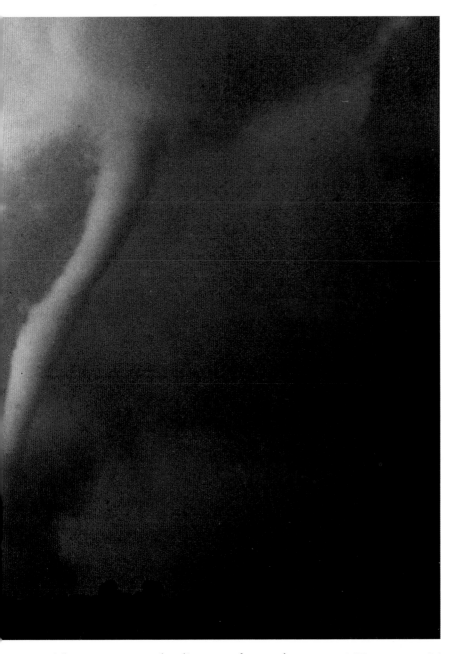

The worst tornado disaster of 1991 began at 4.57 p.m. on 26 April, south–southeast of Clearwater, Kansas. The funnel travelled 24 miles intensifying and developing a multi-vortex structure. Spotters could sometimes observe three vortices revolving around each other. It then moved across McConnell airbase, destroying two apartments, several homes and an elementary school, injuring 16 people. As it moved northeast (the classic direction for US tornadoes), it grew in intensity. Four people, including two children, died while trying to reach shelter in a housing complex. At about 5.40 p.m., the tornado moved into the southern part of Andover, destroying 84 houses and 14 businesses. It reached maximum intensity as it hit a mobile home park, killing 13 people, although 200 survived in the park's tornado shelter. The tornado finally weakened north of El Dorado, Kansas. It had travelled 69 miles.

One of the spotters was Tim Marshall, a meteorologist, civil engineer and dedicated storm chaser. He and a fellow chaser had driven up from Dallas, Texas, in search of tornadoes. At about 5 p.m., they were approaching Argonia, Kansas, when the sky darkened and a rain-free cloud base – ragged and turbulent with a tail cloud extending off to the north – came into view just ahead. 'In an instant, I knew it was the classic tornado storm structure', Marshall wrote later. 'White-hot lightning bolts zagged through the darkening blue sky in increasing tempo.' They pulled off the road and began filming with video cameras. At 5.15 p.m., a funnel like an elephant trunk dipped towards the ground. 'Immediately, the sirens sounded in nearby Argonia. My heart rate quickened and my breathing became shallow – the tornado was heading right at us!'

But after ten minutes the tornado shrivelled and dissipated. When it reappeared, it was heading northeast. They gave chase, but lost the tornado in a curtain of rain. Then, passing through Clearwater, the rain ended and they saw a large cloud lowering on the east side of the town. '"Multi-vortex tornado!" I shouted. The tornado crossed the road in front of us and hit a house. The roof disintegrated and a plume of attic insulation was sucked up into the vortex, appearing like smoke from a fire . . . In seconds, homes disappeared from their foundations. Broken plumbing lines created water geysers where homes had once stood.'

The tornado turned east. When it struck McConnell airbase it just missed rows of parked fighter planes. Marshall tried to keep pace, but had to give up; the twister had toppled power lines across the road. 'The town of Andover was next on the hit list. We could hear spotters frantically telling emergency officials to look to the southwest. A policeman in the town responded, confirming that a large tornado was bearing down on them. With no operational sirens, one officer tried in vain to warn residents of the Golden Spur Mobile Home Park on the edge of town to evacuate. Unfortunately time ran out for many of them at 6.35 p.m., when the tornado obliterated hundreds of homes'.

Scientists from the National Severe Storms Laboratory at Norman, Oklahoma, spend a considerable amount of their time chasing tornadoes. With them goes TOTO, the 400-pound (180-kg) Totable Tornado Observatory, named after the small dog in *The Wizard of Oz* that tackles a tornado. The idea is to drop this robust barrel of instruments in a tornado's path to measure its temperature, atmospheric pressure, and wind speed and direction. TOTO can be unloaded from its truck in less than a minute – but frequently tornadoes give the team insufficient time. There is as yet very little reliable scientific data about what goes on inside a tornado.

The most promising technology for tornado detection is Doppler radar. This exploits the Doppler effect: the well-known fact that the pitch of a sound approaching or moving away from an observer – such as an ambulance siren – rises or falls. The Doppler radar compares the frequency of radar waves emitted towards a moving object with that of waves reflected from the object, and is thus able to calculate the speed of the object. Pointed at a tornado, the detector may show an abrupt change on the radar screen from, say, yellow (winds moving away from the detector) to green (winds moving towards it) – indicating the direction of rotation. Research has shown that Doppler radar may be able to identify incipient rotational circulations within a storm as much as 30 minutes before the formation of a tornado. During the 1990s, a network of such Doppler radars is to be installed across the US as part of a series of experiments and studies aimed at observing storm systems on a nationwide scale, the so-called STORM programme. The existing network of tornado spotters will remain essential for the foreseeable future, however. In the cautionary words of the American Meteorological Society,

> many tornado-bearing storms do not have clear-cut radar signatures, while other storms give false signatures. Signature detection is often a subjective process and a given display could be interpreted in several ways.

Satellite images may help too, though not nearly as much as they can in the detection and monitoring of hurricanes. One of the cloud shapes known as a signature of potential tornadoes is a bright V-shaped cloud wedge with overshooting towers of convection. The satellite sees these clouds as bright against dark wave-like areas: the illuminated tops of the unusually vigorous thunderstorms poking through the cirrus anvil and casting shadows on it. Such images were recorded in May 1983, when violent and destructive tornadoes struck eastern Texas, including Houston. Another cloud signature of tornadoes is the mammatus cloud, a peculiar, pendulous formation that hangs udder-like – the Latin word means 'having breasts' – below the anvil-shaped tops of thunderstorms. Caused by the sinking of moist cold air, mammatus clouds are ample hints of inner turmoil. A third typical cloud condition that presages a tornado is rotary circulation in wind-tattered cloud bases (such as described by Tim Marshall in Kansas).

Tornadoes to come? Pendulous mammatus clouds that develop beneath the anvil-shaped tops of thunderstorms often presage tornadoes in the American Midwest. These particular mammatus clouds produced a total of 37 twisters in Kansas, Nebraska, Iowa and Missouri.

What is likely to be the mechanism that allows a thunderstorm to conceive its devilish offspring? Only 1 per cent actually do so, as we have seen. The giant storms known as mesocyclones, shown in the satellite images of Texas, may reach heights of ten miles or more, and have updrafts of 100 mph – remember the experience of US pilot Rankin, who was caught in one – but still they may not generate a tornado. 'Only half of all mesocyclones result in tornadoes, and we cannot explain yet why one does and another does not,' according to one researcher. When a tornado does appear, it usually comes out of the storm's rear side, near where a stream of cool air from a vertical downdraft spins into the warm, low-level horizontal inflow. Horizontal winds are apparently capable of assisting the formation of the violent vertical updraft characteristic of a tornado; indeed tornadoes do not form without them.

It is hard to be more precise than this. Tornadoes do not offer themselves for study, and laboratory simulations are of severely limited use. Tornadoes are remarkably complex, as the many photographs of them show. Very often they consist of more than one vortex; sometimes one of these mini-vortices spins clockwise, in the opposite direction to the main vortex. There are even a few instances of the main vortex spinning clockwise in the northern hemisphere, against all known laws of nature. (No hurricane of this kind is on record.) Consider this extraordinary testimony by one of the few people to have looked a tornado in the funnel and survived. His name was Will Keller, a Kansas farmer, and he was tending his fields on 22 June 1928 when he saw the tornado coming. Calling to

A supercell thunderstorm. Supercells are long-lasting storms that separate into updraft and downdraft regions. Beneath a rain-free part of the updraft, strong upwards motion and winds flowing inwards may produce a lowered, collar-shaped 'wall cloud'. Tornadoes frequently come out of a wall cloud, as has happened here. Radar can sometimes detect the birth before the tornado actually appears. 'Hook' echoes in the rainfall pattern of a storm on a radar screen are associated with tornadoes. But judging this evidence is often 'a subjective process', according to the American Meteorological Society. In the inset image, two hook echoes are visible, one at the far left and the other at the upper right.

his family, he ran to his cyclone cellar, but just before slamming the door, for a few seconds he took a good look:

> At last the great shaggy end of the funnel hung directly overhead. Everything was as still as death. There was a strong gassy odor and it seemed I could not breathe. There was a screaming, hissing sound coming directly from the end of the funnel. I looked up and to my astonishment I saw right up into the heart of the tornado.
>
> There was a circular opening in the center of the funnel, about 50 to 100 feet in diameter, and extending straight upward for a distance of at least one-half mile, as best I could judge under the circumstances. The walls of this opening were of rotating clouds and the whole was made brilliantly visible by constant flashes of lightning which zig-zagged from side to side.
>
> Around the lower rim of the great vortex small tornadoes were constantly forming and breaking away. These looked like tails as they writhed their way around the end of the funnel. It was these that made the hissing noise. I noticed that the direction and rotation of the great whirl was anticlockwise, but the small twisters rotated both ways – some one way and some another.

The magnitude of a tornado's rotation, its complexity and its severe effect on atmospheric pressure – all vividly suggested here – account for both the destructiveness of tornadoes and the pranks they play. When a tornado attacks a house, the structure behaves like an aircraft wing. A wing is shaped so that the air flowing over the underside becomes packed and at higher pressure than the air above: this creates lift. Similarly, the tornado wind rushes at the front wall, and this barrier (assuming it does not collapse) forces the wind over the roof and the side walls of the house. The air inside is now at higher pressure and exerts a thrust on the roof, on the side walls, and to a lesser extent on the leeward wall. According to calculations by structural engineers, a 160-mph wind will produce a lifting force of over 30 tons on a typical house. If the wind speed doubles to more than 300 mph, which is quite conceivable in a tornado, the lifting force is 100 tons.

The usual effect is that the roof lifts up, weakening the walls. Then the front wall blows in, the side walls blow out, and the rear wall falls down and out; finally the roof falls in. But neither roof nor walls are necessarily swept away. They are much harder to lift when lying flat on the ground than they are when upright, as one can easily see by blowing over a card held lightly between one's thumb and forefinger as compared to a card laid flat on a book.

On this basis, the advice to home-owners threatened by a tornado used to be: open the windows to equalize the pressure.

Today's advice is: keep them closed. The theory has not changed, but scientists now feel that if the windows are opened on the windward side – and how can one predict where the wind will strike – the updraft inside the house, not to speak of the wind-driven rain, could be even more disastrous than the tornadic lift on a sealed house (and of course most houses have copious air leaks anyway).

The explosive pressure difference in tornadoes accounts too for the curious way in which they sometimes pull apart masonry, brick by flying brick, leaving the interior of a house untouched. One would normally expect wind to blow the bricks inwards, scattering them over the floors. Instead, the brick walls crumble outwards, and panels and cladding fly off, creating killer missiles among anyone unfortunate enough to be caught outdoors.

One cannot as a rule design against tornadoes, unlike hurricanes: tornado winds are simply too strong, too freakish and too uncommon for such design to be economically feasible. 'Any building in their direct path is likely to suffer severe damage', according to an expert at the Building Research Establishment in Britain, where tornado damage accounts for about a twentieth of observed wind damage. Essential public structures, however, such as bridges, must attempt to take into account tornadoes – and waterspouts, tornadoes' ocean equivalents. Waterspouts were responsible for Britain's worst bridge disaster, the crumbling of the famous Tay Bridge in 1879, when the Edinburgh mail train plunged into the River Tay, killing 75 people. A severe gale was blowing at the time, but it was the waterspouts, more than 260 feet (over 80 m) high according to an engineer watching, that triggered the collapse. In 1981 a tornado-like waterspout travelling at up to 92 mph passed through the Severn Bridge between England and Wales. It remained intact. But a firm of consulting engineers later estimated that the bridge might not survive a waterspout of speed exceeding 100 mph. According to TORRO, Britain's Tornado and Storm Research Organization, such a waterspout is well within the bounds of probability in the next few decades.

Lightning is one of the few forces of Nature against which humans and property do have effective protection. It is therefore ironic that lightning kills more people in the developed world than any other natural phenomenon. Accurate figures are not available, but it is estimated that in the US twice as many people die from lightning strikes as from tornadoes. About 70 per cent of fatal lightning strikes kill a single person. Three-quarters or more of those struck are men, who spend more time outdoors than women. The peak time is in the afternoon, when thunderstorms have built up; only

'Loop-the-loop' lightning.
Instead of discharging itself into the ground, lightning sometimes discharges into a mid-air pocket of positive charge.

about a fifth of strikes take place at night. The largest single category of deaths is those who have taken shelter from a storm beneath a tree; perhaps a third of these are golfers. Nevertheless, about two-thirds of those involved in a lightning strike subsequently make a complete recovery, most likely because they were not directly hit.

Aircraft are especially vulnerable. Worldwide there are about 100 lightning discharges per second. One of these hits a commercial aircraft once in every 5000 to 10,000 hours of flying time on average. Besides leaving pit marks or burn marks on the wings and nose-cone, lightning can fuse, burn away or otherwise destroy aircraft parts, both electrical and mechanical; it can blind a pilot temporarily; and it can ignite the aircraft's fuel. Mostly, however, the damage is slight. There have been only two commercial aircraft disasters known to have been caused by lightning: near Milan, Italy, in 1959, and in Maryland, USA, in 1963. In both cases fuel ignition was the probable culprit.

The space programme has also been affected several times by lightning. It struck a rocket taking off from Cape Canaveral in 1987, and destroyed the mission. In 1983, it almost hit the space shuttle. And in November 1969, it twice struck Apollo 12 in the first minute after lift-off, once at 6000 feet (about 1800 m) and again at 13,000 feet. Since the clouds above the space centre had not produced lightning earlier, the rocket and its plume of exhaust were the likely cause of the flashes. The mission survived, but Apollo 12 sustained damage to its fuel cells and primary inertial guidance system, and the permanent loss of certain measurements of the rocket's skin temperature and the quantity of propulsion fuel remaining.

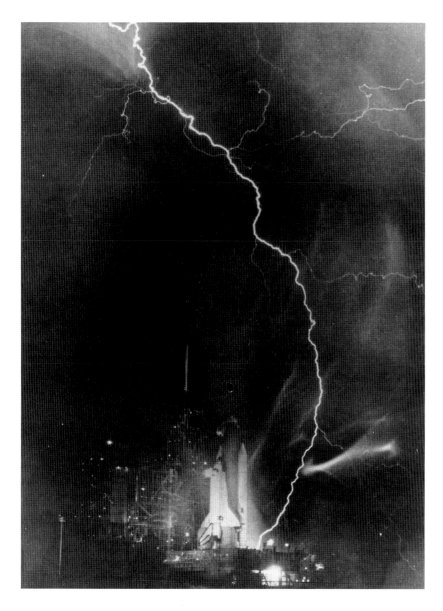

Prelaunch lightning. In 1983, lightning almost struck the US space shuttle at the John F. Kennedy Space Center in Florida. The storm passed and the shuttle took off on schedule. Lightning is also known to accompany some rocket launches, even when no storm is present. In 1969, it twice struck Apollo 12 in the first minute after lift-off, with serious consequences.

The thunderstorm is the most common source of lightning, but there are a number of other sources. Rocket exhausts appear to be one, as we have just noted; violent tornadoes are another; and so, as we already know, are erupting volcanoes. Lightning occurs in snowstorms, sandstorms and in rain and ice clouds that are not thunderstorms. It is also found near the fireballs created by nuclear explosions. It even appears to strike out of a clear blue sky: a so-called 'bolt from the blue'.

Benjamin Franklin was the first to establish that lightning was electricity. In 1750, he suggested an experiment with an iron rod buried in the ground that became the basis of the lightning rod. In 1752 he flew history's most famous kite into a thunderstorm and

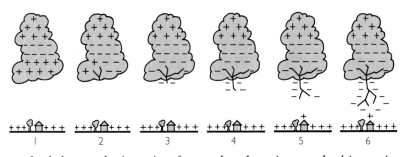

How lightning strikes. A thunder cloud is tripolar, with a region of negative charge sandwiched between two regions of positive charge (1). A lightning discharge generally (though not exclusively) begins in the negative region of the cloud (2) and propagates towards the ground as a negatively-charged 'stepped leader' (3–7). Near the ground it meets an upward-moving positive charge (8) and at that point a 'return stroke' jumps from the ground to the cloud with a flash (9–11). The stepped leader is not visible to the naked eye, unlike the incandescent return stroke; it is also far slower than the return stroke.

watched the sparks jumping from a key hanging on the kite-string to the knuckles of his hand. Luckily for him, his kite did not receive a direct strike; if it had, he would most probably have been killed.

A lightning flash typically lasts a few tenths of a second. It may consist of a single stroke, 3 or 4 strokes (the most common incidence), or as many as 20 or 30 strokes. The strokes are typically 40 or 50 thousandths of a second apart, which accounts for the flicker: the less time elapses between strokes, the less flicker one sees. The electric current in the bolt is generally 10,000–20,000 amperes, but it may reach hundreds of thousands of amperes. It jumps in a few millionths of a second between a cloud-to-ground potential difference of several hundred million volts. (Compare this with the filament of a 100-watt light bulb, which in Britain carries less than half an ampere at 240 volts.)

How this happens is only partially understood. It is certain – because it has been photographed by special cameras – that the process begins from the cloud and advances in steps: the so-called 'stepped leader'. Not far from the ground the stepped leader contacts a travelling spark that is sent up by the object to be struck, and produces a 'return stroke'. It is the dazzling return stroke, not the weakly luminous stepped leader, that we actually see. We therefore assume that lightning travels from ground to cloud, not from cloud to ground. In fact it does both.

Each step in the leader is about 50 yards (almost 50 m) long and occurs in less than a millionth of a second. Moving at about 75 miles per second, the leader reaches the ground in about a fiftieth of a second. The return stroke, with all its branches and forks, is orders of magnitude faster: 20,000 to 60,000 miles per second, nearly one third the speed of light. The electric current that flows, astronomically high and virtually instantaneous, heats the air in the leader channel to a temperature greater than 30,000 degrees C (55,000°F), four or five times the temperature of the surface of the Sun. The initial expansion of the air produces a pressure 100 times normal atmospheric pressure and a shock wave heard as thunder.

By measuring the travel time, duration, loudness and pitch of thunder claps, peals and rumbles, estimates can be made of the length, orientation, altitude and energy of the leader channel. A

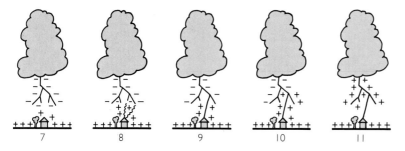

rumble, as opposed to a single clap, indicates a channel pointing away from the observer, for example; the deeper the rumble, the more energy has been released. The width of the channel can be estimated directly by photography, though the brightness overexposes the film making the recorded image broader than it should be. According to the best photographs, the channel is 2 to 7 inches (5–18 cm) wide (these figures are probably overestimates). Objects struck by lightning can provide channel widths too. Spiral furrows on tree trunks are between about 0.6 and 5.0 inches (1.5–12.7 cm) wide. Fulgurites (from *fulgur*, Latin for lightning), the fused hollow tubes with corrugated glassy walls formed when lightning strikes sand, are usually between 0.5 and 2 inches (1.3–5 cm) in length.

How does the stepped leader 'know' to strike a lightning rod, rather than the house it is attached to? 'It is thought,' writes Martin Uman, a leading US expert on lightning, 'that the stepped leader is "unaware" of objects beneath it until it is some tens of yards from the eventual strike point. When "awareness" occurs, a traveling spark is initiated from the point to be struck [the lightning rod] and propagates upward to meet the downward-moving stepped leader, completing the path to ground.' He adds disarmingly, 'there is an awful lot we still don't know about lightning.'

Among the mysteries of lightning are flashes inside clouds (difficult to photograph); why the lightning channel is so infinitely tortuous; bead lightning in which the channel appears to break up into luminous fragments; and – most mysterious of all – ball lightning. Incandescent balls of lightning that fall to earth and behave bizarrely have been reported from all over the world, sometimes by reputable scientists. Here is one of many present-day eye-witness accounts sent to Uman:

> I was standing in the kitchen of my home in Omaha, Nebraska while a terrible thunderstorm was in progress. A sharp cracking noise caused me to look toward a window screen to my left. Then I saw a round, iridescent (mostly blue) object, baseball size, coming toward me. It curved over my head and went through the isinglass [mica] door of the kitchen range, striking the back of the

oven and spattering into brilliant streamers. There was no sound and no effect on me except a tingle as it passed over my hair. Later examination showed a tiny hole with scorched edges in the screen and isinglass, and scorch-like marks on the back of the oven.

Ball lightning has been seen by 5–10 per cent of the population of the United States. But despite much scientific discussion, there is no adequate theory to account for the aspects of its behaviour common to several hundred accounts.

The embarrassing truth, admitted by all scientists of lightning, is that we cannot even properly explain how a thundercloud becomes electrostatically charged. Nearly 250 years ago, Franklin observed that 'the clouds of a thunder-gust are most commonly in a negative state of electricity, but sometimes in a positive state.' No light was shed on this fact during the 19th century. From the 1920s, it became a point of controversy. C. T. R. Wilson, inventor of the cloud chamber and Nobel laureate, observed a number of thunderstorms from a distance and concluded that the upper region of a thundercloud was positively charged and the lower region negatively charged: a positive dipole. Other scientists, measuring the charge on rain falling from thunderclouds, concluded the opposite: a negative dipole.

In recent decades it has turned out that a true picture can be obtained only by measuring the charge distribution at various levels in a thundercloud. We now know that thunderclouds are tripolar, not dipolar. They consist of a 'pancake' or layer of negative charge sandwiched between two positively charged regions, the lower one, nearest the ground, being smaller than the upper one. The region of negative charge is located at around 3.7 miles above ground, at a temperature of around minus 15 degrees C (+5°F). The lower, positively charged region is warmer; the upper region, also positive, is colder, its temperature as low as minus 65 degrees C (−85°F).

The explanation is incomplete and not universally accepted. It depends on the microphysics of the large (i.e. millimetre-to-centimetre-sized) ice particles within the thundercloud. Experiments carried out in various laboratories from the late 1960s have shown that ice at very cold temperatures is negatively charged, while ice as it begins to melt is positively charged. Between minus 20 and minus 10 degrees C (−4° to +14°F), a reversal of the charge takes place. Crucially, this charge-reversal temperature coincides with the temperature of the negative 'pancake' in the thundercloud.

In a mature thundercloud, these ice particles are in a perpetual state of growth, contraction and movement: shot upwards by

Benjamin Franklin. In 1749, Franklin noted 12 similarities between electrical sparks and lightning. He further noted that sparks were attracted by points and wondered whether lightning was too. 'Let the experiment be made', he wrote. In 1752, he himself performed the experiment with the most famous kite in history – and was lucky not to have been electrocuted.

convection, they are then pulled downwards by the gravitational forces of precipitation (and by downward convection) in ways not well understood. As they move, they collide with the cloud's mist of ice particles and supercooled water droplets, and become electrically charged, as shoes do when one walks across a carpet. In the upper, colder regions of the cloud, the particles become *negatively* charged and, falling, leave behind a positively charged mist. When they reach the middle of the cloud, and pass through the region at the charge-reversal temperature, collisions make them *positively* charged, while the mist becomes negatively charged. Falling further to the bottom of the cloud, they form a region of positive charge. From there, they may either precipitate or shoot upwards once more, where the process repeats itself.

The reason why thunderclouds, seen from the ground, seem capable of being both positively and negatively charged, should now be somewhat clearer. Most lightning begins with a stepped leader from the highly charged negative 'pancake', but sometimes the stepped leader may start from the less highly charged positive region. (In the first instance negative charges, electrons, flow into the ground along the return stroke; in the second, they flow into the cloud.) But the exact microphysical processes that might explain how ice can become both positive and negative and change its sign at a certain temperature, remain almost entirely unknown. In the words of one lightning researcher, Earle R. Williams, writing in *Scientific American* in 1988,

> The intractability of the problem [of lightning] stems from the fact that the physics of lightning and thunderstorms spans 15 orders of magnitude in scale. At the one end are the atomic phenomena that initiate the electrification of the storm cloud and that take place on scales of 10^{-13} kilometer [0.0000000000001 km]; at the other end is the air motion of the full thundercloud, which completes the charging process and may take place over scales of tens or hundreds of kilometers. At each scale significant physics is not understood.

It is a curious fact that Man should be so ignorant of lightning and yet be so comparatively successful at detecting and controlling it. The steeple of St Mark's Cathedral in Venice was badly damaged by lightning in 1388, 1417, 1489, 1548, 1565, 1653, 1745, 1761 and 1762. The traditional belief that tolling the church bells during storms would 'break' the lightning, was obviously not well-founded. Then in 1766, 14 years after Franklin's invention, a lightning rod was installed. The steeple has been safe ever since. Today in France an electronic lightning detection network, Météorage, measures the impact of every one of the 800,000 or so

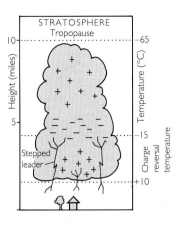

Inside a thunder cloud. A thunder cloud has three regions of electrical charge. The reason why the cloud changes its charge with increasing height and fall in temperature is largely unknown.

lightning bolts that strike France each year. Within seconds, subscribers know where and when the impact occurred, its amplitude and polarity, and the number of return strokes. The information enables Electricité de France, the national power company, to select the best paths around the country to shunt supplies so as to avoid storms; and it allows Euro Disney to cancel outdoor parades using electricity if a storm is coming. Stored on a data base, it helps insurance companies too. 'Lightning struck my cow' is a common insurance claim in France. Now, after checking with Météorage, the insurers reject half the claims as false.

And yet that traditional belief about tolling the church bell, for centuries inscribed on the metal of the bells – *fulgura frango* ('I break the lightning') – died hard. Many people still believed it in the early part of this century; perhaps some still do. Certainly many buildings today, judging from the harsh statistics of lightning-related fires, do not have lightning rods. Franklin was lucky to survive his experiment, as he soon came to realize when a fellow experimenter, G. W. Richmann, electrocuted himself the following year. The philosopher Kant called Franklin 'the modern Prometheus', after the Greek god who stole fire from heaven, bestowed it on Man and came to a nasty end. A big thunderstorm with forked lightning and thunder claps remains a frightening, awe-inspiring sight, lightning rod or no lightning rod. Do we still – some of us more than others, of course – feel a frisson of doubt about the wisdom of tampering with this particular force of Nature?

CHAPTER

—6—

FLOODS, DAMBURSTS AND TSUNAMIS

I do not know much about gods; but I think that the river
Is a strong brown god – sullen, untamed and intractable,
Patient to some degree, at first recognised as a frontier;
Useful, untrustworthy, as a conveyor of commerce;
Then only a problem confronting the builder of bridges.
The problem once solved, the brown god is almost forgotten
By the dwellers in cities – ever, however, implacable,
Keeping his seasons and rages, destroyer, reminder
Of what men choose to forget. Unhonoured, unpropitiated
By worshippers of the machine, but waiting, watching and
waiting.
T. S. Eliot, 'The Dry Salvages', 1941

IT is no accident that a flood is the pivotal force of Nature in the
Bible; or that it gained such a grip on the imagination of western
man, including that of scientists. Flood myths are common to
almost all societies. One compilation lists over 500 of them,
belonging to over 250 peoples or tribes. In most cases there is a
survivor, a Noah-like figure, who is the progenitor of a new race of
men. Floods have always been calamitous, certainly; but they have
also been bringers of new life.

Though not as dramatic as a hurricane nor as spectacular as a
volcanic eruption, floods are the most frequent and the most lethal
of natural disasters. They account for 40 per cent of all such deaths,
a fact that tallies with a second important fact: more than half the
world's population lives on sea coasts, in river deltas or along
estuaries and river mouths.

Very few regions of the Earth are absolutely immune from
flooding, perhaps only the Gobi Desert, the central Sahara and the
Atacama Desert of northern Chile. The scale and duration of floods
are often small, but sometimes they are dauntingly vast, almost of

biblical dimensions. The record of just the last few years bears grim witness. Bangladesh experienced its worst floods this century in 1988, in which half or more of the country – one estimate was 62 per cent of its 56,000 square miles – was under water brought down from the Himalayas by the Ganges and the Brahmaputra. Over 2000 people died and 45 million people were uprooted; Bangladesh was at a standstill for a month. As if this was not enough, in 1991 there was sea flooding caused by a cyclone from the Bay of Bengal; some 150,000 people perished. In China, perhaps the world's worst sufferer from flooding, 77,000 square miles around the lower Yangtze – an area four-fifths the size of the United Kingdom – were submerged in 1991. Again, 2000 people died; a million were made homeless. In Pakistan, it was the same story when the Indus and its tributaries deluged its floodplain in 1992. In Australia – southern Queensland and northern New South Wales – an even larger area was submerged in 1990, necessitating the biggest airlift in Australian history (but causing only four deaths). And in Britain, that same year, there was widespread flooding – some said the most extensive this century: many towns were inundated, among them Inverness, Worcester, Hereford and Shrewsbury.

Nevertheless, floodwater as a proportion of total rainfall on land is fairly small, and a very small proportion indeed of the total water on the planet. In fact, most of the Earth's water (97.41 per cent) is in the oceans. If it were spread evenly over the Earth, it would be

The flooding of a nation. In Bangladesh, floods frequently drown more than half the nation. In the early 1990s, a Flood Action Plan was started that aimed to control the rivers. But while it may improve life in the cities, especially the capital Dhaka, the plan is likely to leave the rest of the country even more vulnerable. (The umbrella in the photograph is a party political symbol. Umbrellas, ironically, are used mainly as sunshades in Bangladesh.)

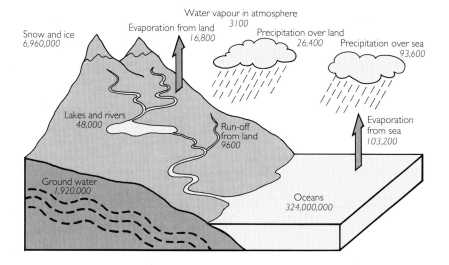

The global water cycle. Figures given are in cubic miles.

almost 2 miles deep. Of the remaining 2.59 per cent, the largest fraction is locked up in the icecaps and in glaciers; a smaller fraction is stored as ground water; and only 0.014 per cent exists in lakes, rivers, soils, living things and in the atmosphere. If the water in the atmosphere were distributed over the Earth, it would lie but a fraction of an inch deep; which suggests that a 'universal' flood of the kind described in Genesis, is rather an unlikely event.

After rain has fallen, it either evaporates immediately into the air, or it is absorbed by the ground, by soils and plants, or it runs off into rivers and lakes and thence reaches the sea, where it eventually evaporates back into the atmosphere. In addition, some returns to the atmosphere through the transpiration of plants. The quantities of water involved in each part of this global water cycle are not accurately understood, but the estimated total annual rainfall on land (more rain falls at sea) is 26,300 cubic miles. Almost two-thirds of this evaporates. Of the remaining 9600 cubic miles, just over one third is controllable runoff (but only some two-thirds of that falls in areas inhabited by humans); the rest, that is 6200 cubic miles, is floodwater. Thus floodwater is less than a quarter of total rainfall on land, but three times the amount of water easily available for human exploitation. (The latter would still be ample to sustain the Earth's present population, if it fell evenly; but of course it does not, as we shall see in Chapter 7, on deserts and drought.)

To channel the flood has therefore been Man's dream since the beginning of civilization. First, so as to use it for irrigation; later, at the same time as irrigation, to free its floodplain for settlement; and finally, in this century, to generate hydroelectric power and stored water for arid and semi-arid areas far from the river. The ancient Sumerians of southern Mesopotamia and the pharaohs of Egypt both owed their prosperity to the flooding of rivers. Each

Rivers change course. In the Fens of eastern England, a former meandering river has left its ghostly signature: a trail of light soil across the chequerboard of modern fields. When vast rivers such as the Ganges, the Yellow and the Mississippi change course, the effects are catastrophic.

attempted to manage the annual phenomenon in the cause of irrigation and settlement. The Egyptians made a success of it, thanks to the character of the Nile; the Sumerians initially succeeded but appear eventually to have fallen victim to silt and salt deposited by the broader, slower-moving Tigris and Euphrates. The Babylonians and Persians subsequently mitigated these problems, but it was the Romans, with their sturdy bridges and elaborate aqueducts, who had the greatest influence on the hydrological world of today – for both good and ill. In the words of Fred Pearce, a significant critic of large dams:

> The Romans imparted from the ancient to the modern world a vision of nature tamed, remade in the image of engineering, of the land separated from the water. It was a world in which water flowing to the sea was wasted, in which marshes were for draining and floods [were] for controlling.

It was the Romans, let us recall, who gave us the word 'rival', a legal term that originally meant a person who shared with another the water of a *rivus*, or irrigation stream. In Roman times, the rivals were individuals; nowadays they are often nations who share rivers – for example Egypt, Sudan, Ethiopia and others who share the Nile, or India and Bangladesh, who share the Ganges – and who are locked in acrimonious but thankfully not yet armed conflict over how to divide the flow of water.

Rivers that flood cyclically can be harnessed, at least in theory, but this is not true of the majority of floods, which occur unpredictably and abruptly after intense rain lasting anything from half an hour to several days. These flash floods, as they are often termed, are a menace that strikes all over the world under very varied conditions. This makes them difficult to categorize. Lethal and devastating as flash floods are, there are no official statistics.

Frequently they are hardly reported. In 1991, for instance, a torrential rainstorm in Malawi brought down almost the entire western side of a mountain; more than 500 people were killed, and some 150,000 were left homeless. In northwestern Afghanistan, flash floods caused by rainstorms claimed the lives of as many as 5000 people. And in eastern Texas, after five days of torrential downpours, there was massive flooding, with 15 deaths and millions of dollars worth of property damage. Who, beyond a few specialists and affected organizations, and of course the surviving victims, now recalls these disasters?

The following year (1992) in Afghanistan the story was repeated. It merited a mere hundred words in a serious national newspaper in Britain, under the heading 'Killer floods':

At least 3000 people are feared dead after flash floods caused by heavy rain devastated numerous Afghan villages, say mine-clearance workers. The floods . . . destroyed hundreds of homes in three valleys in the southern foothills of the Hindu Kush near Gulbahar, about 55 miles north of Kabul.

Distances of up to 20 miles in each of the small valleys are said to have been swept clean of human existence. Most of the wasted villages were populated by returned refugees, who had just finished rebuilding what was destroyed in 14 years of war.

Three weeks later, the most damaging flash floods for many decades struck southern France. Tens of people were killed or went missing in the Vaucluse region near Avignon in the foothills of the French Alps, following a five-hour storm described as a 'tropical downfall'. As much as 12 inches (30 cm) of rain fell in just three hours, and there were 100 mph winds. The River Ouvèze, a

Nature tamed? The Pont du Gard (*top*) is one of the greatest Roman aqueducts outside Rome itself. It stands south-southwest of Lyon in southern France at Nîmes, one of the richest towns of Gaul in Roman times. The aqueducts of ancient Rome are estimated to have delivered enough water to supply a 20th-century city of 5–6 million inhabitants.

(*Above*) **Flash floods,** southern France, 1992.

Britain under water. Many parts of Britain flood regularly despite long-standing man-made defences. The floods of February 1990 were perhaps the most extensive in Britain this century. Here, the royal castle at Windsor presides over a swollen River Thames. Six months later, the entire Thames Valley was in the grip of drought.

tributary of the Rhône, rapidly swelled and produced a 50-foot (15-m) wall of water that covered the Roman bridge in the town of Vaison-la-Romaine for the first time since 1616. Downstream, in another town towards Avignon, the water swept away every bridge except the Roman one. *En route* it devastated a campsite – carrying away camper cars and their screaming occupants as if they were toys – and inundated industrial and housing estates built on the river banks during the past three decades: a practice formerly avoided in favour of land high above the river. Within hours about 1600 policemen, firemen and rescue workers, some drawn from the army and the Foreign Legion, were searching the area for bodies; the same day the French interior minister toured the stricken area and declared it a disaster zone. The French president announced his sympathy for the families affected by this 'natural catastrophe of extreme violence'. French ecologists – as if to mark a final distinction between floods in western Europe and floods in distant Afghanistan – announced that they would start lawsuits against the local authorities for permitting construction in areas prone to flooding.

But perhaps the most famous flash floods ever were those in Florence on the night of 3/4 November 1966. The Florentines were soothed to sleep by hard, steady rain – and awoke to find the River Arno raging through their streets with a low, terrifying rumble. Normally the river flows 20 feet (6 m) below the landmark Ponte

Vecchio; at midnight it was rushing only 3 feet (1 m) below the bridge. The night watchman telephoned the owners of the gold and jewellery shops on the bridge. One of the jewellers, Tebaldo Piccini-Risaliti, dashed to the Ponte Vecchio with several suitcases, along with his wife. She later described the scene:

> The floor was shaking terribly under our feet, and outside I could see tree trunks looking as if they were going to crash in through the window. We collected up some things, but then the bridge started shaking so violently that we thought it was going to collapse at any moment, and we ran for it.

In fact it held, and so did all the other bridges in the city. But the art treasures of Florence, many of them thoughtlessly stored in basements, were less fortunate. In the low-lying 13th-century church of Santa Croce, 13 feet (4 m) of water (made oily by the explosion of fuel tanks) swirled over the tombs of Galileo, Michelangelo, Machiavelli, Rossini and Ghiberti. Next door, in the museum, it smeared the massive *Crucifix* of Cimabue. More than a million books and manuscripts in the Biblioteca Nazionale Centrale, Italy's largest library, were soaked and soiled. In the Piazza del Duomo, the celebrated 'Doors of Paradise' (Michelangelo's name for Ghiberti's ten bronze panels of Old Testament scenes on the portals of the Baptistery) suffered badly: five of the panels were torn off. At the Institute and Museum of the History of Science, the director made 28 perilous trips along a third-floor ledge to the adjacent Uffizi gallery. Among the 35 or so precious objects she rescued were several of Galileo's telescopes.

Responsibility for the flood lay with Man rather than Nature – and with the Florentines in particular. Mismanagement of water releases from two dams 25 and 29 miles upstream of Florence undoubtedly contributed, but very little had been done by the city authorities to protect the city. And that despite many centuries of recorded floods in Florence, at the rate of one every 26 years.

In Etruscan times, before Rome's glory, the River Arno's catchment area was lush with forest. It was gradually denuded as Florence grew and has never been adequately reforested, leaving an almost impermeable surface of naked clay. The first recorded flood, in AD 1117, ripped out the Ponte Vecchio; as did the flood of 4 November 1333. Between 1500 and 1510 Leonardo da Vinci drew up plans for a complex diversion of the Arno involving a large retention basin, a canal, a tunnel and floodgates. With due prescience, he identified the Santa Croce district as especially vulnerable and wrote a letter warning a nephew against living there. Leonardo's plans were ignored. In 1557 there was another flood: this time the Ponte Vecchio survived, but all the other bridges were

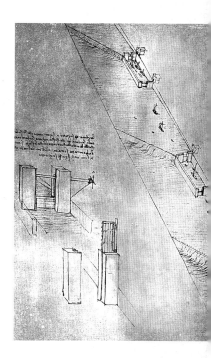

The science and prescience of Leonardo da Vinci. Leonardo spent ten years designing a flood control system for the River Arno to protect Florence. But his plans came to naught.

swept away. The situation today is not much improved: the Arno is simply enclosed between 25-foot (7.6-m) embankments, the northern one topped by a 4-foot (1.2-m) wall of concrete and brick. It seems that the Florentines prefer to forget their 'strong brown god' (T. S. Eliot's phrase) rather than to attempt mastery over its tendency to wreck their homes and treasures.

Really only in the United States, which experiences regular and devastating flash floods, has a sustained effort at forecasting them been made. The loss of 109 people in 1969 when the remains of hurricane Camille passed over Nelson County, Virginia (Chapter 5), provoked the National Weather Service to begin issuing watch and warning bulletins for flash floods, as it was already doing for hurricanes and tornadoes. The hope was – and remains – to devise a workable system based on the combination of data from ground measurements of river level and rainfall with 'bird's eye' measurements by radar and satellite, to be jointly interpreted by experienced and shrewd operators.

There are many obstacles. Automatic rainfall gauges malfunction and require regular maintenance; humans are more accurate and reliable, but may not be available or able to communicate their measurements quickly enough. 'Stilling wells' that measure small changes in river height – by admitting river water to a monitoring chamber under controlled conditions – work better on an automatic basis, but they are comparatively expensive. Radar, if available, can be a powerful tool but has limited range (not much more than 100 miles) and may underestimate the areas of heaviest downpour that are crucial to a forecast. Satellites have proved rather less useful – partly because their images take time to interpret – though they are a real asset in detecting the extent of river (as opposed to flash) flooding, using infrared imagery at night when the thermal contrast between land and water is greatest. (Such images have been of considerable use to rescue services during major river floods.)

The job of human operators is even harder than it is with hurricanes and tornadoes. Not only do they have to gauge the quality of the data they are receiving, but they must also guess the impact of predicted rainfall on the particular topography and population density of the area beneath the storm – and they must do it fast. A cloudburst over a sparsely populated plain is obviously less potentially dangerous than one over a region of river valleys with towns and villages nestling in them, such as the Vaucluse region of France or many parts of Afghanistan. Virginia's Nelson County was another example, and there, to complicate matters, the hillside surfaces lay on rather impervious igneous and metamorphic rocks. Mud, sand and rocks buried some of the flood victims several feet down. No forecaster could have known the way the

Florence, 1966. Overnight on 3 November, the River Arno raged through Florence. It took 35 lives and destroyed or damaged many priceless works of art, besides wrecking buildings, cars and other large objects. The famous Ponte Vecchio survived the onslaught – but only just. Today, since the defences of Florence have not been strengthened, the story may repeat itself: Florence has recorded floods for centuries, at the rate of one every 26 years.

The basin of the Mississippi River.

landscape would behave; the geology of the region was revealed only later in a report by a team from the US Geological Survey.

On top of all these technical uncertainties, there is the worry about the human response to a forecast of flash floods. Too many false alarms, and a correct warning will be ignored; not enough warnings, and the forecaster will be blamed for a disaster. Often, for whatever reason, people take no notice of a warning and are even attracted to the site of the flood. In Kansas City in 1977, for instance, a flash flood in a major shopping and recreational centre claimed 25 lives – despite a crystal-clear warning in good time by the Weather Service. One police sergeant called his station to say that an unruly crowd of 1500 onlookers was hampering rescue work by climbing onto police cars for a better look.

Of all the world's great rivers, the Mississippi has been the subject of the most comprehensive attack by engineering. Some 2348 miles in length (the longest river in North America), it is fed by an estimated 100,000 streams that include four major rivers: the Missouri, the Ohio, the Arkansas and the Red. It drains all or part of 31 states and two Canadian provinces via a basin of about 1.25 million square miles – more than a third of the United States (excluding Alaska) – that stretches from a point only 225 miles from the Atlantic to within 500 miles of the Pacific. Its rate of flow, averaged over a year, though only about half that of the Congo and less than one-tenth that of the Amazon, is 600,000 cubic feet per second (17,000 cubic metres per second, or 36 million cubic feet per minute).

This is no stream. We tend to forget what forceful stuff water is once it gets on the move. A person standing 3 feet deep – waist-high – in water flowing at 2 mph, will have difficulty keeping his balance. Simple physics says that 1 square mile of water 1 inch deep descending 1000 feet has an energy potential of 60,000 tons of TNT, equivalent to 3 atomic bombs. That is less than $2\frac{1}{2}$ million cubic feet of water. Compare it with the amount of water that falls from the Rocky, Appalachian and other mountains and flows through the Mississippi in one year – 19 million million cubic feet (some half a million million cubic metres) – and you have some inkling of the Mississippi's power.

James B. Eads, probably the most brilliant engineer to tackle the Mississippi – and the man who designed the first ironclad fighting ships (used on the river in the American Civil War), who built the first permanent bridge across the river below the Missouri at St Louis, and who became a member of the first Mississippi River Commission (in 1879) – expressed his feelings towards the Mississippi like this:

If the profession of an engineer were not based upon an exact science, I might tremble for the result, in view of the immensity of the interests dependent on my success. But every atom that moves onward in the river, from the moment it leaves its home among the crystal springs or mountain snows, throughout the fifteen hundred leagues of its devious pathway, until it is finally lost in the vast waters of the Gulf, is controlled by laws as fixed and certain as those which direct the majestic march of the heavenly spheres. Every phenomenon and apparent eccentricity of the river – its scouring and depositing action, its caving banks, the formation of the bars at its mouth, the effect of the waves and tides of the sea upon its currents and deposits – is controlled by law as immutable as the Creator, and the engineer need only to be insured that he does not ignore the existence of any of these laws, to feel positively certain of the results he aims at.

To which Mark Twain, then writing *Life on the Mississippi* (1883), and who was an admirer of Captain Eads, famously responded:

One who knows the Mississippi will promptly aver – not aloud but to himself – that ten thousand River Commissions, with the mines of the world at their back, cannot tame that lawless stream, cannot curb it or confine it, cannot say to it, 'Go here,' or 'Go there,' and make it obey.

A century or so later – with levees, concrete revetments, man-made cut-offs, barrages, reservoirs and spillways, not to speak of dredging, all in continual use against the Mississippi – the jury is still out. There have been long periods without floods; in fact the main problem in the late 1980s and early 1990s was low water and the possibility of drought. But the US Army Corps of Engineers, charged by the US Congress with responsibility for the river, has only to recall the floods of 1927, 1937, 1973 and 1983, to understand the unpredictability of its adversary. The 1927 floods threatened New Orleans itself, which had been regularly inundated since its founding in 1727. The city had to be saved by drastic action: a levee below the city, at a place where the river looped eastward, was dynamited, and the Mississippi drained off to the southeast towards the Gulf of Mexico. The thinly populated parishes in the way were simply sacrificed. A brown and sullen sea formed over 26,000 square miles of seven states, mainly Louisiana, Arkansas and Mississippi. It was 18 feet (5.5 m) deep in places and 80 miles across. There were 246 deaths by drowning, maybe as many as 500; 650,000 people were made homeless.

The construction of the enormous Bonnet Carré Spillway north of New Orleans rescued it from the river in 1937 and has protected

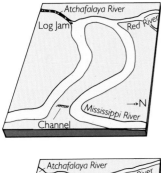

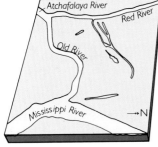

The Mississippi River

SOME 2348 miles in length, fed by an estimated 100,000 streams including four major rivers, the Mississippi is the longest river in North America. It has frequently flooded, with major floods this century in 1927, 1937, 1973 and 1983, as marked on a flood defence wall at Vicksburg in the lower reaches of the river (below). And over a longer time span it has regularly changed course, creating a pattern of old loops and bends visible in this infrared satellite image (right; the red colour indicates healthy vegetation). Over the past century and a half, one of these loops has given particular trouble (left). The problem is: for many decades now, the Mississippi has attempted to divert itself via the Old River into the Atchafalaya, thereby threatening to abandon Baton Rouge and New Orleans. Complex control structures and artificial channels, engineered by the US army, have been required to forestall this shift.

In the diagram (*above*) the top view shows the loop at a point above Baton Rouge where the main river is joined by the Red River and the Atchafalaya River, as it was in 1830. The view below it shows the same area today, after a channel was dug (in 1831) and a log jam was cleared (in 1839).

-----... 602 BC–AD 1194
-----.-- 1194–1288
.... 1288–1324
-----·--- 1324–1855
————— 1855–1887, 1889–1938,
        1947–present
- - - - - 1887–1889, 1938–1947

The changing courses of the Yellow River.

the city – about half of which lies below sea level – ever since. But in the last few decades, a new and extremely serious threat to New Orleans has arisen. The Mississippi is showing signs of changing its course, as it appears to have done roughly once a millennium. Were it to follow its new path, it would spell the demise of New Orleans and Baton Rouge (the capital of Louisiana), and of the intervening stretch of river, sometimes known as the American Ruhr after the great number of chemical companies established there. The Mississippi, noted John McPhee in *The Control of Nature*, had become 'an enemy of the state'.

Ironically, men may have been culpable in triggering the change in the river, back in 1831. Henry Shreve, riverboat captain and founder of Shreveport on the Red River, began the process by having a channel dug through the neck of an irritating Mississippi meander at the point where the Red joins the Mississippi some 80 miles above Baton Rouge. The Mississippi accepted the new channel – but part of the meander continued to operate, becoming known as the Old River. Then, in 1839, the state of Louisiana increased the Old River's flow by burning, blasting and dredging a 30-mile log jam on the Atchafalaya River. Soon, part of the Mississippi diverted itself into the Atchafalaya, flowing towards the Gulf of Mexico 145 miles distant – well under half the distance to the Gulf via the master stream and New Orleans.

A century later, the Atchafalaya was taking almost a third of the Mississippi's total flow, and looked set to capture the majority of the water. In 1950, the US Congress ordered the Corps of Engineers to maintain these proportions – 30 per cent to the Atchafalaya, 70 per cent to the Mississippi – in perpetuity. 'In effect,' wrote McPhee, 'the Corps would have to build a Fort Laramie: a place where the natives could buy flour and firearms but where the gates could be closed if they attacked.' In 1963, the Corps finished its Old River control structure. For a decade, it performed as expected. Then came the 1973 floods. The control structure held – but only just. Scour holes formed on both sides, three of them so deep it took 185,000 tons of rock to fill them in. In 1980 the Corps began work on an auxiliary control structure to relieve some of the pressure on the first one. An editorial in the *Washington Post* commented:

> Who will win as this slow-motion confrontation between humankind and nature goes on? No one really knows. But after watching Mt. St. Helens and listening to the guesses about its performance, if we had to bet, we would bet on the river.

The new structure was not ready for the 1983 floods. The first structure bore the brunt of the water and survived – but only narrowly. The Corps of Engineers, officially at least, like to maintain that they have the Mississippi beat. But others, such as Raphael Kazmann, former professor of civil engineering at Louisiana State University, are publicly sceptical. Like Mark Twain who admired Eads, Kazmann admires the Corps of Engineers, but of their control structure he says:

> It almost went out in '73. Sooner or later, it will be undermined or bypassed – give way. I have a lot of respect for Mother . . . for this alluvial river of ours. I don't want to be around here when it happens.

Chinese peasants know very well what such a breakdown may entail – yet they have no choice but to live in the floodplains of their two great rivers, the Yellow (Huang He) and the Yangtze. It is the fertility of these floodplains that has nurtured Chinese civilization. To protect themselves, the peasants have mainly earthen dikes – precious few pieces of modern engineering. During the last 3500 years, since records were begun, the dikes have ruptured no less than 1500 times. It happened again on the bloated Chu River, north of Nanjing, in mid-1991. In two months of ceaseless rain, 55 inches (140 cm) of water had fallen: the average rainfall over an entire year. Farmers had been toiling for almost a month to fortify a dike, using 150 million cubic feet (4.25 million cubic metres) of earth, 400,000 of rock and more than 40,000 pieces of bamboo. On 11 July they were forced to flee, just ten minutes before the Chu smashed a 70-foot-wide (21-m) hole in the dike and tore across the countryside. 'We ran for our lives,' said a village head. 'Huge logs that we used to support the dike were thrown into the air by the water and rocks and other debris came crashing down. It was the fastest we have ever run and still it wasn't fast enough.'

A century before, in late September 1887, the Yellow River breached its dike further north at a sharp bend near Zhengzhou, 35 miles upstream from Kaifeng. For more than a year Chinese farmers struggled to repair the hole and restore the river to its previous course. By October 1888, when a correspondent from the *North China Herald* paid a visit, the breach was down to 150 yards. Looking down from the top of the dike some 40 feet, the reporter estimated that the current was 100 feet (over 30 m) deep, flowing at 8 or 9 mph, with huge whirlpools in the centre betraying its immense power. 'What now are the materials with which it is proposed to force this body of water, much against its will, into its channel? They are five: sticks, stones, stalks, sand, and bricks.' Somehow, by early 1889, the Sisyphean task was done. But at least 900,000 Chinese, possibly as many as $2\frac{1}{2}$ million, had perished as a result of the floods, through drowning, starvation and disease. No

Floods as a fact of life. Besides being the world's most silty river, China's Yellow River (Huang He) floods more disastrously than probably any other river. During the last 3500 years (since records began), there have been some 1500 floods. Here Chinese peasants in Shaanxi province turn out to rehabilitate their land after flooding by the Yellow. The date is 1963, but the actions of the peasants are immemorially old.

Dambuilding in China.

wonder the Chinese call the Yellow River the Ungovernable, the Scourge of the Sons of Han (the Han dynasty tried to tame the river between 202 B C and A D 220) and, most commonly, China's Sorrow.

The Yellow's course has varied more than any other of the world's great rivers. There have been 26 significant changes during the last 3500 years. For 19 centuries, between 602 B C – the year of its first recorded change – and A D 1288, the river emptied into the Po Sea between Tianjin and the Shandong peninsula (though in some floods it split into two, on either side of the peninsula). Its mouth varied in location by only about 100 miles. Then, during a great flood, it wandered hundreds of miles to the south. For a while it emptied into the Huai, a tributary of the Yangtze, and thence into the Yellow Sea; afterwards it carved a channel across to the Yangtze itself and emptied into the East China Sea almost 600 miles south of its original position. There it remained – more or less – for 567 years, until 1855, when it tore open the dike on its left bank about 30 miles east of Kaifeng. For six years it wandered back again to the northeast, uncontrolled despite the efforts of engineers, until 1861, when it settled into its present channel, emptying into the Po Sea once again, some way south of its northernmost course and way to the north of its southernmost course.

Seen from a distance as it snakes its way across the great plain of north China, the Yellow looks like a massive, elevated roadway. Its course varies enormously because the gradient of the plain is so shallow. The average fall is only 3 inches (about 8 cm) per mile. The smaller the gradient, the slower the Yellow flows, and the more silt it drops. The quantities of silt involved are huge, not to say legion: most of its main channel is between 13 and 26 feet (4–8 m) above the surrounding countryside; when it reaches the sea it is flowing over an 80-foot-thick bed of its own silt. The dikes that contain it – also made chiefly of silt – are up to 100 feet wide (30.5m) at their bases, 50 feet (15 m) wide at their crests, and 30 feet (9 m) in height. Some are even broad enough to accommodate villages.

It is the world's muddiest river – hence its name. It carries over 2.1 pounds (1 kg) of silt per cubic foot, compared to 0.63 pounds for the Colorado River and 0.07 pounds for the Nile. Furthermore, its floodwaters may carry up to 44 pounds (20 kg) per cubic foot, which is *70 per cent* of its volume. The main constituent is loess, a German word originally used to describe fine deposits of mainly quartz in the Rhine Valley, blown by the wind, unconsolidated and therefore easily eroded. A German geologist, Baron Ferdinand von Richthofen, identified the same phenomenon on a much grander scale in the Shaanxi province, through which the Yellow River flows on its nearly 3500-mile journey from its source in the eastern highlands of Tibet. He wrote of the loess:

The Yellow River, Huang He, 'China's Sorrow'.

Everything is yellow. The hills, the roads, the fields, the water of the rivers and brooks are yellow, the houses are made of yellow earth, the vegetation is covered with yellow dust. Even the atmosphere is seldom free from a yellow haze.

Geologists generally agree that the loess has been blown from the Gobi Desert in Mongolia.

For the farmers of the region the loess is a blessing: upon its fertility the exceedingly rich early culture of China was built. But for Chinese engineers hoping to control the Yellow River, the loess is a curse. Not only does it make the bed of the river gradually rise, necessitating ever higher dikes, but it silts up dam reservoirs at an unmanageable rate. The Sanmenxia Dam, located at the point where the Yellow plunges 3000 feet (nearly 1000 m) from the loess plateau to the low-lying plains, had to be rebuilt just two years after it was finished in 1960 because its reservoir had filled with silt more than 65 feet (20 m) deep. After that it needed rebuilding yet again; today its reservoir has less than one-third of its designed storage capacity, and much of the Yellow's burden of silt has to be let through and left to flow down into the plains. The Chinese have made strenuous efforts to establish small check dams in the loess plateau to capture the silt carried by the tributaries. They have also tried to halt erosion with trees and terracing. But by their own admission they are a long way from taming the Yellow flood.

In Bangladesh, the battle with the rivers has only very recently been started. Following the appalling floods of 1987 and 1988, a Flood Action Plan (FAP), funded by 15 donor countries and coordinated by the World Bank, was approved in December 1989. Work has now begun to strengthen old embankments, and to build a series of new embankments and control structures. But there are serious doubts about the FAP's social and political outlook, not to speak of its practicality in attempting to manage a delta three times the size of the Nile's and that has the most complex river system on Earth.

The main criticism is that the FAP will shore up the cities, especially the capital Dhaka, while leaving the rural areas worse off than they are now. In other words, the richer Bangladeshis will benefit, and the poorer majority will suffer further. The poor fared worst in the cyclone of 1991, for instance, because they occupied low ground such as the fertile shifting islands out in the delta. In Chittagong, hundreds of them died in low-lying quarters of the city, while people from the middle classes living on the hills were left unscathed. The latter emerged to watch the bloated corpses float up on the shore. The FAP's proposed embankments are likely to cause increased flooding of such areas. They will also greatly disrupt the fishing and agriculture of the poor, by removing fertile silt and diverting fish, without any compensating advantages.

And why, since cyclonic flooding kills far more Bangladeshis than river flooding (150,000 lives in 1991, 300,000 in 1970), should protection against tropical cyclones not play a much greater role in the FAP? Only one out of the 26 projects approved by the FAP concerns cyclone protection. The Bangladesh government is aware of the criticisms but has refused to modify the plan. Like the Corps of Engineers on the Mississippi, and the panel of western and Bangladeshi engineers in charge of the FAP, the government is in love with the old Roman vision of control over Nature. One of the chief foreign advisors is a Dutchman, Wybrand van Ellen. He says: 'In future, Bangladesh will look more like our country. The only question is when it will happen.' Given the magnitude of the Ganges and the other rivers of the delta – many times larger and much wilder than Holland's Rhine – and given the scale of ignorance of scientists and engineers about the behaviour of these rivers, the answer to such a question must surely be: 'not soon'.

It is widely assumed, for example, that deforestation of the Himalayas, especially in Nepal, is responsible for the apparently greater frequency and ferocity of floods in Bangladesh ('apparently', because there is no certainty that the floods *have* actually increased in frequency – whatever their ferocity). Thus Clive Ponting, in *A Green History of the World*: 'Almost an eighth of the world's population now lives in the area affected by the flooding caused by deforestation and soil erosion in the Himalayan region.' But in fact there is no scientific evidence for this statement, and some scientists doubt that it is true. A US geographer from the University of California, Jack D. Ives, wrote in 1991 that the expansion of the Ganges delta into the Bay of Bengal, while undoubtedly consisting of material eroded from the Himalayas, 'may be nothing to do with human activity.' He continued:

It happens in large part because the Himalayas, the world's youngest and highest mountain chain, are readily eroded. Rates of erosion are generally proportional to the steepness and length of the slopes. But they are increased by torrential rainstorms, by the frequently shattered and faulted nature of the local rocks, and by the high level of seismic activity, which triggers frequent landslides.

Furthermore, it is by no means clear that deforestation in itself *does* promote erosion. If instead of trees a farmer maintains low vegetation, this can often protect soil more effectively. It depends on the height of the trees. According to another US scientist, experiments show that 'raindrop impact on bare soil under tree

An icon of the 20th century.
The Hoover Dam in the American West, completed in 1935, was the world's first superdam. Taller than a 60-storey skyscraper, it contains enough concrete to pave a two-lane highway from San Francisco to New York. Behind it grew Lake Mead, stretching for 100 miles and containing an amount of water twice the average annual flow of the Colorado River that feeds the lake.

canopies greater than 10 metres [33 feet] in height is greater than on bare soil in the open.' Recent studies of Nepalese farming methods suggest that most farmers have an awareness of these facts. So we cannot any longer easily assume that they are the culprits who have increased Himalayan runoff into the rivers and thereby caused the floods downriver in Bangladesh. Paradoxically, says Ives, 'It seems that the more people there are in a region, the fewer the landslides, rather than the reverse as the theory presupposes.'

The world's experience of large dams in the 20th century gives good grounds for scepticism about grandiose engineering schemes such as the Bangladesh Flood Action Plan. Worldwide there are more than 100 'superdams', that is dams more than 500 feet (150 m) high. Three-quarters of them have been built in the past 35 or so years; about 50 were finished during the 1980s, mainly in the Third World. The total capacity of their reservoirs is 900 cubic miles, with a surface area almost 230,000 square miles in aggregate: roughly the size of the North Sea and 15 per cent of the annual runoff of the world's rivers. By early next century, if the dam-builders have their choice, two-thirds of all the flow of rivers to the oceans may be controlled behind large dams.

When the Hoover Dam was completed in the southwestern United States during the 1930s, it was an icon of the age, comparable to the Great Pyramid of Giza or the Eiffel Tower. Newly independent India, which now has more large dams than any other country, embraced dams as a way of lifting itself out of poverty; Nehru, its first prime minister, called them 'the new temples of India, where I worship'. Many people would still agree with him. To the past president of the Austrian Academy of Sciences, delivering the keynote speech to the 1991 meeting of the International Commission on Large Dams in Vienna, large dams were 'a visible symbol of efficient and responsible environmental management . . . the very basis for a civilised existence.' And here is the chief engineering adviser to the power authorities in Pakistan, defending his country's two giant dams, the Mangla and the Tarbela, also in 1991:

> In Pakistan nobody is hungry, nobody is without shoes. This is due to the irrigation network, the biggest in the world. I cannot imagine Pakistan remaining on its own two feet without these two reservoirs. God made Pakistan a desert. Sometimes when people say that deserts and swamps should be protected, they don't know what that means to a country like ours. I don't ever want to see a swamp, whatever rare species live there.

Just over a year after these words were spoken, flood waters

Controlling the Nile. Irrigation permitted the ancient civilizations beside great rivers such as the Nile to grow. But wrongly managed it can lead to the waterlogging of land, salinization and the incubation of disease. In recent decades, the Nile delta has stagnated badly: a layer of algae now covers its waters. As a direct result, Egypt's sardine fishing industry is dead. The cause of the change? – the Aswan High Dam, completed in 1970. The disruption of the river has also affected this Sudanese farmer's irrigation canal above the dam, which has to be cleared of silt.

poured off the Himalayas into the rivers of Pakistan. The flow of the Jhelum River into the Mangla Dam exceeded what the dam could cope with by a third. To save it, the sluice gates had to be opened without warning on two consecutive days. Not only were 400 people living on an island below the dam instantly swept away, but hundreds of villages were swamped. As the waters raced into the Indus Valley, to be joined by waters from four other rivers, army engineers were compelled to dynamite embankments in order to save crucial barrages downstream. Instead of destroying these structures, the water flooded several thousand villages in the plains.

Thus, depending on one's point of view, large dams can be seen as both vital and as disastrous to a country's development. Nowhere has this become clearer than in Egypt during the two decades that have elapsed since the completion of the Aswan High Dam.

'Egypt is the Nile and the Nile is Egypt', said the ancient historian Herodotus. The seasonal flooding of the Nile brought life to the desert. When it failed to flood, people starved. 'For seven years,' one pharaoh lamented, 'the Nile has not risen. There is no grain, the fields are dry. Everyone flees, to return no more, the children weep, the young men faint, the old men wither.'

A 12th-dynasty pharaoh, Amenemhet III, ruling in the 19th century BC, embarked on what is probably the first recorded major attempt to control a river. At a point 60 miles southwest of Cairo, he ordered an irrigation canal 300 feet (90 m) wide and 10 miles long to be dug from the Nile to a natural depression in the land. A dam with sluice gates controlled the flow of water, enabling water to be stored until it was needed for crops during the dry season. There is no record of whether the project succeeded or failed. The latter is more likely, since there is no evidence of similar works for many centuries thereafter. Instead, Egyptian farmers adopted 'basin irrigation': at a certain point in a flood, dikes were opened and the floodwaters were channelled into the lower-lying fields through small canals controlled by gates. There the water was allowed to stand for six or eight weeks. When the flood had receded and the water level in the Nile had fallen, the gates were opened and the water in the fields drained back into the river.

It worked fairly well – in some years wonderfully well – as a way of feeding a population estimated at 1.5–2.5 million people. Now there are more than 55 million Egyptians. Between 1897 and 1946, the population doubled; and then doubled again in the following 30 years. To alleviate the shortage of water for agriculture, the British colonial governors built six dams on the Nile, the largest of which (completed in 1902 and today known as the Old Aswan Dam) stood 90 feet (27 m) above the river at a site 590 miles above Cairo.

But the situation continued to deteriorate. By the 1950s, Egypt's president, Gamal Abdel Nasser, knew that he had to act in order to prevent his country from sliding into chaos.

Work began in 1960. With vital help from the Soviet Union – both financial and technical – and based upon an original design by West German engineers, the Egyptians constructed a new dam at Aswan, 4 miles south of the British-built dam. It spans 11,812 feet (3600 m or 2¼ miles) between the granite wall of the east bank and the sand hills of the west, and stands 364 feet (111 m) high. At its base it is 3215 feet (980 m) thick, at its crest 131 feet (40 m): in bulk, it is 17 times larger than the Great Pyramid at Giza. Its reservoir, Lake Nasser, stretches southward for 350 miles, two-thirds in Egypt and the rest in Sudan. Its capacity is 137 million acre-feet of water, the deepest 26 million of which lie below the level of the dam's spillway and are set aside for the build-up of silt. On present levels of siltation, the dam is expected to have a useful life of 300 years. The total cost was eventually $1.5 thousand million.

'Here are joined the political, social, national and military battles of the Egyptian people, welded together like the gigantic mass of rock that has blocked the course of the ancient Nile', said Nasser at the ceremony to begin impoundment of the dam's reservoir in 1964. Eleven years later, with Nasser dead and the dam fully operational for five years, the British *Economist* magazine published a progress report. It might have been expected to be largely laudatory, instead it laid the following charges against the dam:

> causing the erosion of the Egyptian coastline, killing the sardine industry, depriving the delta of the yearly flood silt that gave Egypt the world's most fertile soil, and spawning a plague of the dangerous bilharzia parasite.

Unquestionably, on the asset side, the dam has controlled the flooding of the Nile. With equal certainty it has generated hydroelectric power, made water available for industry and agriculture at all seasons, and greatly increased Egypt's supply of domestic water. Without it, the modern growth of Cairo, Africa's largest city, would have been impossible. But on the debit side it has also done all that the *Economist* said, and worse. The delta had been static since the building of the first barrages on the Nile a century ago; now it is in full retreat, with one former coastal village already over a mile out to sea (a process global warming may accelerate). Hardly any phytoplankton (microscopic, photosynthetic organisms) or algae on which many fish depend now reach the eastern Mediterranean; hence the collapse of the sardine fishing industry. On the other hand, the Bulinus snail, carrier of bilharzia, flourishes in the year-round water of irrigation ditches. The disease was known to the pharaohs, but it was kept under control by bouts of flooding followed by periods of drought. Today, Nile water has become a general hazard to health. The disappearance of silt from farmland has necessitated the use of chemical fertilizers (made with hydro-electric power). Egypt now uses chemical fertilizers more heavily than most other countries. They have increased the salt concentration of the Nile; combined with salt concentrated by evaporation from Lake Nasser and from waterlogged fields no longer flushed by seasonal floods, this has raised the concentration of salt in Nile delta waters to a third higher than it was before the dam existed. And for the first time in 5000 years of Egyptian history, salinity – the curse of Mesopotamia, that 'satanic mockery of snow' (said the British archaeologist Sir John Marshall) – has begun to damage Egyptian crops.

The impounding of Lake Nasser also required 100,000 Nubians in Sudan to abandon their homes. They moved much against their will. Since then, many people in other parts of the world have faced eviction to make way for a dam. Resistance to such government plans is increasing. At James Bay in Canada (a large, remote, shallow marine inlet on the southern edge of Hudson Bay), for instance, nearly 10,000 Cree Indians and 1500 Inuit Eskimos contemplate the destruction of their hunting grounds by hydro-electric dams. The first stage of the project was completed in the mid-1970s by Hydro Quebec, the utility owned by the Quebec government, on the La Grande River. It comprises 5 reservoirs, 9 dams and 206 dikes. Four rivers have been diverted and 11,600 square miles of land flooded. Nearly 11,000 megawatts of electricity is being generated, enough to supply a city of almost 6 million people. In the second stage, now delayed, Hydro Quebec plan to tame four more rivers that flow into James Bay. The resultant 23 power stations would produce more than 28,000 megawatts, some of which might be exported to the cities of the northeastern United States, including New York. The successful completion of the project could in theory buy Quebec its economic independence.

But in so doing it would complete the destruction of a wilderness described by one US conservationist as 'the northern equivalent of the tropical rainforests'. Besides sheltering seals, whales and polar bears, it is one of the six most important wildfowl habitats in the northern hemisphere and supports the world's largest caribou herd. In 1984, around 10,000 disorientated caribou drowned just downstream of one of the dams on the La Grande River when the sluice-gates opened. Hydro Quebec called it an 'accident of nature'. To the Cree and others, it was a man-made act.

Not only have these peoples lost the territory drowned by the reservoirs, but they cannot eat the fish from the streams. It contains methyl mercury – the same poison that in tuna caused deformation in Japanese children in the 1960s – created by the action of bacteria on drowned soil and vegetation. No one knows how long it will endure, but many scientists estimate 100 years. 'The Cree must put away their fishing-lines', writes Fred Pearce acidly, 'and head for their shopping malls to buy TV dinners.'

In mid-1991, the Cree won a ruling from the Federal Supreme Court of Canada that the second stage of the James Bay project must be subject to an independent environmental review. Hydro Quebec, backed by the premier of Quebec, Robert Bourassa (the progenitor of the entire scheme), planned to appeal. Meanwhile, various power authorities in the northeastern US were persuaded by environmentalists to review their commitment to buy electricity from James Bay. In early 1992, work on the second stage was postponed. The debate between the dam-builders and the conservationists is unlikely to be settled quickly.

In India, such debate has become fierce in recent years. The valley of the Narmada – India's largest westward-flowing river, in the state of Madhya Pradesh – is where Rudyard Kipling set many of his stories in the *Jungle Books*. The Indian government, backed by the World Bank and surrounded by a veil of secrecy, is in the process of turning the valley into the largest integrated development project ever attempted. There will in theory be two super-dams – the first of which, Sardar Sarovar, scheduled to last 200 years, is already under construction – as well as 30 large dams, 130 medium ones and 3000 minor ones. According to the dream, they will feed 20 million famine-plagued people, provide 15 thousand million gallons (68 thousand million litres) of water daily to 40 million drought-prone people and irrigate 4250 square miles of land through the largest canal ever built, protect 750,000 people from downstream flooding, generate 1450 megawatts of electricity, and fuel an industrial boom across the western state of Gujarat. The cost is estimated at $11.4 thousand million; in mid-1992 more than a tenth of this sum had already been spent, about a quarter of it contributed by the World Bank.

What is not so often mentioned by the planners is that up to 1.5 million people – mostly from a diverse community of tribals – will be displaced by the project. They have nowhere to go. Some 1350 square miles of forest and 230 square miles of productive land will be flooded; 80 per cent of the villages in the Sardar Sarovar command area will receive no benefit in irrigation from the dam. And of those that do, 70 per cent are neither drought-prone nor arid. Finally, the projected water flow rates and siltation rates which make the project viable are controversial.

The siltation rate is especially serious. Indian dams have gener-

Blessing or curse? The Sardar Sarovar Dam in western India, partially constructed by 1992, is the centrepiece of the largest integrated development project ever attempted. It may eventually bring water to the parched state of Gujarat. But it has become steadily more obvious that the project may cause environmental mayhem and also function for far fewer years than planned.

ally silted up much faster than predicted. One of the first large ones, built by British engineers in 1931, silted up 16 times faster than forecast. Two Himalayan dams completed in the 1970s became silted to the crest of the spillway within two years. The giant Tarbela Dam on the Indus in Pakistan has filled at a rate approaching 2 per cent per annum since completion in 1974. If the Sardar Sarovar reservoir did silt up three to five times faster than currently projected, as one study suggested, it would last not 200 years but perhaps only the working life of its designers.

Just as the World Bank began publicly to admit misgivings about the Narmada project, particularly in relation to its human and environmental impact, the Chinese government decided to revive another long-running scheme to construct a gigantic dam. First suggested by the republican leader Sun Yat-sen in the 1920s, and actively pursued after the great floods of 1931 and 1954, it was dropped by Mao Tse-tung in 1960 in favour of irrigation and drainage projects. But stimulated by the Yangtze floods of 1991, the National Peoples' Congress voted in early 1992 to approve the Three Gorges Dam. Even so, there was much opposition, some of it courageously outspoken, and only two-thirds of the deputies

Damburst. During this century, dams have failed at the rate of about three a year, but failures of large modern dams have been extremely rare; most failures are of earthen dams, such as the dikes that gave way on China's Yangtze River in 1991. When this dam on the Côte d'Azur in southern France burst, 500 people died.

voted in favour (the rest either abstained or voted against the plan). No date was announced for the start of construction.

If built, the dam will flood over 300 miles of river valley and destroy a tourist region some compare in grandeur to the Grand Canyon in the United States. The government admits that three-quarters of a million people will be forced to move; other estimates exceed a million. Up to 19 towns and counties, including the city of Wanzian, population 140,000, will be inundated. Moreover, 60,000 acres of arable land will be lost. In compensation, says the government, 18,000 megawatts of electricity will be generated – eight times the power output of the Aswan dam, and more than $1\frac{1}{2}$ times that of James Bay's first stage. Navigation on the river will be improved. And most important of all, devastating floods will be prevented.

Few engineers, Chinese or foreign, who have studied the problem are convinced. A British hydrologist, Philip Williams, said in 1992 that the dam operators, in the event of a major flood, would have to choose between flooding land on the margin of the reservoir occupied by half a million people, or flooding large numbers of people downstream. He also said: 'The consequences of failure at Three Gorges would rank as history's worst man-made disaster.'

A great flood could cause failure. So could a big earthquake. The Three Gorges region is seismically active and landslides are frequent. In 1985, a gigantic chunk of cliff face slid into the Yangtze where the reservoir is planned to be. The wave it generated was said to have been 120 feet (37 m) high. So could sabotage. 'War is the key fact that determines whether or not we should construct the Three Gorges project,' said a Chinese military expert. 'Are we going to make a Sword of Damocles that will hang over the heads of future generations for decades to come?' Better, said the veteran politician Li Rui (a former vice-minister of water conservancy), to follow Premier Chou En-lai's advice in 1970: 'Leave this project to our children in the 21st century.'

The consequences when a dam does fail are awesome. In this century the rate of failure of dams of all kinds has been about three a year, though failure of modern large dams is, thankfully, extremely rare. The year 1991 may be said to have been typical. One of the breaks, as we know, was in the earthen dike on the Chu River in China: it caused massive flooding and serious loss of life. The other two failures were of small dams: one in India (475 dead, 425 missing), the other in Romania (over 100 killed).

The usual reasons for failure are either poor maintenance or a poor grasp of the geology in the foundations and area around the dam, rather than poor construction of the dam. Earthquakes are a persistent and disturbing source of concern, but so far they have caused no major failures. (There is however talk of having to demolish a 900-foot (274-m) dam built in Georgia in 1980, because of earthquakes; and the risk from earthquakes may yet abort India's planned Tehri dam in the Himalayas.) The nearest miss came at Koyna, in India, in 1967 (see Chapter 3) – and that was brought about by the impounding of water in the reservoir, not by the seismicity of the region.

Poor maintenance lay behind the worst damburst in the United States. The South Fork Dam near Johnstown, Pennsylvania, was originally built to feed water into the Pennsylvania Canal during dry spells. By the time it was completed in 1853, however, it was redundant: railways had taken over from canals. And so, for the next 36 years, what was then the largest man-made lake in the US was left slowly to decay. During its final ten years, it became the site of the South Fork Fishing and Hunting Club, and was patronized by entrepreneurs, mostly from Pittsburgh, such as Andrew Carnegie, Andrew Mellon and Henry Clay Frick.

Nemesis struck on 31 May 1889, after a torrential storm in the mountain region of western Pennsylvania. At 3.10 p.m., watched helplessly by the president of the club, a wall of water at least 150 feet (45 m) high (according to a lucky survivor) crashed through the village of South Fork. An hour later, laden with debris, it hit Johnstown. A tangled, heaving mass stood 30 feet (9 m) above the water and extended into Johnstown for a distance of 30 city blocks. What it did not destroy, fires, such as a blaze started by a railway car full of lime reacting with the water, finished off. Some 2209 people lost their lives; 565 children lost one or both of their parents; and in the Grandview Cemetery in Johnstown today, there are the graves of 777 unidentified victims.

Tsunamis demonstrate the terrifying strength of moving water even more graphically than floods and dambursts. Recall for a moment that a tsunami – cause unknown – was responsible for most of the deaths produced by the eruption of Krakatoa in 1883. It did not sink any ships in the Sunda Strait, but it washed away 165 villages on the coast without trace, killing more than 36,000 inhabitants. Its height was said to have exceeded 115 feet (35 m) along the shore. When it reached Port Alfred in South Africa, it was still higher than a foot; there was even a 2-inch (5-cm) surge in the English Channel.

The term 'tidal wave', often used instead of tsunami, is inaccurate since tsunamis have nothing to do with the action of tides. 'Seismic sea wave' is more satisfactory. There has to be an impulsive disturbance of the Earth's crust to produce a tsunami. 'Large earthquakes with epicentres under or near the ocean and with a net vertical displacement of the ocean floor are the cause of most catastrophic tsunamis', according to one expert. The San Andreas fault does not therefore produce tsunamis, because it moves mainly horizontally. Volcanic eruptions and submarine landslides are also

The Johnstown disaster. The collapse of a dam above Johnstown, Pennsylvania, in 1889, was the worst damburst in the history of the US. Some 2209 people lost their lives. Thousands of sightseers flocked to view the rubble; one of them is shown in the photograph perched on a tree driven clear through a house by the wall of water. People around the world contributed $3 million to the city's survivors.

Tsunamis in Hawaii Transfixed by a tsunami (*centre below*), a man stands on the pier at Hilo in Hawaii on 1 April 1946, just before he is engulfed by tsunami waves 30–55 feet (9–17 m) high. The tsunami originated in the Aleutian Islands near Alaska some 2700 miles distant. The photograph was taken from a ship in the harbour that managed to ride the onslaught. The tsunami took 159 lives and swept every house on the main street facing Hilo Bay into the buildings on the other side (*right*). It also ripped up railway tracks, buried coastal highways and washed away beaches. Afterwards, the waters around the island were dotted with floating houses.

The Great Wave off Kanazawa. This celebrated print, produced in the 1820s by Katsushika Hokusai, includes his favourite motif: the snow-capped peak of Mount Fuji. The wave, with its menacing crest, is *not* a tsunami wave. Tsunami waves, by contrast, approach Japan stealthily, moving at terrific speed but with crests so low and far apart they are hardly visible in the open ocean. As they reach the coast, however, they rear up and crash down with shattering force.

Tsunamis move fast. This 1957 sequence of photographs shows the arrival at the island of Oahu in Hawaii of another tsunami originating in the Aleutian Islands. Frequently, a tsunami consists of more than one wave: a fact that has often proved lethal when people try to return to their homes after the initial wave in the hope of salvaging their belongings.

responsible, but unless they are accompanied by movements of the ocean floor, their effects are usually localized. Possibly this was true at Krakatoa; the course of the eruption and the exact cause of the tsunami are still not certain (see Chapter 4).

The deeper the water, the lower the tsunami and the faster it moves. In the open ocean, it travels at about 435 mph, but being so low (seldom more than 3 feet in height) and with a distance between crests that may be greater than 60 miles, a tsunami often passes a ship unnoticed. This is what happened in 1896 during Japan's worst tsunami, the result of an undersea quake about 93 miles off the Sanriku coast of Honshu, the main island of Japan. More than 22,000 people were drowned onshore by an 80-foot (24-m) wave, while fishermen far out to sea did not notice the waves passing beneath their boats; when they returned, they found their villages in smithereens.

Such large tsunamis are rare, luckily – though this of course inhibits their understanding by scientists. In recent times Japan has twice suffered seriously, in 1968 and 1983. The last Pacific-wide tsunami was in 1960. It was triggered by a giant earthquake in southern Chile, magnitude 8.5. The waves reached Hawaii about 15 hours later; and the coast of Japan 22–23 hours after the quake. They were up to 20 feet (6 m) in height. On top of the 122 people who perished, 20 went missing, presumably sucked into the ocean.

Tsunamis work their havoc in complex ways. Much depends on the topography of the ocean floor near the coastline and of the coastline itself. Some pounce on coastal settlements like large breakers, the weight of the water crushing buildings and maybe hurling ships and seaside structures onto buildings further inland. Other tsunamis may produce a gentle wave that floats buildings off their foundations. But then a violent backwash, following on, may sweep buildings and anyone unlucky enough to be caught in it out to sea. The tsunami that wrecked Hilo, Hawaii in 1946, killing 159 people, was so forceful it bent parking meters double. Originating near the Aleutian Islands, it consisted, like many tsunamis, of more than one wave: a fact that has often caused needless deaths when people have chosen to return to save their belongings and got caught between the waves. 'Remember,' warns the Japan Meteorological Agency, 'a tsunami is not just a single wave but a series of waves.'

The Hilo disaster prompted the first attempt to establish a Pacific-wide tsunami warning system. The Pacific nations are particularly vulnerable because many of them are prone to earthquakes, many are islands, and most have long exposed coastlines. (Nevertheless, Atlantic tsunamis are frequently reported: the 1755 Lisbon earthquake produced a tsunami that struck not only

Portugal but Spain, Madeira, the Azores, France, the British Isles, and the islands of the West Indies.) Whenever a large earthquake occurs, its details are immediately cabled, radioed, or phoned to Honolulu from earthquake observatories in the US, Japan, Taiwan, the Philippines, Fiji, Chile, Hong Kong, New Zealand and Samoa. This information, combined with measurements of water levels in the region of the earthquake made by tide gauges, provides the basis for issuing a tsunami alert.

The system works well for areas sufficiently far from the source of the tsunami, but it is useless for the majority of tsunamis originating near the coast of Japan: in these cases the tsunami itself reaches Japan before the tsunami alert. In addition to the close monitoring of earthquakes, the Japanese have therefore installed two strings of ocean-bottom tsunami gauges, one off Cape Omae-zaki south of the Tokai district, the second off the Boso peninsula, southeast of Tokyo. The quartz pressure transducer in these gauges can measure the height of a tsunami wave to an accuracy of 0.02 inches (0.5 mm), far out to sea where it is not distorted by the topography of the coastline.

First an earthquake, then a tsunami. In 1992, an offshore earthquake produced a tsunami that devastated a 200-mile stretch of coastline in Nicaragua. The photograph shows the remains of a beachside hotel. Most of the dead were children, whose bodies were swept out to sea by 50-foot (15-m) waves.

The Aegean Sea is another area where tsunamis have regularly occurred, though by no means so frequently as near Japan. In A D 365 a tsunami struck Crete and was reported in Alexandria, where ships were carried inland and left in the streets of the city. In 1650, an earthquake accompanied by an underwater explosion from the Colombo volcano, whose crater lies in the sea to the northeast of the island of Thera, produced a devastating tsunami on the island of Ios, north of Thera. Waves of up to 52 feet (16 m) were reported. Then in 1956 an earthquake near the southwest coast of the island of Amorgos killed 53 people, destroyed hundreds of houses and produced a tsunami with a reported height of 82 feet (25 m) at Amorgos.

If these are the tsunamis produced by comparatively small earthquakes and eruptions, what must the tsunami have been like that accompanied the mega-eruption known to have shattered Thera, probably around 1600 B C? Could it have been part of the catastrophe that devastated the Minoan civilization on Crete? Spyridon Marinatos, the archaeologist who in the late 1960s excavated the remains of a city on Thera destroyed by the eruption, thought so. So does George Pararas-Carayannis, the Greek-born director of the International Tsunami Information Center in Honolulu. In 1992 he wrote: 'There is conclusive evidence that Minoan cities on the north and east coast of the island of Crete were struck by huge tsunami waves.' Some have gone further and linked Crete with legendary Atlantis. It is thus conceivable that a titanic tsunami, following an eruption and earthquakes, produced a giant flood, and that together they annihilated Atlantis. The debate is a lively one, and we are unlikely ever to know the answer definitively. But whatever else it may throw up in the future, it continues to demonstrate one absolute certainty: great floods have a uniquely tenacious hold on the human mind.

CHAPTER

—7—

DESERTS, DROUGHTS, WILDFIRES AND DESERTIFICATION

Our land, compared with what it was, is like a skeleton of a body wasted by disease.
Plato, on the deforestation of Attica, 4th century BC

This area, where today the houses are standing, was once like a forest. You could barely see that village in the distance through the trees. Now they have all gone, and we can only blame God for the crisis. Of course, we do not say that we have not played a part but we are not the main factor. After all, is it man who makes rain?
Farmer, Mali, west Africa, 1990

THE earliest civilizations grew up beside great rivers: the Tigris, the Euphrates, the Nile, the Indus and the Yellow. But the land that supported them – the Fertile Crescent, for instance – was mainly desert. Deserts gave birth to two great religions, Christianity and Islam, and infiltrate much of the imagery of the Bible and the Koran. Western civilization, however, perhaps because Europe lacks deserts, has tended to underestimate their size and importance in the global picture. Fully one-third of the Earth's land surface is arid. It provides at least a fifth of the world's food supplies, over half of the world's production of precious and semiprecious minerals, and a substantial proportion of its oil. In 1991 it was the scene of a major war.

Scientists universally bemoan their ignorance of deserts. 'The truth is that dry lands are probably the least well understood environment on earth', two of them wrote in 1988. Even to define the concept of a desert proves tricky. The most obvious criterion has to be rainfall: a desert is simply a region with less than 10 inches (25 cm) of precipitation per year. But this definition takes no account of temperature, of the rate of evaporation (the higher the temperature, the faster the rain returns to the atmosphere); nor does it recognize the fact that much of the rainfall may be useless to life if it falls in a violent shower, being lost as runoff. The concept of the aridity index has therefore come into use. There are many ways to calculate it, but in essence it expresses a ratio between the amount of precipitation an arid area is capable of evaporating annually and the amount that actually falls. At the high end of the scale are the driest places on Earth, the eastern Sahara and the deserts of Peru, both with an index of 200; at the low end lie the great plains of the United States east of the Rockies, with indexes ranging from 1.5 to 4. Death Valley, north of the Mojave Desert in southeastern California, has an index of 7: lower than one might expect because it receives occasional flash floods.

There is a certain rough symmetry in the way that deserts are distributed around the Tropic of Cancer in the north and Capricorn in the south. Wherever land straddles the equator, there are pairs of deserts, north and south of the humid tropics. In the Americas, the Mojave and Sonora Deserts of the southwestern US and Mexico are matched by the Atacama Desert of South America. In Africa, the Sahara has its equivalent in the Kalahari and Namib Deserts. And in Asia, the deserts of Turkestan and India (though not, significantly, the Gobi Desert, which lies further north) are paralleled by those of the Australian Outback.

Each one is different, bewilderingly so. They are not all flat, stony, monotonous wastes – or even endless rolling sandy dunes. (In fact, just 12 per cent of deserts have dunes.) The only feature common to all deserts is scarcity of water. Compare the bare statistics of the Gobi and the Sahara. The Gobi – which is Mongolian for 'pebbly plain' – is a 500,000-square-mile expanse of mountains and tablelands with an average elevation of 4000 feet (1220 m). It is numbingly cold, with temperatures below freezing throughout much of the year. The Sahara – Arabic for 'desert' – is more than 3.5 million square miles (about the size of the US) of rock, pebbles, salt flats and (20 per cent) sand, with only occasional outcrops of mountains. Much of it is low-lying: as low as 436 feet (133 m) below sea level in the case of the huge Qattara Depression in northern Egypt. Its temperature is oven-like by day, and bitterly cold by night: it can drop almost 40 degrees C (100°F) to as low as minus 7 degrees C (19°F).

Both deserts are extremely inhospitable places, of course, generally lacking in features. With the possible exception of Timbuktu, a fabled name still synonymous with remoteness, 'there has never been for the desert explorer something to parallel the race to the Poles, the search for the source of the Nile, or the desire to scale

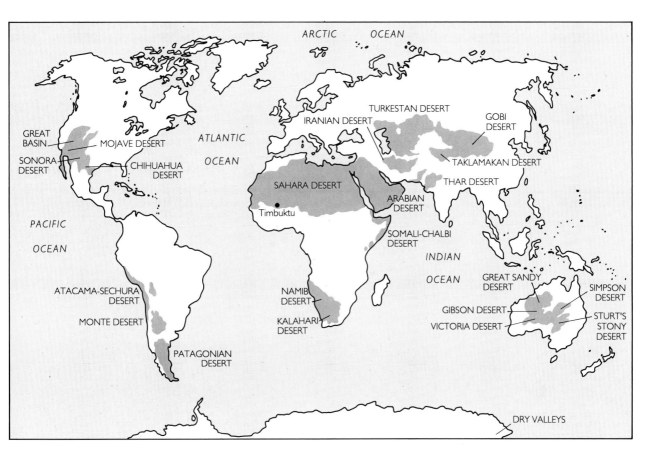

Earth's deserts. Note that there are few deserts on the east coasts of the continents.

lofty peaks simply because they are there', according to Andrew Goudie, Oxford University's professor of geography. 'Conquest has, in general, seemed less dominant than the thirst for comprehension.'

The Arab Ibn Battuta was the first desert traveller in Africa to chronicle his journeys in detail. During some 30 years in the 14th century he voyaged an estimated 75,000 miles in north Africa, Arabia, Asia Minor, China and the South Seas, including the caravan route to Timbuktu, on which he almost died of thirst. Timbuktu at this time was approaching its zenith as an Islamic cultural centre where, as a 16th-century traveller would write, 'doctors, judges, priests and other learned men . . . [are] bountifully maintained at the king's cost'. By the time European travellers set off in search of the city in the early 19th century, it had degenerated into near-desert, like so much of today's Sahel (the belt of troubled drylands that stretches from the Atlantic to Ethiopia, of which Timbuktu was once unofficial capital). The 'Queen of the Desert' by 1828 'consisted of nothing but badly built houses of clay, surrounded by yellowish-white shifting sands. The streets were monotonous and melancholic like the desert. No birds could be heard singing from the roof-tops.'

The words are those of René Caillié, the young Frenchman who became the first European to reach the city and return. (The Scotsman Alexander Laing had got there three years previously, in 1825, but had been strangled by his guide.) Caillié too had nearly perished of thirst, after attaching himself to a caravan that went eight days without reaching water. In the decades that followed until 1880 – the heyday of exploration in Africa – some 200 European travellers attempted to reach Timbuktu. Of these, 165 died of fever or were murdered; most were turned back; and only one, Heinrich Barth, achieved his goal. He had wandered for five years in the wilderness, observing and measuring obsessively, and had been given up for dead.

In the Gobi the pioneer was the Venetian, Marco Polo. He joined the court of Kublai Khan, the Mongol emperor, then in Peking (Beijing); travelled in the East between 1271 and 1292; and later, in a Genoese prison, wrote his famous account. In fact, Polo had been preceded by a Franciscan friar, sent by the Pope a quarter-century before to convert an earlier Mongol emperor; the friar, however, was not at all interested in the Gobi. Polo was: he carefully counted 28 places to obtain water along the short section of the desert he personally traversed. The water holes were still there 600 years later, when the next European travellers made the same crossing. So, of course, were the Gobi's grim bare hills, blown clean of the loess that fertilized China's early civilization and gave the Yellow River its name. Francis Younghusband, an English army officer travelling out of curiosity from Peking to India in 1886, encountered these hills and noted that some of them, nearly 900 feet (275 m) high, were 'composed of bare sand, without a vestige of vegetation of any sort'. He theorized that the sand had been blown from elsewhere. The theory was corroborated by the presence of an immense sandy tract further west in which, according to Mongol legend, there lay a Tartar army, interred in the sand by a mighty storm while forming to invade China.

The deserts of Arabia and Australia have been no less inimical to human existence. Bertram Thomas, the first westerner to cross Arabia's Empty Quarter, in 1930, learnt that even the rare water holes could be lethal. While pausing at one such well, he heard from a Bedouin companion that four of his brothers lay at the bottom. Two of them had descended to clean it out and been overwhelmed by slipping sand. The others, following to rescue them, were engulfed also. 'The well is a tomb. We have abandoned it.'

Charles Sturt, a veteran of Waterloo sent to Australia as an escort for a group of convicts and later secretary to the New South Wales

Waterless but not identical.
Africa's Sahara Desert (*above*) and Asia's Gobi Desert (*left*) differ in many respects. Besides being more than seven times larger than the Gobi, the Sahara is mainly low-lying, whereas the Gobi has an average elevation of 4000 feet (1200 m). During the day, the Gobi is numbingly cold, while the Sahara is furnace-like; at night, however, the Sahara too is bitterly cold, with a drop in temperature of almost 40 degrees C (100°F). About 20 per cent of the Sahara is sand; in the Gobi – which is Mongolian for 'pebbly plain' – sand is much less common.

governor Ralph Darling, got stuck at a water hole for six months in 1844, afraid to go further into the parched Outback. The mean shade temperature was more than 100 degrees F; sometimes it soared to 119 degrees (48.3°C). Sturt later recalled:

> Under its effects every screw in our boxes had been drawn, and the horn handles of our instruments, as well as our combs, were split into fine laminae. The lead dropped out of our pencils. Our hair, as well as the wool on the sheep, ceased to grow, and our nails had become brittle as glass. We found it difficult to write or draw, so rapidly did the fluid dry in our pens and brushes.

Amazingly, when the weather turned cooler Sturt pressed on, until eventually turned back by the dreadful expanse of what is now known as the Simpson Desert, 43,500 square miles of scrub and dunes. He was the first European to penetrate the sere heart of Australia. Sturt's Stony Desert celebrates his achievement on the map of the subcontinent. It remains devoid of habitation.

Why is Australia so dry? And why do deserts form? There appear to be four general causes, that may operate singly or together depending on geographical area. (In Australia, it appears that three of them have joined forces.)

The first is the movement of tropical air from the equator towards the poles mentioned in Chapter 2: one half of the cell named after Hadley. As we know, hurricanes are the escape-valves in this cell. Under normal conditions, the moist tropical air rises to a height of 5 or 6 miles, cooling as it does so; it then spreads laterally north and south, divesting itself of moisture in the form of storms and rainfall. Then it begins to sink. It becomes compressed again and its temperature therefore rises: increasing about 2 degrees C (3.5°F) for every 1000 feet (305 m) it descends. Around the latitudes 30 degrees N and S – not far from the Tropics of Cancer and Capricorn – this warm, desiccated, high-pressure air presses down on the Earth's surface, producing deserts on land and little rainfall at sea. Much of it then flows back towards the equator, to fill the void left by the rising tropical air.

Two of the other three causes are more straightforward. Some deserts are found at the foot of mountain ranges, in what is known as the rain shadow: clouds do not reach them because they have dissipated themselves on the far side of the mountains that face the ocean. The American West and central Australia are good examples. California receives rain, but the Great Basin, separated from the Pacific by the Sierra Nevada and the Cascades, does not. In Australia, the eastern seaboard is well-watered, but the Great Dividing Range leaves little water for the continent beyond. The same holds true for the Patagonian Desert and the Andes. But it is not true of the Gobi. The Gobi is dry not because of mountain ranges blocking moisture, but chiefly because it is in the middle of a landmass, too far from the ocean to receive rain. The same applies to some of the Australian deserts.

This leaves the puzzling fact that much of coastal Chile and Peru is desert, while none of coastal Brazil is; and that the southwest coast of Africa (Namibia) is extremely arid, while the southeast coast is not. The explanation (and the fourth general cause of deserts) lies in the behaviour of the ocean beside the western coasts. The prevailing winds on the western edge of each continent push the surface currents out to sea, and the warm surface water is replaced by a cold upwelling from the ocean floor that reduces the capacity of the coastal air to hold moisture. Fog, instead of rain (if any moisture at all), is what the coastal deserts receive.

These four theories are generally accepted, even if they beg questions about the precise position of actual deserts that cannot be properly answered. What is *not* generally agreed is the history of

The less-than-eternal desert.
The Sahara contains considerable
evidence that it has enjoyed periods
of higher rainfall. Rock paintings at
Tassili-n-Ajjer in Algeria, deep in the
Sahara, show tropical and other
animals (*top*). Their date is likely to
be 5000 BC or earlier. (*Above*) In
the Western Desert of southern
Egypt and northern Sudan, one type
of satellite image shows an
apparently featureless desert, but
(*right*) radar can penetrate the sand
sheet to reveal the landscape of 35
million years ago, which includes
deep river valleys.

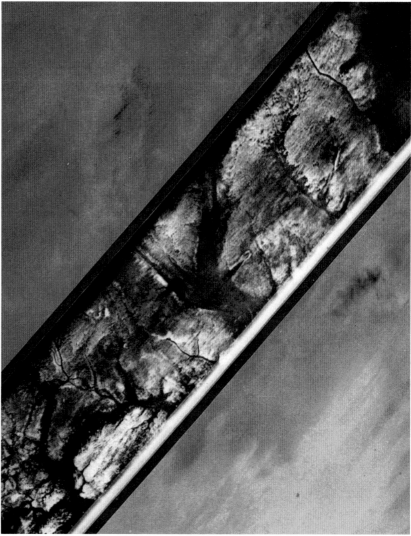

deserts, both in the short term (thousands of years) and in the long term (geological time). How have they moved, if they have moved? All that is certain is that deserts have not always been as hostile to life as they are now. Deep in the Sahara, for instance, at Tassili-n-Ajjer, there are rock paintings showing hippopotamuses, giraffes, buffaloes and cattle. The dating of them has not been settled, but it is likely to be 5000 BC or earlier. Sand-covered antiquities two or more thousand years old, including Roman ruins, demonstrate earlier human habitation too. Shrunken lakes, dry river beds, the stumps of dead trees, and the presence of snappy diminutive crocodiles in remote water holes prove that once there was water where now it is scarce. And in the heart of the Gobi, dinosaur skeletons and dinosaur eggs have been dug up.

As striking, in its own way, was the evidence from radar images made by the scanner on board the space shuttle *Columbia* in 1981. They showed a portion of the Western Desert that stretches from southern Egypt into Sudan, known as the Selima sand sheet. It is one of the driest places in the Sahara. Being so desiccated, the sand is transparent to microwaves: instead of imaging the sand, the radar picks up the bedrock beneath it, as far as 15 feet (4.6 m) down. When these images were shown to the scientists at the US Geological Survey, the first reaction was: 'My God. Where is the sand sheet?'

The concealed bedrock turned out to have hills, valleys, streams and large river channels, some of the valleys being well over ten miles wide – as wide as that of the Nile. It was the landscape of 35 million years ago. In the intervening period, presumably because the whole Africa–Arabia configuration had been altered by plate tectonics, the rainfall had declined. By about 2.5 million years ago, scientists suggest, the rivers and streams had dried up, and sand had started to fill the valleys. Since then, the area has had about 20 climatic reprieves, the last one some 10,000 years ago when it was savannah (grassy plain). But for the past 5000 years, the climate has been static, bone-dry.

Based on these images, the Egyptian General Petroleum Corporation selected a site to explore for groundwater. Eleven wells were drilled and all brought up fresh water from depths between 30 and more than 300 feet (10–100 m). 'As a schoolboy in Egypt,' commented Farouk El-Baz (former scientific adviser to the president of Egypt), who has been involved in studying the images,

> I read that the region west of the Nile used to be the 'granary of the Roman Empire', and became a desert because of misuse. My own work contradicts this and proves that the desert has remained as dry as it is today for 4500 years, long before the

Roman Empire came into being. The 'granary' may have been the fertile land of the Nile River and its Delta, but not the desert to the west.

So it seems that in the past water, ironically, was the primary sculptor of deserts. Perhaps surprisingly, given the obvious power of wind, it still is. Water acts openly by erosion during flash floods, visibly wearing down hills and valleys; but it acts still more effectively in secret, combining forces with the tremendous temperature differential in some deserts between night and day. There are various mechanisms for this process of weathering. Rain or dew first seeps into small fissures in the rocks. Over time it dissolves some of the minerals, thereby weakening the rock, or it can be absorbed into the structures of the minerals making friable compounds. Salts that absorb water swell and may exert pressure on surrounding rocks; if the water then evaporates as the rock bakes in the sun, the salts shrink, only to expand once more when further water seeps in. The expansions and contractions are very small, but over a long enough period they can scar rock with complex pitting called honeycomb weathering. The damage this has done to the face of the Sphinx at Giza is well known.

In extreme cases water may even fracture a boulder. According to Uwe George, a German naturalist who explored the Sahara during the 1960s and 1970s, a 3-foot-wide (1-m) rock near him on a hot summer day 'suddenly gave a loud report, like a cannon being fired, and shattered into several pieces. Not long before, a brief but violent downpour of rain had cooled the heated stone so abruptly that its surface steamed.' Perhaps this accounts for some of the many stories desert travellers have told of so-called 'shooting rocks', that were once attributed with appealing simplicity to over-rapid thermal expansion or contraction. Laboratory experiments have proved that sun and shade alone are not enough; but they could be sufficient in tandem with water.

Of course wind – 'aeolian' force, in scientific discourse – is a vital designer of deserts too. Saharan winds are so powerful and searing that some of their names, harmattan and sirocco, have entered the English language. The harmattan is a northeasterly that creates dust storms up to 20,000 feet (6100 m) high; it blows more than 100 million tons of dust westward into the Atlantic every summer. Reddish dust from the Sahara often settles on the rooftops of Paris and even reaches Sweden. In 1982 a cloud more than 1000 miles long arrived in Florida and pushed up pollution levels precipitously before it dispersed.

In the Sahara itself, these winds can be sandblasters. Uwe George, encountering winds of hurricane strength, had all the paint

The power of wind and sand.
Palmyra (today's Tudmur), an ancient Syrian city on a caravan route, was destroyed by the Romans in AD 272. Ever since, wind and sand have been eating away the pillars of its ruined temples.

The infinite faces of sand. Just 12 per cent of the world's deserts are sand dunes, but dunes – especially the dunes of the Sahara (shown above) – have come to symbolize deserts at their quintessential. Dunes have many names and may move, if driven by strong winds, as fast as 50 feet (15 m) a year. The photograph on the right shows *barchans* marching across new plantations at El Gedida in Egypt; (*far right*) blade-sharp *seifs*.

stripped from his vehicles and the glass in the windshields made so pitted and abraded that it had to be knocked out to allow the drivers to see. The aeolian impact on rocks is equally merciless but far more destructive over long periods. Ventifacts are rocks that have been abraded by wind-blown sand and ablated by the wind itself. Their shapes are wonderful and grotesque. They include the fortress-like buttes of the American West, staple dramatic back-drop of countless films, the undercarved *yardangs* of the Sahara that resemble toadstools and upside-down hulls of boats, and the nameless rounded boulders that neatly dot stretches of yellow sand

in the Tibesti plateau of the central Sahara, resembling nothing so much as burnt buns stuck in congealed custard.

The majority of these strange formations – the boulders especially – cannot be fully accounted for. Probably both wind and water have played a role. In the case of the most famous desert formation of all, sand dunes, there are also many mysteries, but they are definitely a phenomenon of wind in which water is largely irrelevant. Ralph Bagnold, a British army officer, studied dunes in Egypt's Western Desert from the mid-1920s and later in London under laboratory conditions, thereby revolutionizing our knowledge of sand movement by wind. He had this to say about their peculiar attraction:

> In places vast accumulations of sand weighing millions of tons move inexorably, in regular formation, over the surface of the country, growing, retaining their shape, even breeding, in a manner which, by its grotesque imitation of life, is vaguely disturbing to an imaginative mind. Elsewhere the dunes are cut to another pattern – lined up in parallel ranges, peak following peak in regular succession like the teeth of a monstrous saw for scores, even hundreds of miles, without a break and without a change of direction, over a landscape so flat that their formation cannot be influenced by any local geographical features.

Generalizations about sand dunes are plainly difficult to make. Everything about a dune depends on the type of sand, the direction and strength of the wind and, probably, the underlying topography. *Barchans* are transverse dunes: they form across the wind when its direction is generally uniform and the amount of sand moderate. They have a graceful crescent shape, with the horns of the crescent pointing downwind. More abundant sand may produce longitudinal *seifs*, named after the Arab word for sword. *Seifs* have blade-sharp crests, run in the same direction as the wind, and are made sinuous by its variation. If the wind is strong and steady enough, it may, instead of sculpting *seifs*, cut deep troughs in the desert floor and produce parallel dunes of great length, as Bagnold wrote. But if it veers in direction and does not settle, the result may be a graceful star dune, as if two or more *barchans* had come together.

Star dunes do not migrate, for fairly obvious reasons. They remain in roughly the same place for centuries and become landmarks with names, by which travellers in the desert find their way. While longitudinal dunes do move, it is the transverse *barchans* that are the principal moving dunes. The wind blows sand grains up and over the more compacted windward side. They gradually pile up on the leeward side, increasing its slope until it exceeds 35 degrees. A mini-avalanche follows, and the 'angle of repose' is restored. Through an infinitude of such episodes, the dune shuffles forward. *Barchans* in Baja California move as much as 50 feet (15 m) a year. The average dune moves much less, a bare 10 feet (3 m). The fastest dunes have been known to move as much as a foot a day under a strong and steady wind. If they threaten human habitations, it may be possible to stabilize them by covering them and planting them to cut down erosion.

Only in recent decades has this been generally attempted. Until then, every kind of desert dweller – human, animal and plant – had

A ventifact. Winds in the Sahara, such as the harmattan, can be sandblasters. Ventifacts are rocks that have been abraded by wind-blown sand and ablated by the wind itself. Their shapes are often wonderful and grotesque.

followed the basic law of life in deserts: adaptation, rather than confrontation. Cacti have spines, not leaves, that both act as radiators and permanently surround the cactus with 'an invisible jacket of still air' (in David Attenborough's phrase), thereby reducing evaporation; they also grow white hairs that reflect heat away from vulnerable growing tissue. Camels, famously, are capable of converting part of their reserves of fat into water; they also have thick coarse wool on their upper surfaces as protection against the sun, but are virtually naked elsewhere, so as best to radiate excess heat. As for human beings, the ability of Australian Aborigines and Kalahari Bushmen to locate and extract water from wizened-looking plants, is legendary. An equally remarkable example comes from Arabia. Bedouin in the Arabian desert could establish the direction of Mecca for their prayers and find their way even during the dust storms that blot the sky and their own feet from view. 'We felt the stones on the ground,' explained an elder from Kuwait. 'Their pitted surfaces always faced north because this is the direction from which the *shemal* wind blows.' This distinctive pattern has been recognized by researchers both in the pebbles of today and in the geological record.

To stay alive, an average human needs to drink at least a fifth of a gallon (1 litre) of water per day. That is, if he or she is adequately fed. To grow an adequate diet for a human being requires about 300 tons/cubic metres of water per year – nearly a ton a day. 'There are many, many places where there is not nearly enough water to do this,' according to Robin Clarke in his 1991 study, *Water: The International Crisis*.

Drought is a concept not easy to delimit satisfactorily. Like floods, which can occur in dry areas as well as wet ones, drought can affect countries with high rainfall as well as arid lands. (In fact Bangladesh suffered from drought in 1992, a year after massive floods caused by a cyclone.) In Britain, *absolute drought* is a period of at least 15 consecutive days with less than 0.01 inches (0.25 mm) of rain on each day; *partial drought* is a period of at least 29 consecutive days with mean daily rainfall less than 0.01 inches. In India, drought is declared if the annual rainfall is less than 75 per cent of average. In Libya droughts are recognized only after two years without rain.

The point is, shortage becomes drought not at some definite point on a scale, like the boiling point of water or even the amount of water needed to stay alive, but when a society or government decides that there is drought. Malin Falkenmark, a Swedish hydrologist, has provided a useful analysis of the problem and is one of the few scientists who has attempted to quantify world

Drought in Africa. Research suggests that drought has been a feature of the African climate since before the dawn of history. Devastating scourges though they are, 20th-century African droughts are probably mere blips on the graph of long-term climatic change. Many Africans, such as this Dogon boy in Mali (*above*), have adapted to drought by learning how to find water-bearing roots in the desert. But others, such as these women in Zimbabwe in 1992 (*opposite*), have been forced to dig deeper and deeper wells, often without finding a sustained supply of water.

water shortage. She distinguishes four different causes of water scarcity:

aridity, a permanent shortage of water caused by a dry climate;

drought, an irregular phenomenon occurring in exceptionally dry years;

desiccation, a drying up of the landscape, particularly the soil, resulting from activities such as deforestation and over-grazing; and

water stress, due to increasing numbers of people relying on fixed levels of runoff.

Her assessment of water need and availability makes sobering reading. (If the quantities available seem generous, remember how much water it takes to grow only the *food* needed by one person per year: about 300 tons/cubic metres.) Countries that have more than 10,000 cubic metres (10 million litres, 2.2 million gallons) of available water per person per year have 'limited problems' (e.g. the US); those with less than 10,000 but more than 1670 cubic metres have 'general problems' (e.g. China, India); those with less than

1670 but more than 1000 cubic metres are 'water stressed' (e.g. South Africa, Poland); those with less than 1000 but more than 500 cubic metres have 'chronic water scarcity' (e.g. Kenya); and those with less than 500 cubic metres are 'beyond the water barrier'. Tunisia, Israel, Barbados, Libya, Malta, Egypt and Saudi Arabia fall into the last category. In Europe, according to the UN Economic Commission, Cyprus, Romania and the Ukraine are already inadequately supplied; by the year 2000, Bulgaria, Greece, Hungary, Luxembourg and Turkey are likely to have joined their ranks.

This is no empty threat. The 1970s and 1980s were unquestionably decades of drought, with water scarcity reported in California, Mexico, Peru, India, China and, most of all, in large portions of Africa. During 1990, in France, frustrated farmers sabotaged water-pumping stations, anxious to divert domestic supplies to irrigate their holdings; in Greece, the water shortage was the worst for 50 years and the government declared it a 'national disaster'; in Italy, it was the worst for 250 years, with precipitation totals down nearly 50 per cent, crops in the south shrivelling in the fields, domestic water in Naples rationed to two hours a day, and bottled water in Sicily selling for more than beer.

Drought in the Outback.
Australia has experienced six major droughts since 1950. During the drought that began in the late 1980s, more than six million sheep perished.

Australia too was experiencing drought. This was nothing new in itself: there have been six major droughts in Australia since 1950. But by late 1992, there had been no let-up. In parts of three eastern states, covering a region ten times the size of Britain, it had not rained properly since 1989. Six million sheep had died, their bleached bones flecking the vast stretches of red dust with white, and thousands of wool producers, for nearly a century the unofficial aristocrats of Australia, were facing absolute ruin. Many farmers had lost 90 per cent of their flocks. It was doubtful whether great swathes of the Outback would ever be returned to farming.

But no one in Australia was dying from the drought. In Africa, there was a desperate shortage of food. In southern Africa, crops were ruined by drought in nine countries, including parts of South Africa, which decided to freeze all maize exports despite being normally the world's third largest exporter. In Zimbabwe, almost half the deep wells and more than a quarter of the boreholes had dried up; the largest dam reservoir, Lake Kyle, was almost empty; and the country, from being a net exporter of sugar, had become a net importer. Throughout southern Africa, 17 million people were threatened with famine. In the Horn of Africa, particularly in war-torn areas such as Somalia, things were even worse: 23 million people were facing starvation.

Rainfall in Africa is notoriously unpredictable. This, combined with the generally poor and fragile soils of the continent, leaves Africa more at the mercy of drought than any other continent. African rainfall is not only seasonal, it also varies greatly in space and time within one season. When it comes, it often falls in short, intense storms rather like summer thunderstorms in Europe. The edge of such storms can be remarkably precise. One can drive from a wet to a dry road in only a few yards, or stand in the dry while rain falls close by. In the Sahel, which has been historically drought-prone, 4 inches (10 cm) of rain – perhaps the entire annual amount – may fall in a month on one farmer's land but none on another's land only a mile or two away. Furthermore, it may fall in three or four days and at any point during the month. As an extreme example of African variability, the city of Cairo has an average annual rainfall of 1.1 inches (2.8 cm). Between 1890 and 1919, it received rain in only 13 of the 30 years; during one particular day, 1.7 inches (4.3 cm) fell.

To establish what is 'normal' rainfall in the Sahel (or indeed in most of Africa) and what is drought, is therefore tricky. Apart from the intrinsic variability, there is an acute shortage of records. Researchers in the mid-1980s could find only five rainfall stations with records for as long as 50 years. Many former stations have fallen into disuse, some within the last few years. Even where

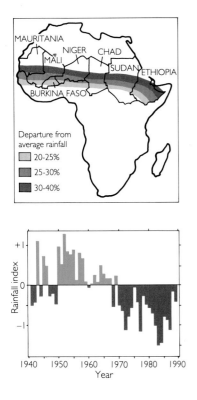

Departure from average rainfall
- 20-25%
- 25-30%
- 30-40%

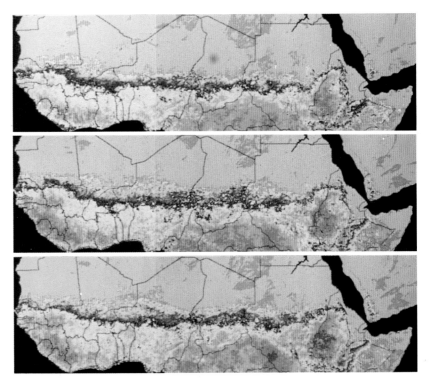

What is desertification? Are spreading deserts entirely forces of Nature, or can people and animals too make deserts? In west Africa including the Sahel, the graph of rainfall (*above*) over the past half-century shows that for the whole region since 1968 rainfall has been below average, with one exceptional year. The nearer to the Sahara a region is, the greater has been the (negative) departure from normal rainfall, as the map (*top*) indicates. The shaded bands on the map show the average annual departures from normal rainfall for each region. The rains were particularly poor in 1983 and 1984, the beginning of the great famine in Ethiopia. Vegetation disappeared from the northern Sahel in 1984, then gradually returned during 1985 and 1986 as rainfall improved. This is clear from the three satellite images (*right*) made in August and September of 1984 (top), 1985 (middle) and 1986 (bottom), in which light green represents the least vegetation, dark blue the most.

reliable records do exist, how sensible is it to regard the 50 or 60 years in which expatriate Europeans have been observing African rainfall, as 'normal' for Africa in the longer term? Much of the planning of Africa's water supplies, especially its dams, has been based on these records, interpreted by experts trained in more temperate climates. 'To someone judging semi-arid Africa by the standards of what is normal in a temperate environment, the variability of the climate is both bizarre and incomprehensible', commented William Adams, a British geographer with personal experience of water management schemes in the Sahel.

The only meteorological record in Africa before the end of the last century is that of the level of the Nile measured by the Roda Nilometer at Cairo from AD 641. It is hard to interpret, but it seems to show periods of high flow in a series of years (most recently 1950–74), and periods of low flows, such as today. Drought appears to have been a feature of African climate for many hundreds of years: recurrent, but not, so far as scientists can tell, regular.

The Sahel encompasses 20 per cent of the African landmass, a semi-arid belt below the Sahara 3000 miles long and between 200 and 700 miles wide, with rainfall averaging 4–24 inches (10–60 cm) per year. It includes Mauritania, Senegal, Mali, Burkina Faso (the former Upper Volta), Niger, northern Nigeria, Chad, southern Sudan and much of Ethiopia: a total population of perhaps 100 million people, with average life expectancies nearer 45 than 50.

What causes desertification?

Many experts believe that grazing goats and cattle, the collecting of firewood, and the erosion of land around waterholes, greatly exacerbate the vanishing of vegetation, leading to sandstorms and the spread of deserts into homes, such as photographed here in Mauritania during the 1980s. Other experts are less persuaded of the connection.

Dune fixation in the Sahel. Most attempts to control the movement of African dunes have failed, but there have been some notable successes (pages 221–22).

This century's records for the Sahel show dips in average rainfall in the 1910s, 1940s and from the late 1960s until today. Colonial officers have described the resulting famines in the first two periods. The drought that still persists (despite occasional wetter years such as 1988, but in the southern Sahel only) is burned into the memories of the millions who have somehow survived it. In 1989/90, 500 older Sahelians spoke about their lives in a unique oral history project, *At the Desert's Edge*, organized by a London-based voluntary agency, SOS Sahel. As the editors of the interviews remarked, 'we can assert with confidence that to be old, in the Sahel, is an achievement, and an achievement well worth recording.' Here are the words of one woman in Chad, Nizela Idriss (age not given):

> We have suffered four major famines during my lifetime. The first was called Amzaytone, meaning 'the time we sold our necklaces', in the 1950s. The second, about 10 years later, was El Harigue, 'the year when everything burnt', when our crops shrivelled under the heat of the sun. The third, in 1982, was Alchouil, 'the year of the sack', when traders came with sacks of millet for us to buy. As long as you had the means, you did not starve during this famine. Finally, in 1985 the big famine came upon us. We called this Laitche, meaning 'the year when everyone fled from the area'.

We shall never know how many people died of drought and famine in the Sahel during the 1970s and 1980s. Where there are statistics there is no malnutrition, and where there is malnutrition there are no statistics, it has been said. Estimates for the 1968–73 period, in which the world first became aware of the disaster, range from 50,000 to 250,000 deaths, with the loss of 3.5 million cattle (in Upper Volta, not one cow in six survived). Nomadic herders and subsistence farmers migrated to cities in tens of thousands. Nouakchott, the capital of Mauritania, had 20,000 people at Independence in 1960; now there are well over 350,000, over half of whom are refugees. Saharan sand had literally overrun their villages. But perhaps most shocking of all was the effect on children, permanently retarded by disease and brain damage traceable to malnutrition. In the words of one writer, 'a beard of flies on the chin of a suffering child became the indelible face of desertification.'

Drought and malnutrition have also caused deaths in the American West within living memory. During the westward expansion of the 1860s and 1870s, when rainfall was above average, Americans convinced themselves that divine providence was behind their push: the motto was 'Rain Follows the Plow'. Some scientists backed the theory. One, a noted climatologist, declaimed:

Since the territory [of Colorado] has begun to be settled, towns and cities built up, farms cultivated, mines opened, and roads made and travelled, there has been a gradual increase in moisture ... I therefore give it as my firm conviction ... that as population increases the moisture will increase.

The first serious drought began in 1888. By 1890 it was clear that the theory was a preposterous fraud. Settlers left the region in droves: the population of Kansas and Nebraska declined by as much as a half. In the 1890s, among those that stayed there were widespread reports of deaths. Two decades later, when the drought returned, such reports were repeated. In fact, there have been major droughts in the great plains of the US about every 20 years during the past century. But until the 1930s, little was done for the victims by the government.

The Dust Bowl storms of the mid-1930s, which ultimately affected 756 counties in 19 states, triggered the first serious attempt to control the effects of drought and erosion. The storms blew for days at a time, shooting dust high enough to catch the jet stream, which carried it to Europe. In Washington DC, in 1934, members of Congress took time out from a debate on a bill to control overgrazing on public lands to crowd the Capitol balcony and see the sky darken at noon. 'From the look of the western horizon, half the continent could have been on fire', wrote Marc Reisner half a century later in *Cadillac Desert: The American West and Its Disappearing Water*. The bill was passed, against attempts by some western members to weaken it, 'even as their states were sailing over their heads.'

A few years later, two soil scientists, Hugh H. Bennett and Walter Clay Lowdermilk, were asked to testify on erosion before a committee of Congress. Without a word they placed a thick towel on the committee's polished table and tipped a large cup of water onto it. Next they removed the wet towel and, still silent, poured a second cup of water on the bare table. The towel, of course, represented the nation's soil. As the water dripped into the laps of the politicians, they were made vividly aware of what America was losing each day through the action of water and wind.

Contour ploughing, windbreaks and the Soil Conservation Service, all introduced in the Dust Bowl years, have prevented a return of the storms. But the degradation of land in the West and the shortage of water remain acute, and they are getting worse. The great plains, according to Reisner, are 'reverting, slowly and steadily, into an amphitheater of natural forces toying with its inhabitants' fate.' Much of the water now used to farm them does not fall from the sky but is pumped up from underground. The

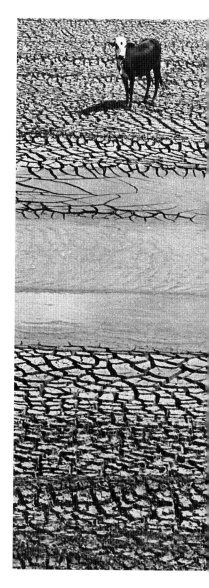

Bovine desertification? Looking at this drought-cracked riverbed in Kenya's Northern Frontier Province, taken in the mid-1970s, one finds it hard to imagine that nomadic pastoralism could be an important generator of deserts. Yet this is the accepted wisdom among many experts on Africa. But others credit nomads with considerable understanding of their environment.

Ogallala aquifer is a body of permeable rock saturated with water that underlies parts of Nebraska, Kansas, Colorado, Oklahoma, Texas and New Mexico. It is the largest discrete aquifer in the world and also the fastest-disappearing aquifer in the world. Pumping exceeds natural replacement at a rate roughly equivalent to the flow of the Colorado River. Within a generation or two, on present calculations by the state water authorities involved, water that took half a million years to coalesce, will be used up.

Across the Rockies, in California, city authorities and farmers are looking very seriously at widespread cloud 'seeding' – a cloud nucleation technique similar to that used (with limited success) against hurricanes – and even desalination of ocean water, to buck the effects of drought. It is not that there have been many fewer storms in recent years – the drought years have produced 80 per cent of the number of storms that occurred earlier – however, the storms during the drought years have produced less water. The main seeding agent is silver iodide, but dry ice and various organic compounds have also produced results. The typical increase in annual precipitation following seeding has been 5–15 per cent, and over the high hills of Santa Barbara, the increase has been 25 per cent. It is at Santa Barbara, where the two main water reservoirs were only 12 and 14 per cent full after five years of drought, that highly expensive but reliable desalination (already important in Saudi Arabia), has proved attractive to the city authorities.

The battle against erosion. Land degradation, whether as a result of Nature or of Man or of both combined, is a common problem in many countries, both rich and poor. Contour ploughing and planting – as in these fields in southeastern Pennsylvania (*opposite*) – have much helped the control of degradation in the American Midwest and West. Around the Aral Sea, in western Asia, in a salty desert created wholly by human action, the fight has barely begun. The light blue of the satellite image (*inset*) shows the Aral as it was in 1960; the mid-blue as it was in 1973; and the dark blue its shrunken form in 1989. Since 1960, the Aral Sea has lost more than 40 per cent of its area (see page 216).

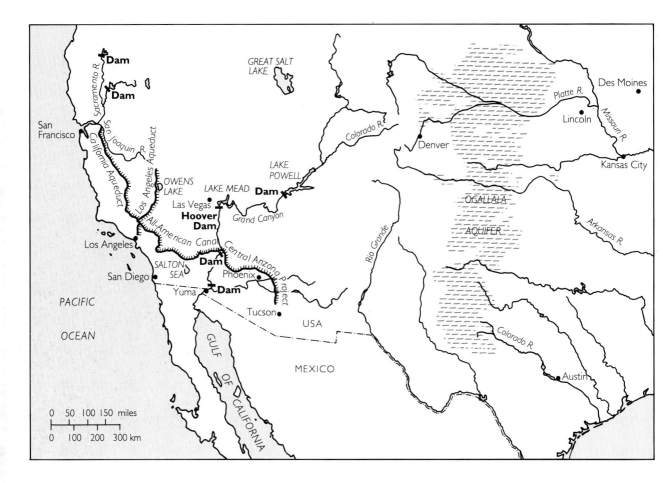

The plumbing of the American West.

Others have far grander, not to say grandiose, solutions to the water crisis of the American West. One talked-about scheme, first proposed by a Californian engineer in 1964 and known as NAWAPA (North American Water and Power Alliance), aims to harness the fresh water of northern Canada and Alaska and divert it to central Canada, the USA and Mexico. Up to 17 per cent of the runoff in ten principal rivers (including the Yukon) would be transferred via 240 new reservoirs, 112 navigation schemes and 17 new navigable canals or rivers. The largest reservoir would be created from an 1100-mile natural gorge in the Canadian Rockies: it would be 500 miles long and contain over 500 cubic miles of water, giving it more than 20 times the capacity of Lake Nasser. Some 160 million acre-feet of water per year would be delivered by the scheme (nearly five times California's annual consumption), and 70,000 megawatts of hydroelectric power.

Mind-boggling. NAWAPA is pharaonic, much bigger than the controversial Three Gorges Dam in China or the Narmada River project in India – and its future is hugely uncertain. In the 1980s, a professor of hydrology at the University of California in Berkeley said of it: 'The environmental damage that would be caused by that damned thing can't even be described. It could cause as much harm as all of the dam-building we have done in a hundred years.' But its supporters include a former US secretary of state and California governor, Robert Finch, and the premier of Quebec, Robert Bourassa, staunch advocate of the James Bay project. In 1992, both the Canadian and the US negotiators for a North American Free Trade Agreement backed NAWAPA. Perhaps, early next century, if the great plains and the American West continue to dehydrate through global warming, NAWAPA will get the crucial boost. Said one US senator from Utah, a long-time lobbyist for NAWAPA, in 1985: 'It may be fifty years or it may be a hundred years, but something like it will be built.'

Given the aridity and drought conditions prevailing in large areas of the United States and Australia, it comes as no surprise that both countries are extremely fire-prone – Australia even more than the US. Australia, at least its most populous southeast crescent, is rich in forest fuel. Most Australian forests accumulate a great deal of fuel on the floor, mainly by bark shedding. The dominant tree is eucalyptus, which is itself fire-promoting. Its oils greatly aid combustion, and its ignited bark is carried ahead of a fire for distances of up to 20 miles, creating 'spot' fires. Australian eucalypts have the longest spotting distances in the world. Bush fires in Australia therefore cover large areas, typically 250,000 acres, and move with frightening speed: in half an hour they can engulf 1000 acres, where a fire in a slower burning coniferous forest might engulf only an acre and a quarter.

In the biggest bush fire of recent times, the so-called 'Ash Wednesday' fire of February 1983 (during the 1982/83 El Niño), 180 fires started in Victoria and South Australia in one day when temperatures went up to 40 degrees C (104°F). Fanned by winds blowing at 40–50 mph, 10 fires raged out of control. They burnt almost 900,000 acres, claimed 72 lives and made as many as 8000 people homeless. One fire tornado shot up to 1250 feet (380 m) in height.

Forest fires in the US burn between 1 and 2 million acres of the 225 million acres of forest land every year. But most fires are small: more than 95 per cent of the area burned annually results from 2 to 3 per cent of the total number of fires. Often, particularly if the cause is lightning, the burnt area is just a quarter of an acre.

But however small the area, if it is populated, a fire can be catastrophic. Californians, particularly southern Californians, live in perpetual awareness of fire. As the detective Philip Marlowe puts it in Raymond Chandler's final novel *Playback*: 'I got out of the car and stamped on the cigarette. "You don't do that in the California

A vision of the desert tamed.
The Central Arizona Project, a computer-controlled aqueduct costing $4 thousand million, zigzags from the Colorado River across the desert for some 300 miles in order to water Phoenix, the capital of Arizona.

hills," I told her. "Not even out of season."' Almost every year, fires destroy homes around Santa Barbara: a particularly bad one in July 1977 reached to within a mile of the downtown area of the city, and reduced over 230 homes to ashes. Oakland/Berkeley, near San Francisco, also suffers badly. In October 1991, a fire thought to have been extinguished reignited the following day and burned 1800 affluent acres of drought-stricken hillside over some three days. When it was finally got under control by more than 1000 firefighters – some of them attacking it from the air – 24 people were known to be dead and 13 others missing; more than 3000 homes and apartments had been wrecked; and damages were estimated at more than $1.5 thousand million. One of the firemen told a reporter: 'I haven't seen anything like this since Vietnam.' In San Francisco terms, it was comparable only to the great fire of 1906 following the earthquake.

Forest fires on a grand scale have struck the US a number of times in its recorded history (and probably similarly before that). One of them, the Tillamook fire in Oregon, burned for long periods – 18 years between 1933 and 1951 – as well as ravaging a huge area. The most lethal and destructive one was centred on Peshtigo, Wisconsin, near the Great Lakes. It is probably the world's greatest wildfire disaster. Fire broke out on 8 October 1871, the same night as a fire in Chicago that killed 250 people, following 14 weeks of drought in the Midwest. Strong winds generated spot fires within the firebreaks that had been built around the settlements. Some 1500 people, perhaps many more, lost their lives, and about 4.25 million acres burned. The fire stimulated the creation of the National Forest System.

Disastrous though it was for human beings and property trapped in its vicinity, the Peshtigo fire, like all forest fires, was to some extent necessary. So far as we know, it was natural in origin and development. All societies have recognized that fire can rejuvenate land by clearing it of choking vegetation, and releasing chemicals via the ash, vital for plant growth: sometimes it is Nature that is incendiarist, other times human beings deliberately decide to take a hand (and all too often they take a hand accidentally). The problem for human beings has been where to strike a balance. In the flaming hot US summer of 1988, the difficulty became fiercely acute.

That year, in the West and across the US, including Alaska, more than 6 million acres burned. Nearly a million of them were in Yellowstone National Park: fire burned or singed nearly half the park, 45 times more than in any year since its founding in 1872. The flames filled the television screens of millions of Americans, provoking criticism of the park authorities. But they left scientific opinion somewhat divided. The basic issue was whether to attempt to suppress the fires, or whether to abandon them to burn, provided that they did not threaten human habitation (such as the Old Faithful Inn). The park's policy until the 1970s had been to suppress where feasible. For more than a decade after that, however, they had followed a policy of 'let it burn'. How effective the earlier suppression had actually been was a matter of debate, but in principle it seemed that it could have helped to stoke up fuel for the inferno of 1988.

To some extent yes, agreed two scientists, who had watched Yellowstone over some years. But seen in a longer perspective, the suppression probably had relatively little effect. They had found evidence from fire scars of major periodic conflagrations in the park. As they reported in *Scientific American* a year after the great fire: 'Data from our study area indicate that the fires of 1988 in fact probably did not behave very differently from the ones that burned across the same area around 1700.'

This hints at the complexity of fire's role in the environment. Even more suggestive was the experience of the astronauts in *Skylab 3* when crossing the Sahel in January 1974. They could see pervasive and extensive cirrus clouds floating over west Africa and also over the coast of Somalia extending into the Indian Ocean. They reported: 'The particular character of the cirrus clouds is that they are dirty-looking, and appear much darker than other clouds in the same area.' Several days later, the clouds were identified. They came from fires set by slash-and-burn cultivators, by nomadic herders wishing to improve pasturage, and by hunters flushing out game and sustaining preferred habitats. 'Like the pillars of fire and dust that guided the Hebrews, the fires showed as flames by night and as ash clouds by day', wrote Stephen J. Pyne in his cultural history of wildfire, *Fire in America*. Such fires have surely been a major element in the ecology of semi-desert regions such as the American West and the Sahel for millennia – one that is by no means simple to categorize as beneficial or destructive.

The idea that deserts can threaten human beings by spreading into their lands and homes is probably as old as Man. The converse notion, that Man can turn Nature into a desert is at least as old as Plato (as his comment at the beginning of this chapter reveals), and was probably known to the earliest civilizations.

But the word 'desertification' is of much more recent provenance. It was coined in the late 1940s and has yet to appear in many dictionaries. One reason is that there is little agreement about its meaning. Scientists, engineers, aid workers, politicians and laypeople disagree with each other and between themselves. Some see it as a purely climatic process, others as a human process, many

Fire in America. In 1988, across the United States including Alaska, the record heat caused more than 6 million acres of forest to burn. The worst fires were in the West, such as the blaze that burnt nearly one million acres at Yellowstone National Park. This fire was in California, one of the most fire-prone states.

as a product of both changing climate and human misuse of land, with proportions according to taste. Some of those who emphasize human misuse widen the term to include not just deserts of the usual kind, but all land degradation, such as that caused by deforestation, salinity and even waterlogging. To them, desertification may take place far from deserts, in humid lands or in river valleys – wherever land is losing its value through misuse.

Thus, according to UNCOD, the first Conference on Desertification, organized by the United Nations in Nairobi in 1977, desertification was primarily the result of human impact, with drought acting as a kind of catalyst speeding up the land degradation that had begun long before the drought. A 'repeated mistake', according to the Egyptian scientist Farouk El-Baz, 'that has created one of the most prevalent misconceptions of modern times: the notion that people make deserts.'

Most people who are not specialists would probably accede to a meaning based simply on the idea that deserts are spreading at their edges. This is the 'commonsense' notion appealed to by two British ecologists, Andrew Warren and Clive Agnew, who reviewed the literature on desertification in 1988 and came to the wry conclusion that the word had suffered 'an erosion of meaning'. They defined desertification as unambiguously as possible, as 'the notion that the extent of deserts – dry areas with few plants – is increasing, usually into the semi-arid lands.'

This leaves the magnitude of the extent and the reason why it is increasing uncertain: as uncertain, if not more so, as the keenly debated extent and cause of global warming (see Chapter 9). It does not leave room for complacency, however. If we care to look, whether into the past or at the present, there is ample disturbing evidence that human societies can and do make deserts.

Five and a half millennia ago, in the floodplain of southern Iraq, the Sumerians cultivated equal areas of wheat and barley. A thousand years later, around 2500 BC, the salt in the water had increased so much due to excessive irrigation that the saline-tolerant barley had taken over more than 80 per cent of the farmland; by 1700 BC no wheat at all was grown. Today, much of the land that once supported Sumer and its successor civilizations is abandoned, the rest is so poor that crop yields are among the world's lowest: some 20–30 per cent of all potentially irrigable land in Iraq cannot be used. In the words of the soil scientist Daniel Hillel, writing in 1992:

Each and every one of the insidious man-induced scourges that played so crucial a role in the deaths of past civilizations has its mirror image in our contemporary world. Salinization, erosion,

The spread of a desert. The striated longitudinal dunes of the Namib Desert in southwest Africa have been thwarted in their northwards march by the course of the Kuiseb River. Evidence comes from the fact that they are expanding into the Atlantic Ocean south of Walvis Bay, slowly modifying the coastline of Namibia and leaving the 1912 wreck of a cargo ship high and dry in drifting sand.

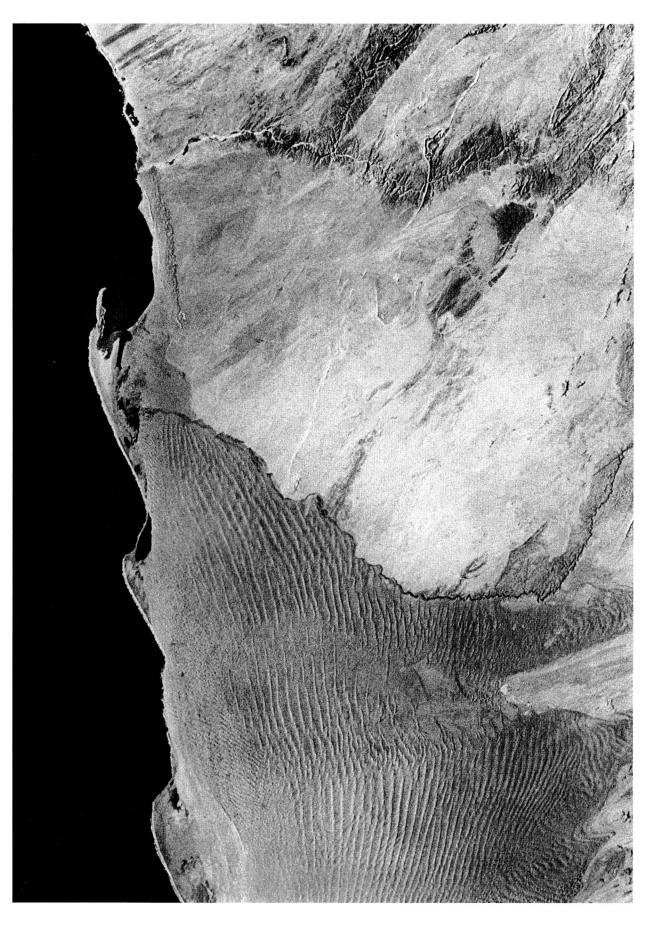

denudation of watersheds, degradation of arid lands, depletion and pollution of water resources, abuse of wetlands, and population pressure are still with us, but on an ever larger scale.

Every one of these diseases has blighted Asia's second largest body of land-locked water, the Aral Sea. Lying at the edge of Uzbekistan, some 500 miles northwest of Tashkent and Samarkand, it is fed by two rivers, one of which, the Amu Darya, was known to Alexander the Great as the Oxus. But for more than 30 years, these rivers have run very low. Since 1960 the Aral has lost more than 40 per cent of its area; and what remains is so salty that its once-vital fishing industry is finished; anyway, its chief fishing port, Muynak, is now stranded 20 miles from water. The hot salty grit that remains, unanchored by vegetation, is whipped up by winds at the rate of 43 million tons a year, and distributed as far afield as the coast of the Arctic Ocean. But mostly it falls on the fields and people of the region, fouling the already inadequate water supplies, clogging the carburettors of cars, inducing throat cancers and producing the highest infant mortality rate in the former Soviet Union.

'You cannot fill the Aral with tears,' said a young Uzbek poet, Mukhammed Salikh, in 1989. He was angry that though the disaster had been admitted at last – its root cause had not been. Lake Chad, in the middle of the Sahel, dwindled in the 1970s and 1980s to practically nothing. Very little blame, if any, attached to Man. But in the Aral's case, the culprit was definitely not Nature. Soviet planners, beginning in the 1950s, diverted the flow of the Aral's two rivers in order to irrigate cotton fields further south. The plan worked, but at huge cost to the 35 million people of the region. And now, ominously, as in ancient Mesopotamia, salt is encrusting the soil of many cotton fields waterlogged by excessive irrigation. The 'white gold' is under threat from a white plague. In 1992, an Israeli team was trying to develop a more efficient 'drip irrigation' system. It was expensive, far more than the government of Uzbekistan could afford. The government's hope was that it could pay for installation in cotton.

Satellite images have proved a most effective means of monitoring the slow death of the Aral. They clearly show the great new deposits of salt and sand exposed along the shores of the lake. Similarly, images of the Sahel made in successive years during the same season graphically portray the advance and retreat of vegetation. They are almost too graphic: accurate interpretation of their meaning has turned out to be much harder than first expected. Desertification does not lend itself to quantification, unlike deforestation.

In mid-1984, for instance, satellite images showed light vegetation on the hills of the Wollo region of Ethiopia, following the rains. The World Food Programme assumed that there would be a harvest and underestimated Ethiopia's requirements during the famine that followed. In fact, on the ground, the rain had bounced off the farmers' fields and washed away soil and rocks into the valleys. The vegetation was a thin, sickly grass, according to Lloyd Timberlake, author of *Africa in Crisis*, who visited Ethiopia at this time. It 'bloated the drought-constricted stomachs of the nomads' cattle, killing many of them', and the rain simply made the drought-weakened old people and children wet and cold at night.

In general, increases and decreases of vegetation may not signify what they seem to the satellite scanner. In Mali, for instance, the pastures of the Sahel are of far better quality for grazing cattle than the savannah immediately to the south. But on a satellite image, they show up as much *less* vegetated. And in the southwest United States, pastures invaded by thorny mesquite are unpalatable to cattle, whereas on a satellite image they appear to be comparatively *well* vegetated. Thus the series of Sahelian satellite images made in the 1980s could be seductively misleading. What did they mean 'in terms of the long-term productivity of the ecosystems of the Sahel?' asked William Adams, the Cambridge University geographer.

> To what extent [were they] evidence of land degradation? What implications did [they] have for agriculture or pastoralism? More importantly, what did [they] imply for the complex social and economic systems (for example reciprocal trade between pastoralists and farmers) on the ground?

So is the Sahara actually advancing? Will it remorselessly encroach on the frail domain of human beings and ultimately bury all trace of their fields and dwellings, as the popular picture of it insists? Most scientists are wary of giving definite answers, despite the apparently incontrovertible evidence of many satellite images – not to mention the ocean of sand that has swamped Mauritania. ('We used to say that in Mauritania there were three things to prevent you feeling sad: the water, the grasses and the beautiful views. Today, if we want to lift up our hearts, we have to search hard for these things', said a man in Nouakchott, quoted in *At the Desert's Edge*.) Scientists are worried about the lack of 'ground truth' for satellite images, so time-consuming to acquire. They are concerned that they do not have precisely comparable series of images taken over many years. Most of all, they are cautious about muddling short-term fluctuations in vegetation with long-term changes.

Nevertheless, US researchers concluded from a study of satellite images that in the 1980s the Sahara did grow, but unsteadily. In 1980, the desert covered 3,333,462 square miles, and in 1990 3,579,041 square miles, with a boundary 80 miles south of its 1980 position. Between 1980 and 1984 it expanded; after that, in 1985 and 1986 it shrank; then it expanded in 1987, shrank in 1988, and expanded in 1989 and 1990. Over the decade, its greatest annual boundary shift was from south to north, by 68 miles between 1984 and 1985.

These figures appeared in *Science* in mid-1991. A few months later they were followed by a paper based on a series of Swedish studies carried out in the Sudan between 1962 and 1984. Ulf Hellden, a professor at Lund University (not far from Malmö), concluded that there had been *no* creation of long-lasting desert-like conditions in the Sudan. Nor had there been any trend towards the growth of desert patches around 103 examined villages and water-holes: favourite candidates as causes of desertification. He wrote:

No major shift in the northern cultivation limit was identified, no major sand dune transformations or Sahara desert encroachment trend was identified. No major changes in vegetation cover and crop productivity were identified which could not be explained by varying rainfall characteristics.

Plainly the experts do not agree. In the desertification debate, leaving aside climate change, rainfall and wind for the moment, just about every conceivable element in society has been implicated at one time or another. Colonial officers, and in many cases the African officials that inherited their jobs, tended to blame nomads more than cultivators. They saw them as deeply irrational: 'cowdolaters' committed to building up their herds regardless of the consequences, and stubble burners hidebound by antiquated custom (remember the cirrus clouds floating above the Sahel). Nowadays, with greater pressure for land, farmers have joined the criticism too. A farmer in Senegal told SOS Sahel: 'During the colonial period there were rules of compensation about how much the pastoralists should pay to cover a farmer's losses. Now there is no formal system: all we do is row and fight with each other.' But many scientists who have studied the nomads and their herds in detail are impressed by their understanding of their environment, inarticulate though it may be. They see the nomads as 'natural ecologists' who, in the words of Goudie (Oxford University's professor of geography), 'might have been destabilized by colonial rule, but who, given a chance, would be able to balance the vagaries of the climate and the requirements of their stock to achieve a long-term equilibrium of humans, beasts, and pasture.'

There is much in this view. In many ways, not nomads but cultivators, and behind them government policies, are responsible for land degradation in the Sahel (and in some other parts of the world). With a falling death rate and an extremely high and barely falling birth rate, village cultivators need to farm more and more land, and so they encroach on land traditionally used for pasture. Furthermore, they have lost some of the best land to large farms growing cash crops, established around the time of Independence. These cash crops earn precious foreign exchange. Their harvest was therefore maintained and even increased during the droughts of the 1970s and 1980s, while the food crop declined and became a harvest of dust. As Timberlake wrote caustically in 1985:

> African governments feel the need to grow more cash crops in much the same way African peasants feel the need to have more children. If children are dying, more – not less – children are needed. And if crop prices are falling, more – not less – cash crops are needed.

The cotton grown south of the Aral Sea is one such cash crop. So are peanuts. During the 1980s there was a television jingle in New York: 'Our peanuts are fresh from the jungle.' But the joke is, peanuts do not come from the jungle; trees must be cut down first so that you can plant. Then you get the peanuts. You also get land degradation and – if nothing is done to halt the degradation – you may create a desert.

Cash crops, fertilizers, irrigation schemes, boreholes, dams – in a word, development – have proved a decidedly mixed blessing, especially in Africa. Most western scientists who have studied the results carefully, feel humbled. 'After World War II, "development" usually meant transferring western technology without adaptation to developing countries, and many aid agencies essentially tried to take Texas to the Sahara,' writes Alan Grainger, a British specialist in desertification.

> There must be a greater scepticism about the capacity of Northern science to second-guess nature in Africa, and caution must replace gung-ho confidence in the ability of technology and engineering to remove constraints on rural production and on the livelihoods of rural people,

wrote William Adams in 1992.

The truth, underlying the human mismanagement, is that Africa's climate is ill understood. It is possible that African droughts and El Niño events (see Chapter 2) may be connected. Drought

Success in the Sahel.
Development in Africa, especially in the Sahel, is chiefly a dispiriting record of failure. In Mali (*right*), fertile land has been degraded by the encroaching desert. (*Above*) By contrast, at El Kumir near Shendi in Sudan, north of Khartoum, a village nursery and adjacent community woodlot have been established in defiance of the desert. Irrigation is from a well. In every case in Africa, success in a project has depended on marrying science with local knowledge and needs; imposing a solution from outside, however rational an expert may find it, seldom works.

struck the Sahel in 1982–83 during a strong El Niño – and also Australia, India, northeast Brazil and the United States. It happened again in the Sahel in 1987, when there was another El Niño, and in India there was a very weak monsoon. But in 1990, when there was again drought in the Sahel (especially in the areas close to the Indian Ocean), there was no El Niño; in parts of India, record rains brought flooding to the Thar Desert that borders Pakistan.

Sea surface temperatures in the Atlantic seem to be important too. The drought that affected northwest Europe in 1975–76 coincided with abnormally low sea surface temperatures over the

Atlantic Ocean north of latitude 40 degrees. There is a statistically significant link between low rainfall in the Sahel, warm sea surface temperatures south of the equator, and cold temperatures to the north. Recent research clearly suggests that there has been an association during the last 14,000 years between Sahelian droughts and injections of fresh water into the western Atlantic. This research, and new evidence accumulated from the analysis of sediments and cores from the ocean bed off Africa, confirm the fundamental picture that there has been extensive climatic variation in Africa. Many dry periods during the last 10,000–20,000 years have been both longer and more intense than any experienced within recent centuries. In other words, according to Adams, drought has been familiar to African farmers and herders since well before the dawn of history. 'The "droughts" of the 20th century, serious though they are today, would be minimal blips on the graph of longer-term climatic change.'

The danger in such statements is that they easily become an excuse for political inaction. If Nature is against the African peasant, what can governments and aid agencies – and indeed villagers – do? What use are the intergovernmental schemes proposed by UNCOD in 1977, and now languishing for lack of political will? 'Certainly,' wrote Goudie in 1985, 'grandiose schemes to plant a cordon sanitaire of trees round the Sahara are most likely to produce an expensive and ineffective Maginot Line.'

There are already so many examples of failed schemes in Africa. For instance, in Niger's Majia Valley, the US voluntary agency CARE tried to stabilize a high sand dune about to swallow a stream bed used to grow crops. The dune was anchored with a chessboard pattern of millet stalks, which had to be bought at steep prices from the very farmers whose land the dune was threatening. The spaces between the stalks were then planted with grass and shrubs, which required protection from sheep and goats. Again, money was needed to pay guards; there were no volunteers. 'How could the villagers be so apparently stupid, selfish and short-sighted?' asked Timberlake, who visited the project in 1982. The answer was that the villagers' existence was already so marginal, they preferred to move elsewhere rather than labour to stop the dune. It was a rational decision, based on long experience.

Yet in the very same valley, CARE had also had success. Working through the medium of a trusted local forester, the organization had overcome suspicion and apathy and persuaded villagers to plant tree windbreaks (consisting partly of the Indian *neem* tree, famously tough and also known for its medicinal properties) across a flat, millet-growing plain. The trees dramatically reduced erosion by the harmattan. No longer did it blow unchecked, desiccating the fields and carrying off the lighter, organic matter in the soil to leave behind the heavier, infertile sand. Crop yields increased by 15 per cent – and that was after allowing for the loss of land in the tree belts themselves. The crops could be marketed relatively easily because the village was near a main road, unlike the village threatened by the dune. And the trees in due course produced vital firewood, which the villagers were given charge of distributing amongst themselves. That was the point when they were really won over by the scheme (unlike the pastoralists, whose animals were banned from the planted areas for three years). The challenge for them then was to maintain the scheme long-term. But the prognosis was hopeful – provided there were not too many years of drought.

So here is the 'ground truth' of desertification: it is susceptible to science and reason, but it is intimately linked with economics, politics and social attitudes. Desertification is a notably complex phenomenon, as the following story told by El-Baz neatly demonstrates. Photographs taken from space in 1975 showed a puzzling area near the northern shores of Lake Chad, which was unusually bright. Such brightness was known to be a signal of land degradation: presumably vegetation had been lost and replaced by drifting sand. Indeed it had. When a research team went to the spot to investigate, they found that it had been eroded by the tracks of countless vehicles. The spot was a favourite show place for representatives of international aid agencies.

CHAPTER

—8—

AVALANCHES, GLACIERS AND ICE AGES

. . . eager to set foot on the new continent so full of promise for me, I sprang on shore and started at a brisk pace for the heights above the landing. On the first undisturbed ground, after leaving the town, I was met by the familiar signs, the polished surfaces, the furrows and scratches, the line engraving *of the glacier, so well known in the Old World; and I became convinced . . . that here also this great agent had been at work.*

Louis Agassiz, 1846 (on reaching America at Halifax, Nova Scotia)

O N 19 September 1991, at a glacier high in the Alps on the border between Austria and Italy, a German tourist on a walking trip stumbled across the head and shoulders of a frozen male corpse. Seeing a hole in the back of the skull, and suspecting foul play, he hurried back to report the find to the nearest hikers' shelter. Police on both sides of the border were telephoned: the Italian *carabinieri*, used to climbing accidents, showed no interest; their Austrian counterparts, who had already extracted eight corpses from glaciers that summer, promised to investigate by the following afternoon. In the meantime, the owner of the shelter, Markus Pirpamer, went to take a look. He was flabbergasted: 'I had seen bodies come out of the glacier,' he said later, 'but this was nothing like them. Bodies trapped in the glacier are white and waxy and usually chewed up by the ice. This one was brown and dried out. I could tell that it was really old.'

Approximately 5200 years old, according to radiocarbon dating. Some scientists have dubbed its owner *Homo tyrolensis*; the Austrians, affectionately, call him Ötzi, after the Öztaler Alps where he died; to the world, perhaps inevitably, he is the Iceman. But whatever his name may be, he is by far the most ancient human being ever discovered virtually intact. (Egyptian mummies, though in some cases older than the Iceman, had their brains and vital organs removed.)

From implements found near his body, the Iceman appears to have been a shepherd. No one can know for sure, but perhaps he ventured into the high Alps tempted by the pasturage; climatologists know that Alpine conditions 5000 years ago were somewhat warmer. He got caught in a storm and took refuge in a basin 10 to 15 feet (3–5 m) deep, ridged on both sides. There, exhausted, he fell asleep and froze to death. Icy winds – or perhaps the föhn, the warm, dry wind discussed in Chapter 2 – dehydrated the body, naturally mummifying it. Heavy snow, maybe an avalanche, soon buried it, and gradually became compacted into ice. The body became locked in the Similaun Glacier, prevented from decay by the frigid temperature, minus 6 degrees C (21° F), and protected from dismemberment by the walls of the basin.

It lay undisturbed for 53 centuries – and would probably have lain many more were it not for the föhn. The 1990/91 föhn delivered tons of sand from the Sahara to the Alpine ridges, thereby increasing the rate of melting. Nothing unusual in that, but it coincided with a winter that produced very little snow; throughout the Alps that summer, the glaciers retreated. Even so, the Iceman almost stayed concealed. 'By the end of September,' noted a climatologist at the University of Innsbruck, where the body was taken, 'he would have been buried under a half-metre of snow. Most probably, he would have remained in his glacial grave for at least another hundred years.'

Even in the last decade of the 20th century, the chance of survival and rescue for anyone caught in an avalanche is not high. A fifth of avalanche victims are dead when the avalanche halts, the rest need to be extracted within an hour at most if they are to live. If found within half an hour, a victim has a 50 per cent chance of survival. But in general, rescue teams do not arrive in time; they find only 5 per cent of victims alive.

Tragically, a victim is often buried just a few feet below the surface. Escape is impossible because the snow of an avalanche becomes densified by its fall. It is not uncommon for skiers caught only ankle-deep to have to abandon their boots in the snow's icy grip. Surprisingly, technology too is often made helpless. Rescue teams have tried advanced detectors of every kind – sonar, radar, magnetometers (which can pick up skis), infrared detectors of body warmth, detectors of change in dielectric constant (the human body is an electrical insulator compared to snow), even lasers – but dogs remain the most effective. Properly trained, a dog can search an area of over 1000 square feet (100 square metres) in as little as 20–30

minutes, compared with the four hours needed by a team of 20 people.

Even better, however, is companion rescue. Avoiding the potentially lethal delay in waiting for a rescue team, members of a group who have not been buried immediately begin searching. Best of all is when a victim has thought to equip him/herself with a small transceiver, set to transmit. The rescuers then set their transceivers to receive and pursue the signal emitted from beneath the snow.

Avalanches in the Alps were first recorded nearly 2000 years ago, by Strabo writing in his *Geography*. Before that, in 218 B C, as many as half of Hannibal's 38,000-strong army are thought to have perished crossing the Alps, many of them no doubt killed in avalanches. Pilgrims travelling to and from Rome have left centuries of accounts of the ferocious Alpine passes. In 15th-century France, avalanches in the Dauphiné area destroyed whole villages. (Not coincidentally, the word avalanche derives from the French *aval*, meaning valleywards.) In Switzerland, many villages have been obliterated several times over. In fact, Switzerland has the largest number of avalanche fatalities in the world. Of the 1210 deaths throughout the Alps between 1975 and 1986 (an average of about 100 a year), 324 (over a quarter) were Swiss. And the figures continue to increase substantially, as more people take part in mountain sports such as skiing.

A similar rise is taking place in the Rocky Mountains in the United States, but the overall figures are lower because the Rockies are not as populous as the Alps. An estimated 100,000 avalanches occur every year in the mountainous west of the US. In the past they affected mainly travellers, and miners living in badly sited mining settlements; now all those who venture into the mountains

Avalanche rescue. The chance of surviving an avalanche is not high. If found within half an hour, it is about 50 per cent, but most rescuers fail to arrive in time; they find only 5 per cent of victims alive. Every conceivable technological aid has been tried, but dogs remain the most successful searchers.

'The Iceman', the oldest virtually intact human being ever discovered. According to radiocarbon dating, he is about 5200 years old. Found in 1991 in the Alps on the border of Italy and Austria, he may have died in an avalanche.

Avalanches in the Alps

*A*VALANCHES *have been recorded in the Alps for nearly 2000 years. Today there are about 100 deaths a year. Switzerland, pictured here, has the highest rate of fatalities; in the past, many Swiss villages have been obliterated by avalanches several times over. The threat is palpable in the Valais, where the Weisshorn (14,780 feet, 4505 m) rears above the village of Randa (right). On occasions, parts of the hanging glacier below the summit have dropped off and crashed onto the glacier in the centre of the photograph. Ice avalanches such as these are especially dangerous in winter when they can set enormous masses of snow and ice in motion. In 1639, 36 people died when this occurred.*

during winter – often ignorantly – are at risk. The worst American avalanche disaster was in 1910, when two snowbound trains near a pass in the Cascades in Washington state were swept into a canyon with the loss of 96 lives.

But in comparison with what happened in Peru in 1962, and again in 1970, this US toll pales into insignificance. Both Peruvian avalanches descended from the glacier-clad Nevado Huascarán, the 22,205-foot (6768-m) peak in the Cordillera Blanca that is the most unstable mountain in Peru. The cause of the first one is unknown, but it prised a gigantic mass of ice – 200 yards long and nearly half a mile wide – off the precipitous north summit. By the time it came to rest, some 13,000 feet (4000 m) beneath its source, and 10 miles from the summit, 4000 people lay dead. The second avalanche was even bigger. Triggered by an earthquake of magnitude 7.8 (the same lethal quake that made the Peruvians so jittery during the failed US earthquake prediction in 1981), it consisted of rock as well as ice. Approximately 65 million cubic yards (50 million cubic metres) of ice, rock, glacial debris and water reached the valley bottom in about three minutes. It spread much further than before, burying the town of Yungay. About 18,000 people perished.

Thankfully, ice avalanches are rare as compared with snow avalanches. But not so rare. If the definition of ice avalanche is broadened to include ice/rock avalanches, the phenomenon becomes an uncomfortably frequent one. New Zealand, like Peru, is especially prone. The mountains of South Island, like the Andes, are young and destabilized by plate tectonics. Since 1979, six large rock avalanches have fallen onto glaciers in the Tasman Valley. In 1991 the top 30–35 feet (10 m) of New Zealand's highest mountain, Mount Cook, suddenly collapsed, tobogganed down 50-degree ice slopes and shot across 3 or 4 miles of a glacier plateau. (Avalanches not involving ice or snow at all – i.e. landslides – are a worldwide menace: over 1000 urban centres in Italy are at risk from landslides, and in the northern Los Angeles area, the San Gabriel Mountains monotonously devastate homes with debris flows.)

Very little can be done to forecast events of such size, and almost nothing to mitigate the destruction they cause, other than to enforce prohibitions on development in areas known to be at risk. Only against the smaller avalanches do control measures stand a chance of success. In Japan, check dams, drainage systems and other controls in combination with development restrictions meant that in 1976 – the country's worst year for sliding rock in some two decades – only 2000 homes were lost and less than 125 people died. (In 1938 nearly 130,000 homes were destroyed and more than 500 people died.) In Los Angeles, the city authorities catch the rock in football-stadium-sized debris basins, that have often to be cleared (sometimes urgently). At least 120 basins line the foot of the San Gabriel Mountains. The system works – most of the time – but at great cost in both dollars, time and energy (as well as lawsuits). One of the engineers involved told a symposium held in 1980: 'Through[out] the district, the residents are battling, but sediment is still winning . . . frankly, it is like trying to hold back the storm tides of the ocean.'

Against snow – as opposed to rock or ice – much more can and has been done, in the Alps at least. Buildings in avalanche-active areas have long been defended by wedge-shaped deflectors. In this century, particularly since 1951 (a disastrous year for avalanches in Switzerland), retarding and deflecting structures have been installed on all three stages of an avalanche's likely path: the so-called starting zone, the track, and the runout zone. Trees to winnow the snow are especially efficacious. Unfortunately, most Alpine forests were cleared as long as 600 years ago, and new forest is both hard to establish on the bitterly cold slopes and time-consuming to nurture before it takes effect. The forest that does remain is therefore so precious it is known as *bannwald* – forbidden forest – and not even children may enter it.

The alternative is to go on the offensive against potential avalanches, using explosives and military weapons. In Swiss legend the chime of a bell, the crack of a whip or the beating of a bird's wing can trigger an avalanche. Carefully aimed explosives enable snow to be cleared in a series of small episodes rather than one major avalanche. Rogers Pass in the Selkirk Mountains of British Columbia has one of the most comprehensive avalanche-control programmes in the world, established some years ago by two Austrian-born brothers working with a detachment of the Royal Canadian Horse Artillery. It protects both the Canadian Pacific rail route and the Trans-Canada highway as it runs a gauntlet of 160 avalanche paths. Over 3 feet (1 m) of snow fall each year. Circular gun positions along the road are used to station howitzers; in more remote areas the recoil-less rifle is employed because it is lighter and more manoeuvrable.

The forecasting of avalanches is also practised. The Swiss Federal Institute for Snow and Avalanche Research, founded in 1936, has for many years offered a prediction service. About 70 observation stations are dotted over the Alps at altitudes of 1000 to 1800 metres (3280–5900 feet), with a few as high as 2500 metres (8200 feet). Trained local people of various occupations work part-time at these stations, transmitting reports in the early morning by telephone, telegraph and telex to the Institute. Avalanche warnings are broadcast two or three times a week by radio and television and published in newspapers.

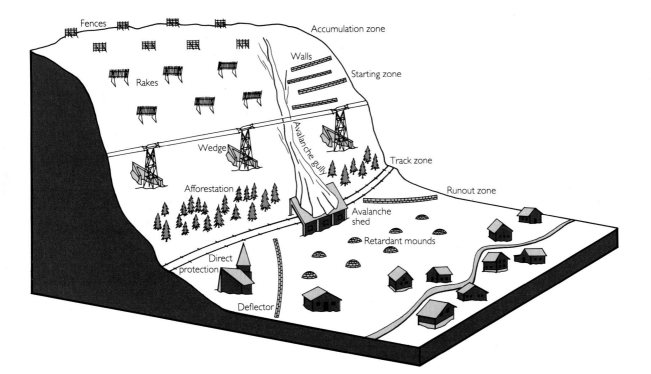

Fences

Accumulation zone

Walls

Rakes

Starting zone

Wedge

Track zone

Avalanche gully

Runout zone

Afforestation

Avalanche
shed

Direct
protection

Retardant mounds

Deflector

Action against avalanches.
Various steps (*above*) can be taken
to reduce the probability and impact
of avalanches on human beings
(*opposite above*) in each of three
parts of an avalanche-active area:
the starting zone, the track zone
and the runout zone. Of course
only one or two of the methods
shown here are likely to be in place
in any given area.

Barriers and trees have been
introduced to this slope (*lower
right*) in the Swiss Alps to protect
the village of Andermatt below it.
And (*lower left*) a church has an
unusual wedge shape which helps to
divert any avalanches.

The method of prediction is basically an empirical one that relies
on field experience and past statistics of avalanches, however
incomplete. Not enough is known about snow structure and snow
transport to anticipate the behaviour of specific snow fields. Only
rather general statements are possible. Scientists know that slope
angle is important. An angle between 30 and 45 degrees produces
the most avalanches; less than 20 degrees is too slight, more than 60
degrees rarely allows enough snow to accumulate. They also have
an idea of avalanche size and power. Fully developed avalanches
may attain a mass of a million tons, and travel at speeds of 200 mph,
twice that of a free-falling sky diver. Their impact pressure varies
enormously: 3 tons per square metre (0.3 tons per square foot)
destroys a wood-frame house; 10 tons per square metre uproots a
mature tree; ten times that moves reinforced concrete structures. In
Japan, monster avalanches have registered impact pressures of 145
tons per square metre (13.5 tons per square foot).

The density of snow in an avalanche is clearly a major factor in its
destructiveness. The denser it is, generally the higher the impact
pressure. In addition, density determines which of two major types
of process generates an avalanche. A 'loose-snow' avalanche (also
called 'pure') arises from low-density snow, as its name implies.
The snow behaves rather like dry sand. A small amount of it, 1
cubic yard or less, slips and starts to move. The sliding spreads –
through a process recently termed 'self-organized criticality' by US

scientists studying sand piles in laboratories – and produces an inverted V-shaped scar. A 'slab' avalanche, on the other hand, occurs when a layer of high-density snow breaks away from a weaker underlying layer, leaving a sharp fracture line. The weak layer may have formed in diverse ways: sometimes it is known as 'depth hoar', hollow, cuplike crystals that result from refreezing of water vapour within the snowpack and which act like ball bearings. The slab – which may be more than 100,000 square feet in area and more than 30 feet (up to 10 m) thick – may bring down as much as 100 times more snow as it gathers speed. Slab avalanches are the most dangerous kind of avalanche (see pages 234–35).

The mechanical properties of snow depend on the presence or absence of water to lubricate its sliding, on its crystal structure, and on its density.* Depending on the precise state of a mass of snow (and of course on the topography over which it travels), an avalanche is believed to move either by saltation, in which the snow particles 'hop' down the slope, or alternatively it may float along by turbulent flow, in which case the particles remain suspended in the air throughout their fall. As yet, neither process is properly documented or defined. As an experimental physicist at the Swiss Federal Institute admitted a decade ago:

> Snow is so complicated, we really know little of its physical properties. As these mysteries unfold, science will come to understand the effects of time and temperature on the snowpack, and how they lead to avalanching.

Glaciers too are made of snow. Although they flow under gravity like rivers, they are not – whatever their sinuous courses and often turbulent surfaces may deceptively suggest – rivers that have frozen. The snow in a glacier has been altered to form ice in four ways: pressure (squeezing from above), stress (shearing from the side), flow, and recrystallization. In many respects glaciers behave like rock. No wonder, given the complexity of rock, that the Inuit (Eskimos) have dozens of words for different kinds of ice.

One might instinctively expect heavy snowfall to be the chief requirement for the growth of a glacier. But a moment's reflection suggests otherwise: there are many sloped areas of the world that receive huge amounts of snow but have no glaciers. Snowfall alone is not enough; for a glacier to form, the snow must not melt, it must be conserved. This is what happens in the extremely cold Arctic

---

* Snow density varies from 20 to 600 kilograms per cubic metre, the densest snow being two-thirds the density of ice and more than half the density of water, 1000 kilograms per cubic metre.

and Antarctic ice sheets: although they receive minimal precipitation – in fact large areas of them qualify as desert – what snow and moisture does fall is hoarded, it does not melt. In high mountains, too, low temperatures (falling with increase in altitude) are important; so is shade and lack of wind. The most likely place for a mountain glacier to grow is a hollow on the lee side of a mountain, sheltered from both wind and sun.

The snow is converted to ice in a number of stages, assisted by meltwater in many glaciers. It may be transformed in about ten years, or it may take hundreds of years where no liquid water is present on the suface, as in most of Antarctica. First, the fragile snow crystals break as they are compressed by the weight of snow settling on top of them, or as they are wetted by meltwater.

Rivers of ice but not frozen rivers. Glaciers, like rivers, move under gravity, but they are formed by the gradual compression of snow into ice, not by the freezing of water into ice. The Barnard Glacier in Alaska's St Elias Mountains consists of at least a dozen principal ice streams, which may be distinguished by dark stripes of rock particles known as medial moraines. Three vigorous tributary streams are shown.

Gradually, the snowflakes change into grains, becoming rounded and granular like coarse sugar; the air pockets between them remain connected. This snow is known as firn (German for 'last year's snow'); it is generally created after one complete winter–summer cycle. The density of firn approaches half that of water, some ten times the density of fluffy snow. (Here is a curious fact about water: it is most unusual in being denser than its solid form.)

After this, the firn begins to recrystallize: the small grains coalesce to form large interlocking crystals of ice, the air becomes trapped as bubbles inside the growing crystals. The flow of the glacier, deforming the ice, aids crystal growth. The final density, that of pure ice with virtually all the air squeezed out (though not quite all – as we shall see), is around 90 per cent of that of water.

The ice may then be coloured 'a gorgeous, brilliant, deep shade of clearest blue' (in the words of Robert P. Sharp, a glaciologist from the California Institute of Technology), instead of the white it started as. Ice is intrinsically blue: red wavelengths in light are absorbed by the ice molecules, leaving blue light transmitted to the eyes. The white colour results from the strong reflection of light by air-bubble/ice interfaces, and also reflection from the rough surface of bubbly ice. (Think of white froth on a fizzy drink.) But with the bubbles gone, and the ice surface smooth, the blue colour wins through.

How much of the Earth is currently loaded with ice? And where are the glaciers located?

Land ice covers 10.8 per cent of the continents; sea ice covers 7.3 per cent of the ocean. During the last ice age, which ended some 10,000 years ago, the proportion of land ice was trebled, rising to 32 per cent of total land area – about the same area as deserts cover today. The formation and melting of the ice-age glaciers caused worldwide changes in sea level, estimated at around 350 feet (107 m), maybe more. If today's glaciers were to melt in their entirety, the sea level would rise by about 230 feet (70 m).

The bulk of this ice lies on Antarctica. Its area is a third bigger than Europe or Canada, twice as big as Australia, 86 per cent of the world's ice cover. Some of the ice reaches a depth of 15,669 feet (4776 m) and rests on bedrock as much as a mile below sea level; entire mountain ranges are inundated by it. The Greenland (Arctic) ice sheet is only an eighth the area of its southern counterpart. Nevertheless, it is up to 10,171 feet (3100 m) deep, and covers most of Greenland; were it to melt, Greenland would eventually rebound some 2000 feet.

The rest of the Arctic areas apart (including Iceland and northern Scandinavia), glaciers are scattered across all the continents, except

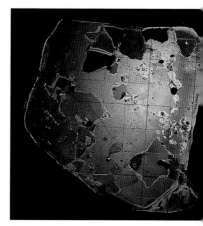

Snow becomes ice. Air bubbles are trapped inside ice as snow is compressed to form ice in a glacier. The thin slice of ice shown here is from a Norwegian glacier. When viewed between a pair of polaroid plates, individual ice crystals are visible, as are air bubbles.

Two types of avalanche. Although real avalanches occur in a multitude of ways, there are two basic types of avalanche. The loose-snow type (also called 'pure' – *opposite*) arises from low-density snow; the slab avalanche, by contrast (*above*), breaks away from high-density snow.

Louis Agassiz, pioneer glaciologist. During the 1830s, working at Neuchâtel in Switzerland, Agassiz studied glaciers and became convinced of the existence of an ice age that had destroyed all life on Earth. Although his idea was not fully accepted, his work on glaciers was the beginning of a new science. The engraving is taken from his first study of glaciers, published in 1840.

Australia (though New Zealand has them). In Europe, there are major glaciers in the Alps and the Caucasus; in Asia, in the Himalayas and associated ranges – the Karakoram in Kashmir, the Kunlun Shan (China), the Hindu Kush (Afghanistan) and the Pamirs in Tadzhikistan – though there is no glacier, curiously, in Siberia (it is too dry); and in the Americas glaciers exist in the Andes, in Alaska and in parts of Canada. There are even small ones near the equator, in the mountains of New Guinea and on Mount Kilimanjaro in Africa. Together, the glaciers of the northern hemisphere contain about 4 per cent of the world's ice. This sounds insignificant, but it amounts to about 10 million gallons (45 million litres) of fresh water for *each* citizen on the planet; it could cause damaging changes in sea level if the glaciers expand or contract substantially, as they have been wont to do.

It was in the Alps that this phenomenon of fluctuation was first observed; there are records as far back as the 16th century, showing how much land farmers had gained from the glaciers or lost to their advances. The earliest mention of glaciers in any form (though not their movement) dates from as recently as 11th-century Icelandic literature. Glaciers do not apparently feature in any of the literatures of the ancient world. If the Romans were aware of them – as we know they were aware of Alpine avalanches – they evidently regarded them as too remote from their concerns to merit investigation.

That was how they remained, more or less, until the beginning of the 19th century. Even scientists regarded glaciers as esoteric and inconsequential – like volcanoes, but more so. The Flood held sway as the explanation of the landscape. True, there were certain puzzles it did not resolve, but these could be ignored in favour of the main evidence. It was difficult to explain 'drift', for instance, the stony debris found in chaotic jumbles in many parts of Europe; if it had drifted in a great flood, should water not have sorted it by size and density, leaving layers? (Curiously, the term persists in glaciology today.) And what about 'erratics', the boulders that dotted the countryside of eastern England whose composition showed them to be of Scandinavian origin? Had the Flood carried them across the North Sea? The geologist Charles Lyell, Darwin's friend, proposed an ingenious explanation in the final volume of his *Principles of Geology* (1833). Erratics, he wrote, had been ferried inside icebergs that had broken off glaciers near the North Pole and been carried south by the waters of the Flood.

In other words, ice could be an important geological force – but only at the Pole, not in Europe itself. No scientist at the time could suggest that ice and glaciers had once covered large parts of Europe, and expect to be taken seriously. The writer Goethe is thought to

have been the first to speak of an ice age (*Eiszeit*) – extent unknown. Well before him, though, it appears that villagers in Alpine valleys had come to accept the idea from the boulders and scratched rocks scattered all around them. But it was not until the mid-1830s that it started to receive sustained scientific attention – from Swiss scientists, as was only appropriate. Its greatest advocate, subsequently known as 'the father of ice ages', was the young, up-and-coming professor of natural history at the College of Neuchâtel, Louis Agassiz.

Initially sceptical of the idea of ice ages (whatever their extent) – which had first been proposed in a lecture by amateur naturalist Jean de Charpentier, who had systematized a theory put forward by Alpine engineer Ignatz Venetz, who had himself first heard it from mountaineer and chamois hunter Jean Pierre Peraudin – Agassiz soon convinced himself of its truth by studies of nearby glaciers. In fact he became so passionate about it that his ice age came to encompass the entire globe, annihilating all previous life. Instead of a great flood, there had been ice upon the Earth, said Agassiz. He described his vision thus:

> The development of these huge ice sheets must have led to the destruction of all organic life at the Earth's surface. The ground of Europe, previously covered with tropical vegetation and inhabited by herds of giant elephants, enormous hippopotamuses, and gigantic Carnivora became suddenly buried under a vast expanse of ice covering plains, lakes, seas and plateaus alike.

The Karagom Glacier, in the central Caucasus Mountains, 1890. The photograph was one of many taken by Vittorio Sella during his magnificent study of European glaciers in the late 19th century.

The silence of death followed . . . springs dried up, streams ceased to flow, and sunrays rising over that frozen shore . . . were met only by the whistling of northern winds and the rumbling of the crevasses as they opened across the surface of that huge ocean of ice.

There were not many takers for this new version of the Creation; nor could Agassiz convince other scientists that the dramatic evidence of glaciation in Europe, Canada and the United States could be generalized to include the whole planet. But by the time of his death in 1873, aged 66, the concept of an ice age – extent still to be determined – and the crucial role of glaciers in geology, had become the orthodoxy. A special monument was brought all the way from Switzerland to Boston, Massachusetts, where Agassiz had settled as a Harvard professor, to mark his grave: a 2500-ton erratic boulder, scarred and polished by ice. It came from the area of Agassiz's favourite glacier.

In Agassiz's day, indeed until the building of large cities and the clearing of land for farming towards the end of the 19th century, geologists could trace a more-or-less continuous series of ridges across the length of the USA from eastern Long Island to Washington state. These were terminal moraines, heaps of debris deposited by glaciers as they began to retreat; these moraines delineated the southern limits of glaciers in the ice age.

In fact, with newly opened eyes, one could see evidence of glaciation all around. On the small scale there were scratched ('striated'), polished or shattered surfaces and boulders. Some of these rocks demonstrated all three processes in one: *roches mouton-nées*, for example, were rocks smoothed and grooved on one side

The impact of glaciers. Ice moving over long periods is an extremely powerful force. In the past it has sculpted: U-shaped valleys (*far left*); *roches moutonnées* (*above*), these from California's Yosemite National Park; drumlins (*below right*), here from the Hirzel area south of Zurich in Switzerland; and today ice is busy sculpting cirques out of the Karakoram Mountains of northern Pakistan (*below left*).

that sloped gently, steep and rough on the other, where they had been plucked by the departing ice. (The name derived from a wavy French wig popular in the 18th century, or perhaps from the back end of a sheep!) On the grand scale, in the United States, Cape Cod was a terminal moraine; Bunker Hill a 'drumlin', its streamlined shape the result of both deposition and erosion as a glacier ground over it; while Yosemite Valley had plainly been scoured out by a glacier that had left behind its tell-tale U-shape and the hanging valley of the Yosemite Falls. In Europe, there were the fjords of Norway and the Scottish lochs; the bowl-shaped cwms of Snowdonia in Wales, where circular glaciers – generally known as cirques – had scoured away the rock; and in the Alps the razor-sharp ridges of the Matterhorn, the product of three or more cirque glaciers eroding backwards in concert (and the source of the glaciological term, horn).

By the late 19th century, then, much geomorphology could be attributed to glacier action and suitably labelled. Subsequently explaining the mechanism of its creation has proved more tricky. Consider cirques, among the most common and recognizable glaciated landforms:

> Inspection of rock exposures on cirque floors provides adequate evidence that they were once occupied by moving ice and owe their origin primarily to glacial erosion. Why erosion has been so effective at the head of a glacier, where the ice is thin and slow-moving, and how it acts to create a theaterlike basin with precipitous rock walls, are questions that furrow glaciologists' brows.

Thus Robert Sharp in his study of glaciers, *Living Ice*.

In order to erode rock, a glacier must have two basic characteristics. The underside of its ice, that is the base in contact with bedrock, must carry abrasive particles of rock cemented in the ice like sand in sandpaper; clean ice will not do, though it may perhaps shatter or pluck rock. And it must move. Generally speaking, the colder a glacier is, the thicker its load of basal debris and the slower it moves. While heavy debris may encourage erosion, slow speed discourages it.

Temperature is a useful distinguishing feature of glaciers. Scientists divide glaciers into two somewhat theoretical categories based on temperature: warm/temperate glaciers, and cold/polar glaciers. The distinction is not rigid, and it is possible for a large glacier to be warm *and* cold in different areas. Even in the heart of Antarctica, where all glaciers are cold/polar, with air temperatures as low as minus 89 degrees C (−128°F), water pockets have been located beneath many thousands of feet of ice; as much as a third of the ice sheet is wet-based. There are two reasons for this surprising observation. First, pressure on ice lowers its melting point, so that it stays liquid at lower temperatures: a fact that enables ice skaters to skate and an ordinary wire to 'saw' through ice. Secondly, the Earth's heat melts the ice. On the other hand, as one might intuitively expect, the temperature of many glaciers falls with depth: throughout, from top to bottom, the temperature is the melting point of ice under pressure (which is minus 1 degree C, plus 30 degrees F at a depth of 5000 feet, for instance). This is the case in all warm/temperate glaciers.

There is a tremendous contrast in the rate at which glaciers move. The Meserve Glacier of Antarctica moves scarcely a quarter of an inch (0.6 cm) per day, and takes three months to travel a yard, while the Jakobshavn Glacier of northwest Greenland – a prodigious calver of icebergs into Baffin Bay – gallops along at over 42 feet per day, 15,400 feet (4700 m or nearly 3 miles) per year. In New Zealand the contrast in speed, though not as great, is especially striking because the glaciers are separated by just a few miles across the mountain divide. The Franz Josef Glacier on the maritime west flank of the Mount Cook range is fed by extremely high levels of precipitation. It descends into rain forest (where snow rarely falls) at speeds averaging 2300 feet (700 m) per year, which in periods of heavy rain may reach 8200 feet (2500 m) per year. But the Tasman Glacier – New Zealand's biggest – receives so little precipitation that it has a maximum speed of just 820 feet per year. Its snout – the term for its front portion – does not leap backwards and forwards like that of the Franz Josef Glacier; instead it thins or thickens along its entire ablation area. (Ablation is the opposite of accumulation. In the accumulation area of a glacier, snow and rain increase the ice; in the ablation area, melting, evaporation and the calving of icebergs decrease it. In between lies the equilibrium line where gain balances loss, and it is here that the ice moves fastest.)

Scientists have devoted much study to the path travelled by ice from the head of a glacier to its snout. The ice in the snout is oldest: 10,000 years old if one believes the tour guide at the Columbia Glacier in Alaska who offers Ice-Age-cooled martinis. (In the Columbia's case, given its speed, the ice is in fact likely to be only a few centuries old.) It has flowed through the glacier in laminations, as one can easily see from photographs of the surface streaks, which do not mix – unlike currents in a river, which flow turbulently. But like a river, the flow is fastest in the middle of the glacier and slowest at the edges, where the friction is greatest. This pattern was first established by Agassiz, who planted rows of stakes in a Swiss glacier, lined up against marks on the rocky wall of the valley.

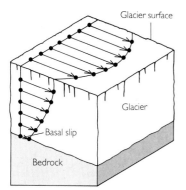

How a glacier moves. A glacier's ice moves by both flowing or deforming and by slipping (*above*). Slippage is demonstrated by this steep mountain glacier in Peru (*right*). The previous evening icicles formed from flowing meltwater, which ceased to flow during the cold of night; those icicles that had become anchored to firm ground became bent as a result of the slippage of the glacier towards the lower right.

Returning the following year, he found that all the stakes had moved down the valley, but not in a straight line: they had created a crescent across the glacier.

Subsequent experiments examined the way the flow changes with depth. A straight pipe buried in a glacier to its bottom becomes bent into a curve, because the bottom of the pipe moves a shorter distance than the top. This proves that glaciers move partly by deformation of the ice and partly by basal slip of the ice over the underlying rock. The ratio was once thought to be about 50:50, but the most recent studies suggest that slip usually predominates. Not surprisingly, the more water there is to lubricate the base, the higher the proportion of slip.

'A glacier can be considered as a small-scale model for the processes that occur deep in the Earth's crust, such as the formation of the Western Cordillera or the Alps as a result of the collision of continental plates', two glaciologists, Michael Hambrey and Jürg Alean, have recently written. (Some geologists have taken the analogy to its logical conclusion in the hope of shedding light on rock fractures and even – who knows? – the mechanism of earthquakes.) Like ancient contorted rock strata exposed in a road cutting, complex and beautiful foliations of ice stand naked near the snout of a glacier or in crevasses where the surface has been torn apart at an ice-fall (the glacial equivalent of a waterfall). Bands/ waves on the surface itself, known as ogives, are among the most fascinating (and mysterious) of all glacier structures. Ogives form only at ice-falls, but for some reason not at all ice-falls. A pair of light and dark bands – the product of dirty ice in summer and snow-covered ice in winter – corresponds to a year's movement of ice through the fall. Measurement of the gap between pairs of bands at the foot of an ice-fall permits an approximate estimate of ice velocity at the fall; further down the glacier the ogives become more closely spaced, indicating that the glacier is moving more slowly. By counting the ogives between an ice-fall and the glacier's snout, one can determine how long the glacier has taken to cover the distance. In this sense, ogives are like glacial tree rings.

Crevasses offer a more direct, if somewhat risky, way to plumb glacier structure. Agassiz was among the first scientists to descend one, and was almost skewered by stalactites on the ascent. He reached a depth of about 100 feet (30 m), which is typical of a crevasse in a warm/temperate glacier. Below that depth, ice flows together faster than it splits. But crevasses in cold glaciers (such as those in frigid Antarctica) can be much deeper: they are often big enough to swallow a house, not to speak of the many vehicles that have fallen into them. There exist few reliable measurements of their depth.

Sometimes a crevasse can act as a – rather macabre – yardstick of a glacier's movement. In 1933, two naturalists making a routine survey of the Lyell Glacier in Yosemite National Park came face to face with what appeared to be a normal mountain sheep. They were astonished, since such sheep had been extinct in the region for at least half a century. This particular sheep had apparently been swept into a crevasse some 250 years before, to emerge in perfect condition after a journey of 1936 feet (590 m). And in 1820, in the Alps, three guides in a climbing party were carried by an avalanche into a crevasse on a glacier near Mont Blanc. Their bodies were disgorged 43 years later from the ice near the glacier's snout, after travelling just under 2 miles.

Nothing so dramatic appears to have happened to the body of the Iceman. It was revealed not because *it* moved but because, as so often occurs in the Alps, a glacier advanced or (in this case) retreated. In North America and Europe almost all glaciers have retreated considerably since the beginning of this century, a pattern partially reversed in the late 1970s and early 1980s, and then, in some cases, reversed yet again during the warm period of very recent years (when the majority of Alpine glaciers were once again on the retreat). One of Switzerland's best known glaciers, the Rhône, retreated a mile and a half over nearly a century from 1818, stranding a hotel famous for having a glacier on its back doorstep. The Unterer Grindelwald Glacier advanced from 1600 (the begin-

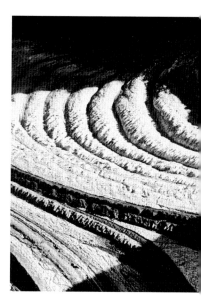

Waves in the ice. Bands or waves formed on the surface of glaciers are among the most fascinating of all glacial structures. Known as ogives, they form only at ice-falls, but not at all ice-falls. A pair of light and dark bands corresponds to a year's movement of ice through the fall: ogives are therefore a kind of glacial tree ring. The ogives shown in the photograph are from the Patmore Glacier in British Columbia.

Advance and retreat of glaciers. In North America and Europe almost all glaciers have retreated considerably since the end of the Little Ice Age in the mid-19th century, but with periods of advance. The Argentière Glacier in Switzerland is shown here in an engraving made between 1850 and 1860 and in a photograph taken in 1966.

A crevasse. Many crevasses are no deeper than about 100 feet (30 m) but some, especially in the coldest glaciers in the polar ice caps, are far deeper. This dramatic photograph of a crevasse was taken in 1888 by Vittorio Sella, at the White Glacier high in the French Alps.

ning of records) until 1860, and then retreated consistently – except for some minor re-advances early this century – until 1977, losing more than a mile of its length. But by 1990 it had recouped over a sixth of its loss, 1000 feet (300 m).

Even without regular documentation, the state of fluctuation of a glacier can usually be determined from its snout. A gently graded, even flat snout, fairly easy to walk on, means that a glacier is retreating; a steep, convex cliff, scalable only by an experienced ice climber, signals an advancing glacier. The difference is graphically suggested by the Three Congruent Glacier in the St Elias Mountains of Alaska. Three glaciers occupy three parallel valleys; but while one is undoubtedly retreating, another is unquestionably advancing.

Alaskan glaciers also show a tendency to surge: a phenomenon of glaciology probably more enigmatic than any other. Leaving aside volcanic surges such as those of Iceland – which rejoice in the name *jokulhlaup*, Icelandic for 'glacier run' – surges have been reported all over the world and show no pattern of occurrence. A surge is no mere rapid advance. The Kutiah Glacier in the Karakoram mountains of northern Pakistan sprinted nearly 8 miles in three months, an average speed of 369 feet (112 m) per day – probably the fastest surge on record. (Surges in the 1980s proved serious hazards in the building of the Karakoram highway between Pakistan and China.) The Black Rapids Glacier of Alaska reached the front page of the *New York Times* in 1937. Almost overnight its snout turned from being smooth and gently inclined into a strongly crevassed ice face well over 300 feet (100 m) high. Crashing along at up to 300 feet (some 90 m) per day, it threatened to dam the Delta River, block the only all-weather highway into the interior of Alaska and demolish a well-known hunting and fishing lodge. (Today it might threaten the Alaska pipeline.) But four months after the surge began, as inexplicably it virtually halted – within a mile and a half of the roadhouse and highway.

In 1982/83, scientists were able to observe close-up the extended surge of the Variegated Glacier in Alaska, which had been anticipated on the basis of four previous surges spaced roughly 17 to 20 years apart. One of these scientists was Robert Sharp, who wrote:

The major surge was not a single simple event. Rather, the glacier behaved like an athlete warming up for an event by taking deep breaths, doing calisthenics, and engaging in short sprints to flex muscles and get in trim for the main effort. Many mini-surges occurred before the big surge, and one even took place afterwards, similar to a warming-down exercise.

Plainly a workable explanation of surges has a lot of explaining to do. Most scientists believe that an imbalance in the ice of the glacier develops and somehow blocks the drainage of its base, thus causing it to skid. But the mechanism is still poorly understood and probably differs between glaciers, depending on 'size, shape, orientation and gradient, climate, bedrock type and thermal regime', according to Hambrey and Alean.

The surging of part of the Antarctic ice sheet as a result of global warming has been seriously mooted, but so far there is little solid evidence that it might happen. Instead, the ice sheets at both poles ablate largely by calving icebergs into the ocean. (Very little melting and evaporation occurs, because temperatures are so low.) The bergs may last for a decade or more before they melt away, disintegrating into progeny known (in order of declining size) as bergy bits, growlers and brash.

New-born, an iceberg has a myriad shapes and sizes beginning from around 20 feet (6 m) in height and 50 feet (15 m) in length, but glaciologists have settled on five broad categories: tabular, blocky, drydock, pinnacle and domed. The one that probably sank the *Titanic* in 1912, drowning 1503 people, was described as standing 80 feet (24 m) above the water, having a length of 60 feet (18 m) and an estimated weight of 200,000 tons. One of the biggest icebergs ever recorded broke away from the Ross Ice Shelf in 1987; it was 100 miles long with an area of nearly 2500 square miles. The US National Science Foundation announced that it contained enough water to supply Los Angeles for 675 years: a reference to US interest over the last three or four decades in harnessing and towing icebergs to thirsty, drought-ridden lands. During the late 1970s, one of the Saudi royal family sank considerable sums into a feasibility study. But so far, as with NAWAPA, the North American Water and Power Alliance (see pages 210–11), the fantastic project has not taken off. Nevertheless, it might be technologically feasible, particularly if the icebergs are towed from the Antarctic only as far as, say, Australia or South Africa, avoiding the predatory warmth of tropical waters.

'Ice ages have always provoked argument', wrote the astronomer Sir Fred Hoyle in *Ice*, published in 1981. This was true when Louis Agassiz first popularized the concept a century and a half ago; it is even truer today, when we have abundant scientific evidence for the existence of ice ages. The problem is, the more we know about them, the more complex they appear.

One thing is quite clear: there have been many periods of glaciation in Earth's history, not just one, as Agassiz proposed. Some scientists have even proposed recently that 'ice on Earth may

Simultaneous advance and retreat. Sometimes different parts of a glacier can move in opposite senses. The Three Congruent Glacier in Alaska, for instance, has three parallel streams. In the photograph, the stream on the left has recently advanced; the one in the middle is retreating; and the one on the right has made a very recent advance.

A glacier surges. The Variegated Glacier in Alaska surged in 1982–83, with glaciologists in full attendance. One photograph (*below*) shows the surge; the other (*left*) shows the glacier three years after the surge ended, with the large crevasses and chasms of the surge rapidly ablating away.

Earth's ice ages.

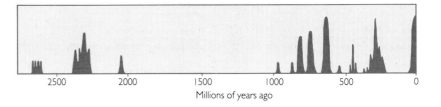

2500   2000   1500   1000   500   0

Millions of years ago

be as much the norm as more temperate conditions' – Michael Hambrey. Are ice ages 'the healthy state of a middle-aged planet, and the brief warm spells the fevered state of a planetary illness?' questioned James Lovelock in 1991.

On the basis of the skimpy evidence available about early Earth, Hambrey has compiled a chronology of glaciations. It shows a major glacial phase between 2500 and 2000 million years ago, a period more or less free of ice for 1000 million years after that, followed by frequent peaks of glaciation during the past 1000 million years. Of these peaks, the two with the most secure claim to be called worldwide glaciations – 'true' ice ages – occurred between 700 and 600 million years ago, and between 250 and 230 million years ago.

Amazing evidence from the Sahara discovered in the 1960s has suggested an episode of glaciation there in a remote period. In the 1960s French petroleum geologists working in southern Algeria stumbled across a series of giant grooves. Rather than wind, glaciers seemed to be responsible, and this was confirmed by an international team. They identified striations, erratics and eskers – long banks of sand typical of those deposited by ice sheets as they melt – all baking in the north African sun. What made the find especially satisfying was that it agreed with the conclusions of a separate study made by other scientists of the magnetic orientation of rocks in many parts of the world. They had concluded that about 450 million years ago what is now northern Africa lay over the South Pole. The rocks in the Sahara therefore were probably glaciated at that time.

If so, it raises a question: was there a worldwide ice age 450 million years ago, or was it just that north Africa occupied the South Pole long enough to be glaciated, assuming, that is, that the poles can be glaciated when the rest of the globe is not? This is a reasonable assumption, for it is known that 13 million years ago there was a large ice mass on Antarctica, and 37 million years ago there was at least some ice – two periods when the rest of the Earth was definitely not experiencing an ice age. It appears likely that several of the 'ice ages' identified by scientists within the past 450 million to 250 million years are not 'true' ice ages, but actually polar glaciations.

The most recent ice era began about 66 million years ago, at the time of the mass extinction that included the dinosaurs. Mild at first, about 55 million years ago small glaciers began to grow in Antarctica. Like the expanding and retreating glaciers of the Alps their growth was not uniform, but gradually they coalesced into a dome-shaped ice sheet that by 20 million years ago covered the whole continent. About 8 million years after that, Alaska started to be glaciated; by 3 million years ago, Greenland lay beneath an ice sheet. Around 2½ million years ago, the geological era known as the Pleistocene began. Since then, the ice sheets of North America and Europe have advanced far into the middle latitudes at least four times, and perhaps as many as ten times. Thus ice ages have alternated with warmer periods (interglacials). Each of these might qualify as a 'true' ice age. And on at least ten other occasions the ice sheets have spread far beyond their present extent.

By 6000 B C they had all retreated to their present positions. The ice age was finally over. But many of today's glaciers are not

An ice age in the Sahara.
Scientists have discovered unmistakeable evidence of glaciation in the middle of the Sahara Desert. About 450 million years ago, what is now northern Africa lay over the South Pole. The photograph shows a water scour, a deep channel that was cut by the rushing waters of an ice sheet as it melted.

shrunken remnants of those great ice sheets; they were formed during a more recent period of worldwide cooling that peaked about 2500 years ago. Some of them even grew substantially more recently still: during the period AD 1430–1850 known as the 'Little Ice Age', of which more in Chapter 9.

The later stages of the last ice age saw the disappearance of a large number of species, including giant mammals such as the woolly mammoth and the sabre-toothed cat. The scope and timing of extinction varied, as the extent and duration of the ice sheets varied. In Europe it took about 20,000 years to eliminate 50 per cent of the megafauna, but in North America a full 70 per cent of them died out within a mere 1000 years. How they had managed to survive previous interglacials has never been satisfactorily explained. The naturalist Alfred Russel Wallace, Darwin's contemporary, was one of the first scientists to contemplate the conundrum: 'We live in a zoologically impoverished world, from which all the hugest, and fiercest, and strangest forms have recently disappeared. It is surely a marvellous fact, and one that has hardly been sufficiently dwelt upon'.

Was the climate change responsible, or did early humans kill the animals? Or did both contribute, along with other factors? An 11,000-year-old mastodon (elephant-like mammal) recovered recently in a well-preserved condition from a peat bog in Ohio shows how complex the riddle is. Scientists had previously hypothesized that mastodons became extinct when their food supply, evergreen forests, moved north at the end of the ice age. But the main diet of the mastodon corpse, according to the remains of its

Woolly mammoth. The extinction of megafauna such as the woolly mammoth that flourished during the last ice age has yet to be adequately explained. Was climate change wholly responsible, or did early human beings play a part, along with perhaps other geographical changes still unknown? This mammoth calf was discovered in Siberia in 1977.

last meal in its intestines, was wetland grasses, not twigs or conifers. Perhaps, scientists now tentatively suggested, it was the draining of the vast wetlands that existed in the late glacial and early post-glacial periods that led to the animal's demise? Maybe Lyell was close to the truth when he wrote in 1863:

> It is probable that causes more general and powerful than the agency of Man, alterations in climate, variations in the range of many species of animals, vertebrate and invertebrate, and of plants, geographical changes in the height, depth and extent of land and sea, or all of these combined, have given rise in a vast series of years to the annihilation of many large mammalia.

One class of organism most certainly not extinguished during the ice ages were the foraminifera, the tiny planktonic organisms whose chambered shells form an important component of chalk and of many deep-sea oozes. They have lived in the oceans for millions of years, some species only in warm waters, others only in cold waters. Innocuous as they are, in the last few decades their shells have provided the most substantial clue so far in the effort to unravel the sequence and ultimately the trigger(s) of the ice ages.

To understand how these protozoa have assisted, we must for a moment digress. The key to the method lies in the isotopes of oxygen concentrated in the shells. These are two: oxygen 16, that has eight protons and eight neutrons in its atomic nucleus, and oxygen 18, with eight protons and ten neutrons. Almost all the oxygen in ordinary water is oxygen 16, but a few water molecules out of every thousand incorporate the heavier isotope oxygen 18. Being heavier, these molecules tend to be left behind when water evaporates. This means that rain and snow, precipitated from ocean water vapour, are slightly *depleted* in oxygen 18; and seawater, conversely, is slightly enriched in the heavier isotope.

When an ice age began, and water was removed from the oceans into the ice sheets, these isotopic ratios became pronounced. An increasing ratio of oxygen 18 to oxygen 16 in seawater mirrored the increasing size of the ice sheets. 'Of course, specimens of seawater from a remote era cannot now be recovered or identified', wrote an expert in *Scientific American* in 1984. But the shells containing the oxygen in that sea water can be – by drilling holes in the sea bed and extracting from them marine sediment cores. The shells of dead foraminifera are made of calcium carbonate, chalk (which contains three atoms of oxygen for every one of calcium). The higher the ratio of oxygen 18 to oxygen 16 in a sedimentary specimen is, the more land ice there was when the sediment was laid down. In the words of US marine geologist William Ruddiman, speaking in

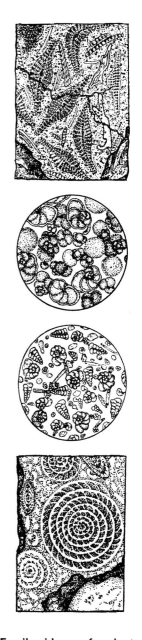

Fossil evidence of ancient climates. Foraminifera are tiny planktonic organisms whose chambered shells form an important component of chalk and of many deep-sea oozes. The remains of ancient foraminifera, when analyzed for their oxygen content, may sometimes prove to be 'our library of the far past', according to one geologist. The drawings show foraminifera in recent and geological marine deposits.

1986: 'Seabed cores are our library of the far past. They tell us the Earth's past climate, the movements of its crustal plates, where the ice sheets lay, and why – in large part – life today is as it is.'

The last few years have demonstrated more limitations in the cores than Ruddiman's enthusiasm suggests – gaps in the library, so to speak – but they remain an exceptionally powerful tool. The core record permits scientists to graph the change in ice volume on land over the past 600,000 years. The graph documents a series of peaks, each corresponding to an ice age. The question now, of course, is what can explain the pattern?

One possibility would be a variation in sunshine at the surface of the Earth. If less sunshine falls on the Earth, we would naturally expect more ice to form; and vice versa. Leaving aside sunspots, astronomers have long been aware that Earth's orientation towards the sun changes cyclically. The seasons are one manifestation of this astronomical pacemaker; there are also others. Early this century, long before the first marine cores were drilled, the Yugoslav astronomer Milutin Milankovitch set out to calculate from first principles exactly how the sunshine should vary.

Milankovitch elucidated the existence of three cycles in solar radiation. He was convinced that these three cycles, with periods of 23,000, 41,000 and 100,000 years, were responsible for the advance and retreat of ice across the Earth. But until the 1950s, there was no way to put his prediction to the all-important test, since there was no detailed record of the ice ages. Then the first marine cores became available. Did calculated peaks in sunshine correspond with troughs in ice volume and vice versa? Yes and no. There is a marked 100,000-year cycle in the ice volume, but much less evidence of sensitivity to the two shorter cycles.

This is surprising because, if the Milankovitch theory is correct, the precession or wobble and the tilt of the Earth's spin axis (which together have the two shorter cycles) are calculated to have *more* effect than changes in the shape of the Earth's orbit around the Sun (which completes a cycle every 100,000 years). Also difficult to reconcile with the theory is the fact that ice volume in the southern hemisphere seems to be synchronized with ice volume in the northern hemisphere – that is what we mean by a 'true' ice age (i.e. a worldwide glaciation) – whereas the Milankovitch theory predicts that sunshine in the two hemispheres will vary *out of step*. (It predicts too that ice ages should have repeated in a regular pattern over much longer than the $2\frac{1}{2}$ million years of the Pleistocene.) Most awkward of all to explain is how such small differences in sunshine between equatorial and polar regions – only about 1 per cent difference – can have so dramatic an effect on climate. Fred Hoyle, as a leading astronomer, wrote sceptically:

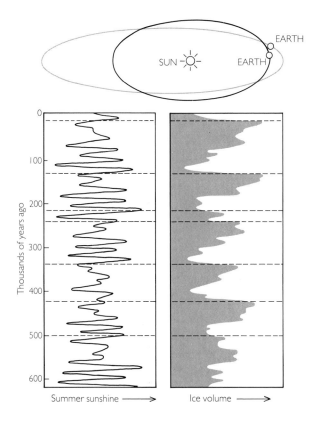

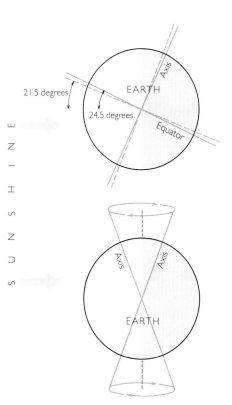

Summer sunshine ⟶   Ice volume ⟶

If I were to assert that a glacial condition could be induced in a room liberally supplied during winter with charged night-storage heaters simply by taking an ice cube into the room, the proposition would be no more unlikely than the Milankovitch theory.

To complicate matters further, recent studies of sediment cores drilled on land – instead of taken from the sea bed – have cast doubt on the dating and interpretation of the marine core record. A single cylinder of carbonate – only the size of the cardboard tube in a roll of paper towels – extracted from a water-filled fault called Devil's Hole in Nevada, has been much more precisely dated than all the marine cores. (The uranium content was used, which is too small in the marine cores to be reliable.) The correlation between the Devil's Hole oxygen isotope ratio and Milankovitch's cycles is looser still than that of the marine cores. According to the marine record, the end of the penultimate ice age corresponds with a peak in sunshine 128,000 years ago – in line, therefore, with Milankovitch's theory; but the land record puts the retreat of the ice at 140,000 years ago, corresponding with a sunshine *minimum* – a clear contradiction of Milankovitch.

Earth and Sun: three astronomical cycles. The shape of the Earth's orbit is not a perfect circle but an ellipse (*top left*), which oscillates between being more and less elliptical over a period of *100,000 years*. The tilt of the Earth's axis (*top right*), which creates summer and winter, fluctuates from 21.5 to 24.5 degrees and back every *41,000 years*. The wobble of the Earth's spin axis resembles that of a revolving gyroscope (*above right*); it traces a complete circle about every *23,000 years*.

Do astronomical cycles cause ice ages? There is a marked coincidence, seen in the graphs (*above left*), of *low* sunshine and *high* ice volume 100,000 years ago, and lesser coincidences roughly every 100,000 years thereafter.

Whiffs of ancient air. Air trapped in glaciers when the ice was formed can be analyzed by drilling the ice caps to great depths and sawing up the ice cores extracted into manageable sections. Great care must be taken not to contaminate the trapped air during extraction and analysis; it is also likely that the air undergoes some change while trapped, for which allowance must be made. Nevertheless, ice cores enable scientists to examine the variation of carbon dioxide and other gases over tens of thousands of years.

Most scientists accept that changes in the Earth's orbit do have a role in causing ice ages, but very few now think this extraterrestrial cause is the dominant factor. Terrestrial triggers are now considered to be crucial. But it is exceedingly difficult to sort them out and give each due weight. Quite possibly, the discrepancy between the two cores has as much to do with their different origins in the sea and on land – with all the intricate chemistry of oxygen in the atmosphere intervening – as it does with the methods used to date the cores. At present, scientists can make only a half-educated guess.

One potential candidate as a terrestrial trigger is volcanism. Ice cores drilled from the Greenland ice cap over the past three decades have been analyzed for bands of acidity that correspond mainly to the sulphuric acid in volcanic fall-out. Danish scientists have identified the bands by testing the electrical conductivity of melted ice samples. There is unmistakable evidence in the ice, increasing with depth as one would expect, of massive eruptions: far-off Krakatoa (1883) and Tambora (1815) and nearby Laki in Iceland (1783), as well as prehistoric eruptions – Thera, Mazama (creator of Crater Lake in Oregon) and seven different great eruptions somewhere on the Earth between 7911 and 7090 B C. By correlating the ice core record of volcanic activity with a temperature index for the northern hemisphere (based on climatic records from England, tree ring widths from California, and variation in precipitation on the Greenland ice sheet), the Danish scientists were able to demonstrate that major eruptions have a considerable effect on climate. Nevertheless, warned Robert Sharp, 'The problem with volcanism as the primary cause of an ice age is the large amount and long duration (tens of thousands of years) of explosive activity required.'

Another candidate is global disruption of the ocean-atmosphere system. There is a salty (hence dense and deep) current that threads the world's oceans and keeps their waters well mixed. Excess evaporation in the north Atlantic drives it; most of it ultimately mixes upwards in the Pacific, compensating for excess precipitation there. Two US scientists, Wallace S. Broecker and George H. Denton, have termed this current the Atlantic 'conveyor' and recently proposed that during the last ice age the conveyor shut down, then suddenly restarted 14,000 years ago towards the end of the ice age. They cannot say why this happened, but are sympathetic to the claims of the Milankovitch theory: 'Our proposal is not a rejection of the astronomical theory of the ice ages but an extension of it.' There is a range of interdisciplinary evidence, including records from marine and ice cores, to support their contention:

The warming of north Atlantic surface waters, the onset of melting in the northern ice sheets and the mountain glaciers of the Andes, the reappearance of trees in Europe and changes in plankton ecology near Antarctica and in the South China Sea – all took place between 14,000 and 13,000 years ago.

How much help do the ice caps themselves give us in trying to work out the cause of the ice ages? The importance of Antarctica and the sea ice that surrounds it can scarcely be exaggerated. As already remarked, the ice sheet is twice the size of Australia; the sea ice, at its maximal seasonal extent (in August), covers an area seven times that of all the tropical rainforests in the world, and twice that of the tropical and temperate forests combined. But at its minimal extent (in February), it shrinks to a mere one fifth of its maximum size. (The maximum area in the Arctic is similar, but it does not shrink as dramatically as its southern counterpart, and the changes happen, of course, at opposite times of the year.)

It is satellite images that give us such information on a regular and reliable basis. But they are not yet capable of answering an equally vital question: are the ice sheets shrinking or expanding? For this degree of accuracy, ground traverses are required. After more than 30 years of intensive field work in the inhospitable wilderness of Antarctica, such traverses are only now being made. In the Antarctic summer of 1990/91, six scientists travelled 775 miles along the 2500-metre (8200-feet) contour line, skirting the Lambert Glacier, in three turbo-charged tractors. For four months, these tractors, pulling 70–80 tons of load, represented home to these men. Every 30 kilometres (nearly 19 miles), the party recorded by satellite the position of a marker placed in the snow. Measured again two years on, these markers would show how the glacier was moving. Poles placed in the snow every 2 kilometres (1.25 miles) were measured on the party's return leg, to determine rates of snow accumulation. Meanwhile, throughout the journey, pulse radar recorded the thickness of the ice.

The glacier itself turned out to be moving no faster in 1990/91 than it was when measured 22 years before; nor had its surface elevation increased. But its rate of melting was much higher than expected, with the production of large lakes and streams extending more than 10 miles down the glacier. The effects of global warming? Not necessarily, said the scientist in charge: 'The actual mass balance of the glacier may not have been affected. There may be more snow falling inland which makes up for the melt.'

Similarly, it is hard to draw conclusions about the melting of ice shelves in Antarctica. These are floating glaciers formed where land glaciers meet the ocean, with thicknesses well over 3000 feet (915

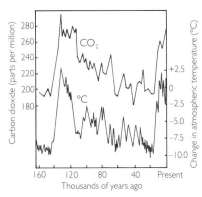

Carbon dioxide and the ice ages. There is a truly impressive correlation between carbon dioxide concentration and Earth's temperature over 160,000 years. In the depths of the last ice age, for instance, carbon dioxide too was at a low point. The reasons for the resemblance are only partially understood.

m) in their inner parts, half that or less at the edges where they calve. The Ross Ice Shelf is twice the size of the United Kingdom and bigger than California. Were it or another large ice shelf to start melting, this would be as worrying a sign as the ozone hole above Antarctica. There is no evidence that melting is occurring, but the small Wordie Ice Shelf off the west coast of the Antarctic peninsula has largely disappeared in the past 30 years. 'If this warming trend continues, other nearby ice shelves . . . may be at risk', wrote two British scientists in 1991, presenting satellite imagery of the Wordie's disintegration in *Nature*. 'But substantial additional warming would be required before similar processes could initiate breakup of the Ross and Filcher-Ronne Ice Shelves, which help stabilize the west Antarctic ice sheet.'

What is beyond doubt from measurements made all over both ice caps is that parts of them are shrinking and other parts are growing. As of now – and certainly for several years ahead, perhaps decades – scientists cannot know the overall picture. It may even be that during past periods of relative climatic warmth, the Antarctic ice sheet *grew* – presumably because increased precipitation in its interior exceeded the increased melting of ice at its edges. That is what an ice core taken from the Lambert Glacier in the 1980s definitely shows. During the period 7000–3000 years ago, after the great northern ice sheets had finally retreated – and when for a few brief years the Iceman lived and died in the Alps – there was a major *expansion* of the Antarctic ice sheet.

During the last ice age sea levels fell 350 feet (107 m), as already mentioned – a figure based on estimating the size of the ice sheets from the extent of glacial moraines and the height of striations on mountains. If, as the world warms, the ice caps actually increase in size instead of diminishing as common sense suggests, the ice-age scenario may be repeated, but on a much smaller scale. In the opinion of one geologist who has studied the evidence – and he is not alone – 'the ice sheets look likely to grow, not melt, in the next few decades, and the seas should eventually fall, not rise.'

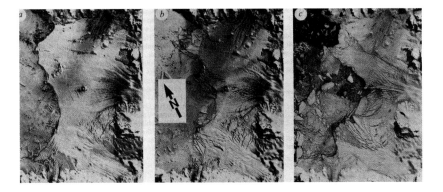

Breakup of the Wordie Ice Shelf, Antarctica. The images (from left to right) show the ice shelf in January 1974, February 1979 and February 1989. Could global warming be responsible?

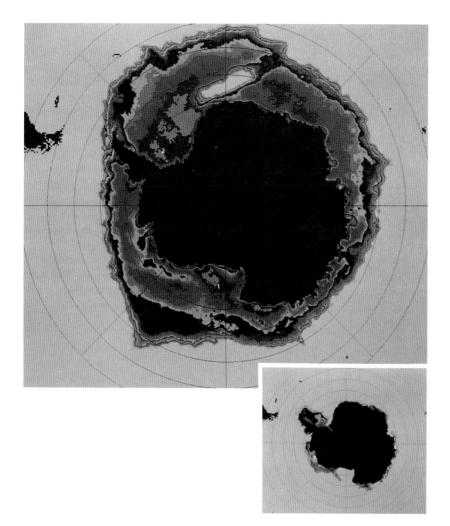

Pack ice in Antarctica. The top image shows the pack ice in August 1974, the Antarctic winter; the bottom image shows it in February 1975, the Antarctic summer.

There is, though, one essential difference between now and the climatic situation some 10,000–15,000 years ago: civilization has entered the scene. Ice transparently demonstrates its impact. Ice cores taken from the Alps on the Swiss–Italian border record – along with Saharan dust storms – nuclear explosions such as the Chernobyl accident, and sulphur concentrations that have risen three times over the last 100 years. Other cores provide a most intriguing chart of carbon dioxide: both naturally occurring and, in recent centuries, human-generated. Ice cores are an 'archive in the ice', said Richard Laws, a former director of the British Antarctic Survey. In the words of two leading core-scientists, a Swiss and an American, Hans Oeschger and Chester C. Langway Jr, introducing the latest research on the subject in 1989:

> Ice core research has significantly contributed to the rethinking of the Earth . . . wherein a wide spectrum of biogeochemical processes are interacting within the purely physical processes.

This ensemble of processes is now often referred to as the organism Earth.

The carbon dioxide the cores contain is trapped, along with oxygen and other gases, within the ice crystals. Carefully released from the imprisoning ice, these whiffs of ancient air are a direct, analyzable chronicle of past atmospheres. (As always, the technique is not quite so simple; scientists must learn to take account of possible changes in the air while it was trapped.) When the concentration of ancient carbon dioxide in the air is plotted against time on the same graph as the changes in temperature (calculated from oxygen isotope ratios), the two graphs resemble each other in a truly impressive manner. When the climate was warm, at the end of the penultimate ice age, carbon dioxide levels peaked; when the temperature reached a minimum in the depths of the last ice age, the carbon dioxide too fell to a low point.

Did a fall in carbon dioxide cause the ice ages? If so, how? Or did ice-age conditions (caused by other factors, including perhaps changes in solar radiation) lead to a reduction in carbon dioxide? And what will the effect be of the extremely rapid rise in carbon dioxide generated by Man since the industrial revolution? Could it put an end to the ice ages? We have no definite answers, only some hopeful lines of enquiry. As Oeschger and Langway willingly confess, despite the flood of data about ice ages gathered during recent decades by astonishingly ingenious means, the ice ages continue to raise 'perplexing questions': they are 'still unanswered today some 150 years after Louis Agassiz presented the first of his ice-age theory papers at a meeting of the Swiss Society of Natural Sciences in Neuchâtel.'

CHAPTER

— 9 —

GLOBAL CLIMATIC CHANGE

We dwell on a largely unexplored planet . . . how many species of organisms are there on earth? We don't know, not even to the nearest order of magnitude. The number could be close to 10 million or as high as 100 million.
Edward O. Wilson, 'The Diversity of Life', 1992

Geophysiology ignores the traditional divisions between the Earth and life sciences, which view the evolution of the rocks and the evolution of life as two separate sciences. . . Geophysiology is at the information-gathering stage, rather as was biology when Victorian scientists went forth to distant jungles to collect specimens.
James Lovelock, 1988/91

WHEN Mount Pinatubo in the Philippines erupted in June 1991, it opened an acid parasol of sulphurous particles over a large portion of the Earth. It also opened a debate among scientists that indicated yet again the interdisciplinary direction in which science must move, both for its own development and for the sake of society that depends on it.

Data on the eruption from the *Nimbus 7* satellite – the satellite that spotted the ozone hole – showed the emission of 20 million tons of sulphur dioxide into the stratosphere: at least twice that of the 1982 eruption of Mexico's Mount El Chichón (and about the same quantity of the gas as US industries emit each year). The haze – technically an 'aerosol' – was dispersed within weeks through the upper atmosphere around the equator in a swathe of sulphuric acid. Within months air currents spread it towards the poles, thus covering the entire globe. There it was expected to remain, shading and cooling the planet by reflecting solar radiation, for two years or more.

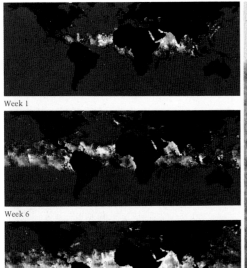

Week 1

Week 6

Week 10

The greatest volcanic eruption of the 20th century.

Photographers flee Mount Pinatubo in the Philippines in June 1991. Having been dormant for 600 years, the volcano blasted two cubic miles of fine ash and some 20 million tons of sulphur dioxide into the atmosphere: two or three times the output of the eruption of Mount Chichón in Mexico in 1982, and about the same as that of Krakatoa in 1883. At stratospheric heights of 12 to 15 miles, the gas became an aerosol of supercooled droplets of sulphuric acid, within weeks girdling the equator, later spreading to higher latitudes. The satellite images (*above*) show the aerosol 1 week, 6 weeks and 10 weeks after the eruption. It reflected sunlight back into space and cooled the planet slightly, by 0.5 degrees C (0.9°F), like the eruptions of Mount Tambora (1815) and Krakatoa. The cooling effect was predicted to last two or more years, thus masking any man-made greenhouse warming. Some scientists speculate that the eruption may also be linked to an El Niño event in the Pacific Ocean. Conceivably, one influence may counteract the other.

The Little Ice Age. Frost fairs, such as this one on the River Thames at London, were a feature of life in Europe from c.1430 to 1850: average temperatures sometimes fell as much as 1.5 degrees C (2.75°F) below the average temperature of the past several millennia. Between 1564 and 1814 – the date of the last frost fair on the Thames – the river froze at least 20 times.

The debate concerned the likely effect of the eruption on temperatures – both global and regional. If the aerosol cooled the Earth, it would mask the much-discussed trend towards global warming. How much cooling could be expected, and at what latitudes? How long would it last? A calculation, though difficult, was possible. But what if the eruption had other, unpredictable effects – for instance on winds, on sea surface temperatures and on the ozone layer? (The aerosol might help to liberate ozone-destroying chlorine atoms, many scientists feared.) Could its knock-on effect cause cooling in one place, and warming elsewhere? To complicate matters further, only months later in 1991, as in 1982 after the eruption of El Chichón, there were signs of an El Niño developing in the central and eastern Pacific: in early 1992 this went on to produce floods on the coast of Peru, three times the normal rainfall in Texas, freak storms in southern California, temperatures 3–7 degrees C (5.5–12.5°F) above normal from Alaska to the Great Lakes, and was thought to be a major cause – in all probability – of the devastating drought in southern Africa. El Niño affects temperature differently from volcanic aerosols: it can heat one part of the atmosphere, but cool another, while its effect on global temperature overall is a temporary fall. Clearly the assessment of temperature trends in the early 1990s, even if we leave aside every other factor but El Niño and Pinatubo, is certain to be an arguable business.

There is no hard evidence for El Niño as an accomplice of Mount Pinatubo but the link seems a reasonable one: as we know from Chapter 2, El Niño has followed the eruption of a volcano for more than a century. Until more research is done, the connection must remain speculative, but the general point, an important one, is now a settled conviction among scientists: they have been compelled to go global in their questions and hypotheses. The forces of Nature, like the tectonic plates, interact worldwide. To understand them more deeply – and perhaps to predict them to a useful degree of accuracy during the coming century – one must think about them unconventionally, as part of systems that operate Earthwide.

Most of us continue to think locally, however. It is hard enough to maintain our interest in global political concepts like the United Nations, let alone global scientific ones, which have a much less tangible presence (space shots apart). In the 1970s, it was global cooling that occasionally made headlines; now it is global warming. A good scientific case has been made for both prospects, but neither preoccupies most of us – until, that is, we experience a particularly extreme winter or summer.

Few Europeans remember the summer of 1988 as a special one; few North Americans can forget it. It was the summer of the worst forest fires in recorded history (when Yellowstone National Park burned); the summer when US grain production dropped below consumption probably for the first time since the days of the Pilgrim Fathers; the summer when the Mississippi dropped so low it stranded thousands of barges and revealed the skeletons of three scuttled Civil War ships; when the Detroit factories shut down their assembly lines; when Harvard University closed its doors – the only time in its 356-year history; when Americans spent an extra $500 million in August running air-conditioners; and when New York City had 32 days above 32 degrees C (90°F) by the middle of August, with a 75 per cent jump in the murder rate. It was during the summer of 1988 that global warming began to feel real – at least to many North Americans.

Yet the 1988 summer's average temperature was barely one degree C above normal for the US. Is the world as a whole warming significantly? What do the climate records actually show?

The meteorological use of the thermometer dates from the 18th century. Before that we therefore have to rely on other sources. In historical time, these include the records of wine harvests and how far north vines could be grown (in Europe), the blossoming of cherry trees (in Japan), the freezing of rivers (in Britain the Thames at London froze at least 20 times between 1564 and 1814), the dates of settlement of Iceland and Greenland by the Norsepeople (A D 874 and 986), and the advance and retreat of glaciers. In prehistory, we have the growth rings of the bristlecone pine, the carbon content of pollen in mud cores, the oxygen content in the shells of marine organisms in seafloor sediments, and the oxygen content of Greenland and Antarctic ice cores. Precision about the temperature is impossible, but there appears to have been a natural climate variability since the last ice age of at least 1 degree C (1.8°F), perhaps as much as 2 degrees C. There was a notable warm period in medieval times, between about A D 1000 and 1300, followed by a 'Little Ice Age' between about 1430 and 1850.

As for actual temperature data, the earliest continuous and reliable records began only in 1850, when national meteorological agencies became active (and even then coverage remained patchy for large areas of the world, particularly the southern hemisphere). Considering the natural variability of climate, this is too short a period for making accurate predictions. Furthermore, interpretation of the data has to take into account the various methods and circumstances of its collection. If a weather station was moved from a valley to a hillside, for example, the data will have been affected; if a city grew up around a station, it will have produced a 'heat island' effect, artificially raising the temperature recorded. Measurements made at sea before 1940 were usually made by

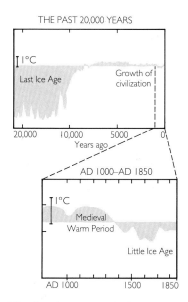

The last ice age and after.

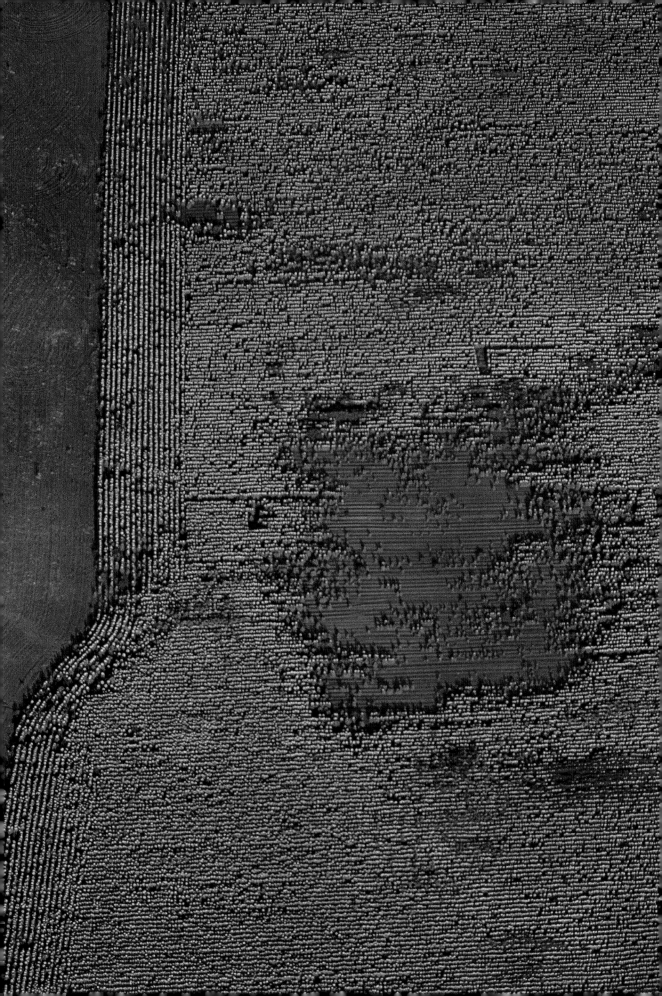

dipping a thermometer into a canvas bucket full of sea water, while those made since 1940 have come from a thermometer placed in the intake pipes of a ship. Comparative studies show that the latter measurement is 0.3–0.7 degrees C (0.5–1.25°F) warmer than the former: the same magnitude, unfortunately, as that of the possible global warming.

Nevertheless, two exhaustive (and independent) analyses of available records performed in Britain and in the United States during the mid-1980s came to the same conclusion about the mean global temperature. It has varied considerably from year to year (a large part of Europe cooled between the mid-1970s and the mid-1980s, for example), but yes, it *has* increased by about 0.5 degrees C (0.9°F) over the past century.

'Global mean surface air temperature has increased by 0.3 degrees C to 0.6 degrees C over the last 100 years, with the five global-average warmest years being in the 1980s', concluded the Intergovernmental Panel on Climate Change in 1990. IPCC was founded in 1988 out of the concern felt about the two earlier temperature studies. It has been an unprecedented instance of scientific collaboration, with 170 scientists from 25 countries contributing papers, which were then reviewed by 200 other scientists. Its first report, *Climate Change* (updated in 1992 after the two warmest years on record), was described by the British prime minister Margaret Thatcher as an 'authoritative early warning'.

That it unquestionably is; but it is also a monument to the awesome complexity of climate change and our current ignorance about it. To quote Sir Crispin Tickell (Britain's former ambassador to the United Nations and a pioneer of the policy implications of climate change), writing in the mid-1980s: '[Climate change] is an area where vital information is still lacking, where scientists can both passionately and plausibly disagree with each other, and where the man with a bee in his bonnet could still turn out to be right' – a view likely to remain true for some years into the future.

The warming of the Earth during the 20th century – comparatively slight as it may seem – is a fact, then. It also lies well within the climate variability of the past several millennia. The question now becomes: is the warming natural, like the medieval warming that unfroze Greenland, or is it man-made? If human beings are responsible for it, how fast will we cause it to increase? And what will a warmer Earth be like? There are formidable obstacles to answering these questions, especially the second and third. Both the likely rate of global warming and its effects are highly controversial, because so little is known about the interaction of the atmosphere, the rocks, the ice caps, the oceans and life (the so-called 'biosphere').

Summer, 1988, in the United States. Drought ate a hole in this field of sunflowers in North Dakota. By sucking up moisture from the subsoil with long taproots, sunflowers can weather most dry spells, but the summer of 1988 was too much for them. US grain production dropped below consumption probably for the first time since the days of the Pilgrim Fathers: the possibility of global warming began to seem only too likely.

But before we tackle the controversy, let us look at two more facts. Besides being incontrovertible, they are interlinked and fundamental to an understanding of the debate about climate change. The first involves an upward-trending graph too; but instead of showing the temperature of the atmosphere, it shows its chemical composition or, rather, its concentration of carbon dioxide. The second fact, which we shall come to a little later, concerns a phenomenon that is now widely known: the greenhouse effect.

The carbon dioxide curve has become a kind of icon of Earth studies. Some call it the breathing of the planet, others the exhalation of industrial civilization. As the obsessive labour of one man, the US chemist Charles David Keeling, it is sometimes known as the Keeling curve. He has measured the concentration high up on the slopes of Hawaii's Mauna Loa, where the air is clean, since 1958. The graph thus brings up to date the final graph of Chapter 8, which showed atmospheric carbon dioxide concentration over the past several hundred thousand years. Its oscillations correspond to the decomposition and growth of vegetation worldwide, the cycling of the seasons, with emission of carbon dioxide in the autumn and winter, and absorption by photosynthesis in the spring and summer. This is the classical 'balance of Nature', as 19th-century scientists conceived it. But why does the concentration now rise inexorably, year after year? The source of the extra gas has long been obvious: human activity, principally. Breathing out, rearing animals, making cement, using wood and – by far the most important (four-fifths of the output) – the burning of the fossil fuels oil, coal and natural gas: all these activities generate carbon dioxide in large quantities. And it is the developed world that is responsible for the lion's share. Until the industrial revolution, carbon dioxide concentration stayed at 275 parts per million, with a variation of 10 ppm either way; today its concentration is over 350 ppm. Human activities have therefore augmented it by some 25 per cent.

To put that in perspective, the average US car, driven the average annual distance (10,000 miles), releases its own weight in carbon into the air. Between 1870 and 1970 fossil fuel burning contributed 400 thousand million tonnes of carbon dioxide to the atmosphere; between 1970 and 1989, another 400 thousand million followed it. In 1991, well over 20 thousand million tonnes of carbon dioxide were emitted, one per cent of them (according to the IPCC) billowing from the burning oil wells in the Gulf.

Other gases have also increased substantially in recent decades: methane, nitrous oxide and chlorofluorocarbons (CFCs, the same gases responsible for the ozone hole). They are present in smaller

Greenhouse gases and their growth

Gas	Concentration (ppm*):	
	Pre-industrial	1989
Carbon dioxide	275	354
Methane	0.70	1.7
Chlorofluorocarbons (CFCs)	0.0	0.00075
Nitrous oxide	0.28	0.306

*parts per million

(This table excludes the greenhouse gases water vapour and ozone.)

Two less familiar contributors to the greenhouse effect.
Cement manufacture generates large amounts of carbon dioxide when limestone (calcium carbonate) is heated. This factory is in Romania: one of the many horrors perpetrated against the environment by the former Communist regimes of eastern Europe. Rice production in paddy fields feeds about half the world's population (a proportion that is increasing); it also produces vast quantities of methane. The gas is generated not by the rice plant itself, but by bacterial decomposition of vegetation under water.

concentrations than carbon dioxide, but a greater proportion of them results from human activity. Methane, which is also known as swamp gas, comes mainly from the decomposition of organic material by anaerobic bacteria. Paddy fields produce vast amounts of it, so do the stomachs of the world's cattle: a healthy cow generates about 1000 times more methane than a human. So do termites: a single termite mound can excrete 5 litres (over a gallon) a minute. And termites are prolific – an astonishing half a ton of termites exists for every person on the planet.

So what? one might reasonably ask. None of these gases is poisonous, and even together they make up less than 0.04 per cent of the air. Compared to nitrogen (78 per cent) and oxygen (21 per

The greenhouse effect and global warming

(*Right, centre*) **Global temperature.** There has been a slight but significant rise in global temperature, about 0.5 degrees C (0.9°F), over the past century. If increased greenhouse gases are responsible and present trends of production continue, global warming will occur on a greater scale. Computer models vary in their estimates of the warming.

(*Right, below*) **Atmospheric carbon dioxide** rises and falls annually with seasonal changes in vegetation, but it also steadily increases. The reason is human activity: carbon dioxide has increased some 25 per cent since the Industrial Revolution.

(*Left*) **Over 20 thousand million tons** of carbon dioxide were emitted into the atmosphere in 1991 by fossil fuel burning, 1 per cent of which came from the smoking oil wells in Kuwait.

CARBON dioxide and other greenhouse gases in the atmosphere act somewhat (though not exactly) like the panes of glass in a greenhouse. They let in visible radiation from the Sun but they do not let out infrared radiation from the Earth's surface; and so the Earth, like the plants in a greenhouse, is kept warm. This is the natural *greenhouse effect* (facing page), first identified in the 19th century. The problem today is: human beings, by increasing the greenhouse gases in the atmosphere, may well be causing a man-made *greenhouse effect*. The slight rise in global temperature this century could be the first sign: we do not yet know for certain. What we do know is that we are vastly increasing the concentration of carbon dioxide, chiefly through the burning of fossil fuels, oil, coal and natural gas.

Incoming solar radiation 100%

25% Reflected by upper atmosphere

25% Absorbed by clouds and radiated as infrared

5% Reflected by lighter areas of Earth e.g. snowcaps

12%

S P A C E

A T M O S P H E R E

Clouds and greenhouse gases absorb infrared and radiate it into lower atmosphere

88%

GREENHOUSE GASES
Water vapour, carbon dioxide, methane, chlorofluorocarbons (CFCs), nitrous oxide, ozone

Outgoing infrared radiation

100%

Solar radiation absorbed by Earth's surface

45%

HUMAN CONTRIBUTION TO GREENHOUSE GASES
From burning of fossil fuels in power stations, factories and vehicles, from cement manufacture, from burning of tropical forests, from agriculture, from spray cans etc.

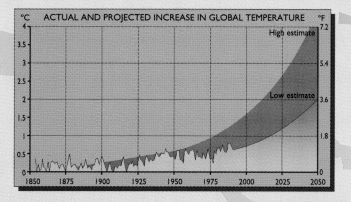

°C ACTUAL AND PROJECTED INCREASE IN GLOBAL TEMPERATURE °F

High estimate

Low estimate

1850 1875 1900 1925 1950 1975 2000 2025 2050

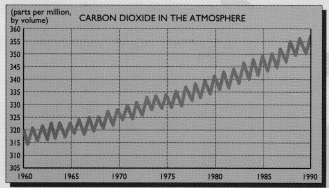

(parts per million, by volume) CARBON DIOXIDE IN THE ATMOSPHERE

1960 1965 1970 1975 1980 1985 1990

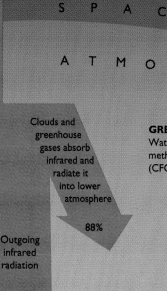

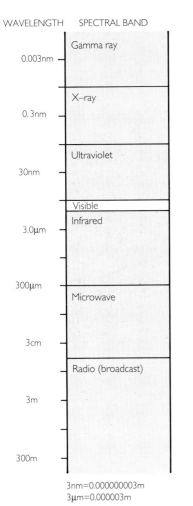

WAVELENGTH   SPECTRAL BAND

0.003nm	Gamma ray
0.3nm	X–ray
30nm	Ultraviolet
3.0μm	Visible / Infrared
300μm	
3cm	Microwave
3m	Radio (broadcast)
300m	

3nm=0.000000003m
3μm=0.000003m

The electromagnetic spectrum.

cent), carbon dioxide is virtually a trace gas, the other gases barely perceptible. This is all true – but it so happens that carbon dioxide, the object of so much recent concern for its potentially damaging effects on the planet, also keeps us alive.

The essential point is, 99 per cent of Earth's atmosphere has no insulating properties. Carbon dioxide and the other gases mentioned above (but not nitrogen or oxygen) act as a blanket and keep the Earth warm enough for life to survive and flourish. Water vapour in the clouds works in the same way (and its concentration is of course far greater than that of carbon dioxide). Along with some other gases they are all known as greenhouse gases because they trap infrared radiation, one form of heat, in a manner similar (though not identical) to that of the panes of glass in a greenhouse. In a real greenhouse, visible radiation – light from the Sun – enters, is absorbed by the dark plants, and is then partially reradiated by them as infrared radiation, most of which cannot escape the greenhouse because the glass is opaque to it. The atmosphere of the greenhouse therefore becomes heated and the temperature inside rises well above that of the outside air. In the Earth's case, solar radiation is absorbed by its surface and radiated back into the atmosphere as infrared, where it is absorbed by the greenhouse gases and clouds and then partially reradiated. A significant proportion escapes into space (unlike in the greenhouse), but a larger fraction radiates downwards, heating both the lower atmosphere and the surface. Without the greenhouse gases, *all* the infrared radiation of the Earth would escape into space, the surface would freeze, and the Earth would be as uninhabitable as the Moon.

This 'natural greenhouse effect' is our second fact (the first was the measured increase in greenhouse gases). It is not a hypothesis, like the suggestion that a volcanic eruption may trigger El Niño, or the Gaia hypothesis of James Lovelock; it is proven. Three interesting bits of scientific evidence give it solidity.

First, there are millions of infrared measurements by satellites, which see the Earth as a whole (including its atmosphere), and which monitor its infrared radiation to space – Earthlight, invisible to human eyes. In physics every radiant body has a spectrum of infrared radiation characteristic of its temperature. (When you switch on an electric toaster and the element heats up and reddens, the peak of its radiation spectrum shifts from the invisible infrared to visible light of shorter wavelength; the hotter an object is, the less red and more blue – hence white – its light is: eventually it becomes white-hot.) If the body in question is Earth, its temperature seen from space is measured to be minus 19 degrees C (−2°F). But when measured from within the atmosphere its average temperature is *plus* 14 degrees C (57°F). The difference of 33 degrees C (60°F), which makes all the difference in the world to human beings, is the greenhouse effect.

Secondly, putting Earth aside for a moment, let us look out into the solar system. Consider again the table of planetary atmospheres on page 42. The surface temperature of Mars is minus 53 degrees C (−63°F), colder than much of Antarctica. It has an atmosphere consisting mainly of carbon dioxide, but more than 100 times thinner than Earth's atmosphere. The surface temperature of Venus, by contrast, is 459 degrees C (858°F), a furnace. Its atmosphere is mainly carbon dioxide too, but the pressure is 100 times *greater* than Earth's. How do we account for this, the so-called Goldilocks phenomenon? Why is Mars too cold for life, Venus too hot, but Earth just right? Again, it is the greenhouse effect at work: minimal on Mars, runaway on Venus, controlled on Earth.

Lastly, we dig into the Earth. As we know, ice cores from Antarctica and Greenland show a remarkable positive correlation between the temperature of the atmosphere and its carbon dioxide concentration during the Pleistocene period. The graph on page 256 could as aptly be captioned 'the natural greenhouse effect'.

It was Jean Baptiste Joseph Fourier, the celebrated mathematician and physicist (and a baron under Napoleon), who first recognized the effect, in 1827. But it was not until a century ago that anyone realized that human activity could contribute to it. In 1896, a Swedish chemist Svante Arrhenius (later a Nobel laureate), published a paper with the undramatic if descriptive title, 'On the Influence of Carbonic Acid in the Air [i.e. carbon dioxide] upon the Temperature of the Ground'. In it he made a remark, now famous, that 'we are evaporating our coal mines into the air', adding to it a few years later (less famously): 'we may hope to enjoy ages with more equable and better climates, especially as regards the colder regions of the Earth'. His idea was ignored, as was a British engineer who announced in 1938 that Earth's temperature was already rising and echoed Arrhenius's hope. Not until the end of the 1980s was the probability of a human-enhanced greenhouse effect widely accepted by scientists. In 1990, the IPCC opened its (mostly deeply uncertain) report, *Climate Change*, with a definite statement of the area of general scientific agreement about climate change. So important is it that it bears quotation in full:

We are certain of the following:
– there is a natural greenhouse effect which already keeps the Earth warmer than it would otherwise be.
– emissions resulting from human activities are substantially increasing the atmospheric concentrations of the greenhouse

Svante Arrhenius. In 1896, the Swedish chemist Arrhenius became the first scientist to recognize that human beings could contribute to the greenhouse effect. He wrote: 'we are evaporating our coal mines into the air'.

'The Goldilocks phenomenon'.
Mars (*left*) is a cold desert (surface temperature minus 53°C/63°F); Venus (*centre*) is a furnace (surface temperature plus 459°C/858°F); the temperature of the Earth (*right*) lies in between (plus 14°C/57°F). Mars is too cold for life and Venus too hot – so far as we know – while Earth is just right. (See table on page 42 for the composition of the planetary atmospheres.)

gases: carbon dioxide, methane, chlorofluorocarbons (CFCs) and nitrous oxide. These increases will enhance the greenhouse effect, resulting on average in an additional warming of the Earth's surface. The main greenhouse gas, water vapour, will increase in response to global warming and further enhance it.

From now on we enter disputed territory. The global temperature trend of the past decade or so *may* indicate the start of the man-made warming, or it may be part of natural climate variability, perhaps the effect of sunspot cycles, among other factors; there is no way to be sure at present, and probably not for another decade or two, maybe longer. Sooner or later, the man-made influence must predominate – the question is when?

Assuming we do not curtail our emissions of greenhouse gases and carry on with business-as-usual, the IPCC makes the following specific predictions. There will be an increase in global mean temperature during the next century of about 0.3 degrees C (0.5°F) per decade (with an uncertainty range of 0.2 to 0.5 degrees C per decade); in other words temperature will increase some 6 times faster than during the past century, faster than at any time since the end of the last ice age. The likely increase by 2025 will be 1 degree C (1.8°F) and by the end of the next century 3 degrees C, but the rise will not be steady. Global mean sea level will rise by about $2\frac{1}{2}$ inches (6 cm) per decade over the next century (with an uncertainty range of $1\frac{1}{4}$–4 inches, 3–10 cm per decade), mainly from the thermal expansion of the oceans and the melting of some glaciers (but *not* the polar ice caps). By 2030, the global mean sea level will rise by 8 inches (20 cm), and 26 inches (65 cm) by the end of the century.

These simple figures – with their grave implications for some low-lying countries in the immediate future, assuming the figures are correct – rest upon a great web of calculations. Using the most powerful computers available, scientists have made mathematical simulations – models – of the Earth, in which the equations of physics and chemistry are combined to reproduce the interactions of the atmosphere, oceans, land, icecaps and biosphere. A well-known simple model in science is the 'ideal' gas of physics, in which atoms are deemed to behave like microscopic billiard balls. How enormously harder it is to model the Earth! 'High-tech crystal balls' is how the present generation of models – known as GCMs (general circulation models) – are described by a leading climatologist, Stephen Schneider, of the National Center for Atmospheric Research in Colorado.

The methods of climate modelling were pioneered by meteorologists, who today depend on models for weather prediction. Adapting some of those methods, climatologists place a grid over the Earth's surface, dividing it into blocks of at least 5 degrees in latitude by 5 degrees in longitude: the size of, say, the state of Colorado or half the size of France. Plainly this cannot take account of fine distinctions in temperature, rainfall, soil moisture

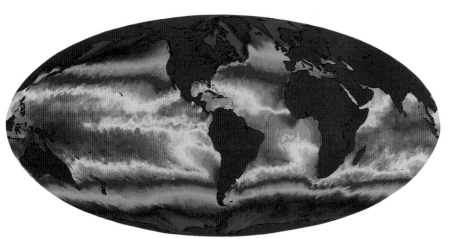

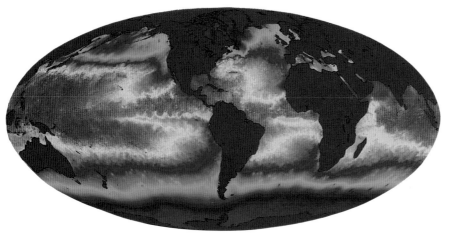

The challenge of climate modelling. These two satellite images of global sea surface temperatures, made in January (top) and July (bottom) 1984, demonstrate the complexity of the ocean. Red indicates a temperature of 20 degrees C (68°F), dark blue 2 degrees C, green 12 degrees C. The temperature patterns are the result of ocean currents, surface winds, cloud cover and solar heating, among other influences. If climate models are to prove accurate, they must be fed with accurate and detailed information about conditions in the oceans, on the land, and in the atmosphere throughout the year. At present, even with satellites to help us, this is impossible, and so some large assumptions must be made.

and so forth, nor can it properly represent cloud cover. The atmosphere is divided into 20 layers. The ocean too has been divided up into cells, though scientists are relatively ignorant of its physics and chemistry and the movement of ocean currents. The initial state of each surface block, atmospheric layer or ocean cell is fixed on the basis of actual climate, past and present, and informed guesswork, then the whole system is set running on the computer and left to reach equilibrium. Even with these rough approximations, it takes a week or more to run a single change of input to the model: say the doubling of carbon dioxide in the air.

Chaotic behaviour, the butterfly effect mentioned in Chapter 1, compounds the difficulties. All scientific equipment suffers from such 'natural variation', usually termed 'noise'. The trick is to design the instruments in such a way that the noise is much less than the all-important 'signal': then the signal – in this case the variation in temperature due to changes made by the modeller – stands out clearly from the unwanted noise. In GCMs, worryingly, the signal does not stand out clearly; it is of about the same magnitude as the noise.

Climate models have nevertheless scored some success in simulating aspects of climate at selected times during the last 18,000 years. They also simulate the temperature patterns in the seasonal cycle rather well. It is important that they should have the ability to 'predict' these large temperature variations – tens of degrees' difference between winter and summer – if we are to put any faith in their ability to forecast the (much smaller) details of the greenhouse effect. A US congressman once challenged Schneider on this point: 'Do you mean to tell me that you guys have spent millions of dollars of the taxpayers' money telling us that winters are cold and summers are warm?' 'Yes, sir,' Schneider replied, 'and we're proud of it – for if we couldn't independently simulate the seasonal cycle well, I wouldn't have the nerve to stand before this committee and argue that rapidly changing climate from human pollution is a serious problem.'

Even so, the most refined models cannot really resolve the relative response to the greenhouse effect of the northern and southern hemispheres. The models expect the northern to warm more quickly than the southern, because land should warm faster than ocean. In fact, between 1955 and 1985 the *southern* hemisphere warmed by about 0.3 degrees C (0.5°F), while the northern hemisphere barely warmed at all; now, however, the latter has started to warm quite rapidly. The reasons are not known, 'though man-made aerosols [e.g. sulphur dioxide emissions] and changes in ocean circulation may have played a part', the IPCC concluded in 1992.

With so many imponderables, only the broadest generalizations about climate change – no regional predictions – are meaningful. The models will require a decade or two of empirical adjustment using the results of ground-based and satellite observations before we shall begin to know how, say, the temperature rise in Tokyo next century may differ from that in Los Angeles (to pick two cities at similar latitudes). In other words climatologists, to be clairvoyant, need a lot more information from the Earth before they can gaze into their crystal balls with confidence. Scientists may now have a fair idea of the physics and chemistry of carbon dioxide in the atmosphere, for instance, but they know much less about the way carbon dioxide is absorbed and released by the oceans that cover more than 70 per cent of the Earth and contain vast quantities of carbon; and even less about the role of living organisms (including human beings) in maintaining the carbon balance on land, in the oceans and in the atmosphere. Obviously, change in carbon dioxide concentration in one part of the system will affect every other part; but the models so far barely reflect this fact. 'Biological feedbacks have not yet been taken into account in simulations of climate change', the IPCC 1992 report admitted.

Nature is rife with feedbacks – physical, chemical and biological. It may be, on the basis of what little we know at present, that the El Niño/Southern Oscillation (ENSO) is a feedback mechanism triggered by great volcanic eruptions and their aerosols: a warming to counteract a cooling. Another current theory backed by calculation suggests that depletion of the ozone layer may have at least one beneficial effect. Ozone is an effective greenhouse gas both in the stratosphere and in the troposphere; a decrease in its concentration should therefore lead to less trapping of heat in the atmosphere. The IPCC took this theory seriously enough to revise its predictions of temperature rise published in 1992.

These are negative feedbacks; other feedbacks could be positive, accelerating a change, like sound waves in the howling of a badly adjusted public address system. Venus, with its furnace-like temperature, appears to have experienced runaway positive feedback. Large-scale melting of polar ice and snow on Earth could be another example. The ice caps reflect more than 95 per cent of incident solar radiation and thus keep the planet cool; melting, they would produce blue-green water, which reflects less than 15 per cent of the Sun's energy and has a heating effect – which would augment the rate of melting. Or consider the chemical fact that carbon dioxide is less soluble in warm water than in cold. An ocean warmed by the greenhouse effect might progressively release dissolved carbon dioxide into the atmosphere, enhancing the effect. Again, the rate of warming would accelerate.

Predicting rainfall with climate models. Three different models, one British, one Canadian and one American, offer three scenarios for mean precipitation in June/July/August, on the assumption that carbon dioxide in the atmosphere has been *doubled*. Increases of rainfall are in blue/purple, decreases in brown/orange. The three scenarios differ drastically – consider Mexico, for example – because our present understanding of Earth systems is still primitive.

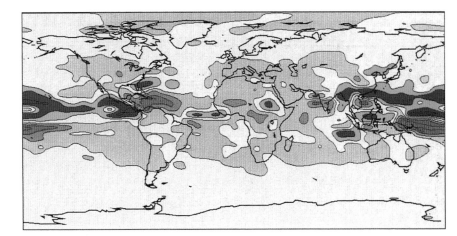

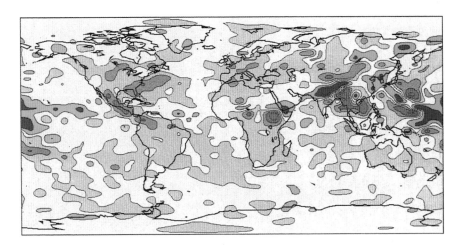

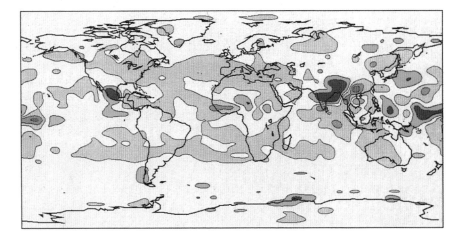

Umbrellas or blankets?
According to some evidence, clouds shield the planet from the Sun's heat; other evidence suggests that they trap heat in the lower atmosphere. Clouds are clearly intimately linked to the temperature, humidity and pressure at the Earth's surface, and they are also affected by the processes of life; but the nature of the connection in each case is not well understood. In the photograph, heat and emissions from the smokestacks of a US power plant in western Pennsylvania have deliberately been made to trigger the formation of a cumulus cloud during a field study conducted by the US Environmental Protection Agency.

At present, it is clouds that are attracting most attention from those studying natural feedbacks. They know that water vapour is a powerful greenhouse gas, but they do not understand at all well its operation. Climate models have grids too coarse to incorporate individual areas of cloud, and so only extremely general – not to say vague – assumptions can be made about the effect of clouds on the surface and on the oceans. Not to put too fine a point on it, there is total disagreement among scientists about the magnitude of cloud feedback and even its direction (positive or negative). On the one hand, there is evidence that clouds act as umbrellas, counteracting the greenhouse effect by reflecting solar radiation back into space; on the other, there is different evidence that they act as blankets, reinforcing the effect by trapping infrared radiation in the lower atmosphere. Many scientists accept that clouds can operate in both ways, depending on their size, water content and altitude. A study of increased Pacific sea surface temperatures in the 1987 El Niño, published in *Nature* in 1991, proposed that the warming of the ocean led to increased evaporation, more cloudiness, less radiation at the surface, and hence a drop in temperature. 'Highly reflective cirrus clouds' were said to 'act like a thermostat, shielding the ocean from solar radiation'. Other scientists disagreed, and dismissed the idea of the thermostat. Given the infinitely variable nature of clouds, the debate is likely to run and run.

Biological feedbacks are, if anything, even more controversial. No one denies their existence, but many deny their active role in making the Earth habitable and maintaining its habitability. Those scientists who hold that the laws of physics and chemistry alone are sufficient explanation of Earth's thermostat, are in the majority. Their view was encapsulated by the comment of a team working for NASA: 'the Earth would still have remained habitable even if it had never been inhabited.' James Lovelock is perhaps the leading exponent of the opposite view: 'except for a mere 1 per cent, the gases of the air are wholly the products of surface and ocean living organisms', he asserts. (The 1 per cent consists of helium, neon, argon, krypton and xenon, the 'noble gases', that are chemically inert.) In the absence of life on Earth, says Lovelock, the nitrogen in the atmosphere would almost all move within a few million years into the oceans; there is little nitrogen in the atmospheres of lifeless Venus and Mars.

Earth's carbon dioxide cycle – which is obviously vital in considering the impact of any enhanced greenhouse effect – looks significantly different when seen from Lovelock's point of view. The 'classical' explanation of the peaks and troughs one sees in the Keeling curve (leave aside the man-made rise) is that vegetation absorbs solar energy and uses it to photosynthesize carbon dioxide and water into sugars and oxygen. This process removes carbon dioxide from the air. Carbon dioxide is returned to the air by bacterial decomposition (fermentation) of vegetation, and by the respiration of animals (which use the oxygen produced by photosynthesis). The removal and the return of carbon (and oxygen) are thus kept in balance – see diagram on page 280.

But this cannot be the full picture, because volcanoes constantly add carbon dioxide to the atmosphere. What stops the carbon dioxide concentration from gradually rising? According to geochemists, in fact most scientists, the answer is rock weathering: the excess carbon dioxide falls as carbonic acid in rain water, reacts chemically with certain rocks and eventually runs off via rivers and other paths into the oceans as dissolved calcium carbonate. Lovelock does not disagree, but says this process cannot proceed fast enough to maintain the balance of carbon dioxide in the atmosphere. Being a geophysiologist he therefore adds *life* into the equation: soil organisms (like the deep-living bacteria mentioned earlier) must accelerate the rate of weathering so that it is fast enough to match the rate of leakage from volcanoes. (And marine organisms like foraminifera build their shells with the dissolved carbonate; their dead shells then form sediments on the ocean floors, and these eventually become the rock strata at continental margins which we know some scientists think may be responsible for plate tectonics.) It is thus partly life that controls carbon dioxide in the atmosphere and keeps it constant at its present low value, Lovelock proposes – not just physics and chemistry. Without the organisms – with only the slow diffusion of carbonated rainwater through the rocks – carbon dioxide would build up to a far greater concentration, he argues, perhaps 100 times what it actually is, before reaching equilibrium. Such a concentration of carbon dioxide would have a massive greenhouse effect: Earth would be uninhabitable.

Lovelock and collaborators published the theory in scientific papers during the early 1980s. In 1989, two other scientists established that, yes, the weathering of basalt proceeds 1000 times faster in the presence of organisms than when the rock is sterile. Soil is the key: 'without life there would be no soil, but only regolith, the rock rubble of dead planets', Lovelock recently remarked.

A testable prediction such as this makes Gaia more than just an appealing metaphor. It has had other successes in suggesting biological feedbacks. Studies by the microbiologist Lynn Margulis and colleagues of mats of microbial life covering the evaporite lagoons along some coastlines (Baja California, for instance), suggest that it is micro-organisms that have maintained the salinity of the oceans at less than 5 per cent salt (sodium chloride): otherwise the constant chloride input from rivers and volcanic processes would have wiped out life. And in the early 1970s Lovelock first suggested the role of marine algae in the sulphur cycle: they transfer sulphur from the ocean back to the land by emitting a gas, dimethyl sulphide (DMS), that is deposited on land as sulphate in rain water (a mild form of acid rain). This was fully confirmed in the 1980s. Lovelock further proposed, in 1987, that the DMS emissions might nucleate cloud formation, forming a 'thermostat' reminiscent of the one proposed for El Niño – with the notable difference that it involves life. Results published by a team of Australian scientists in 1991 appear to support a cloud-algae connection, but they are by no means conclusive; in fact a vocal critic of Gaia, James Kirchner, maintains that the evidence

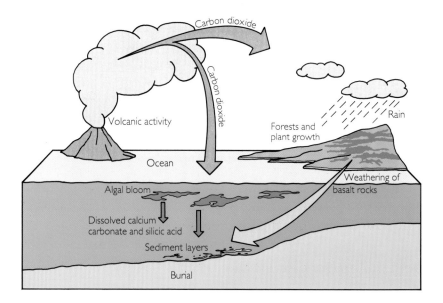

The carbon dioxide cycle.

Volcanic activity generates carbon dioxide in large quantities. The carbon dioxide concentration of the air remains roughly in balance, however, apart from the man-made increase – which is small compared to volcanic output. What keeps the balance? According to James Lovelock and others, it is life: soil organisms speed up the slow inorganic process of rock weathering by carbonic acid (carbon dioxide dissolved in rain); and marine algae pump down carbon dioxide, then eventually die and form sediments of chalk on the ocean floor. Without life, carbon dioxide would increase dramatically and make Earth uninhabitable.

The arrows in the diagram represent *net* carbon dioxide flux: there is also some flow of carbon dioxide from the land and sea back to the atmosphere, but it is less than the flux in the opposite direction.

points in the opposite direction. The IPCC notes cautiously that the bloom processes of these algae 'would most likely respond, although in uncertain ways, to changes in ocean-atmosphere exchanges resulting from climate change.'

If global climatic change is riddled with uncertainty, scientifically speaking, the likely impact of it on humans and their response to it is even more dubious. How on Earth to predict what will happen to man-made emissions of greenhouse gases over the next half-century and more, as the world economy grows (five-fold by 2050, according to many economists)? Imagine trying to predict the world economy of the 1990s back in the 1930s, when computers, modern plastics and nuclear energy were non-existent. The IPCC has perforce settled on four 'scenarios' in which emissions are assumed to be cut back at four different (increasingly draconian) rates, beginning with Scenario A, 'Business-as-Usual' – no cuts at all. Scenario outputs are therefore not really predictions of the future, but models built from a range of assumptions: economic, demographic and political. 'They are inherently controversial because they reflect different views of the future', admits the IPCC. Nothing conveys the complexity of the problem better than a bare list of the developments in 1990 and 1991 that necessitated a revision of the scenarios. They included:

the London Amendments to the Montreal Protocol [signed in 1987 to control ozone depletion by CFCs]; revision of population forecasts by the World Bank and the United Nations; publication of the IPCC Energy and Industry Sub-group

Mats of microbial life. Mats such as these covering the shallow coastal lagoons in Baja California, Mexico, help to sequester salt washed off the land into the oceans in evaporite beds. The oceans are thus prevented from becoming too saline to support life. The salt is formed by solar evaporation of sea water; it then steadily accumulates, rather than being washed back into the ocean, because its surface becomes coated with a varnish – a 'living raincoat' (James Lovelock) – secreted by the microbes.

scenario of greenhouse gas emissions to AD 2025; political events and economic changes in the former USSR, Eastern Europe and the Middle East [including the Gulf war]; re-estimation of sources and sinks of greenhouse gases [e.g. carbon dioxide concentration in the oceans]; revision of preliminary FAO [UN Food and Agriculture Organization] data on tropical deforestation; and new scientific studies on forest biomass.

Scenario A, Business-as-Usual, is the forecast mentioned earlier, in which the average global temperature is predicted to rise by 1 degree C (1.8°F) by 2025, and 3 degrees C by the end of the next century – by which time carbon dioxide concentration will have more than doubled. What will this mean 'on the ground'? There are two ways in which we can derive some idea: by looking backwards to previous climatic changes, and by running computer simulations of the future. First, the past.

The picture is imprecise, but generally discomforting, though this may be because we know much more about the Little Ice Age (*c.*1430–1850) than we do about the medieval warming (*c.*1000–1300) and earlier changes. After 5000 BC a warming appears to have assisted the spread of agriculture across Europe from the Near East as vegetation zones moved northwards (which probably tempted the Iceman into the high Alps), and the birth of civilization in Mesopotamia. The medieval warming enabled vines to be grown in England as far north as the River Severn (so successfully that France at one point wanted to ban imports of English wine), and Iceland to be colonized, followed by Greenland. But the 14th century, when the trend changed from warming to cooling, was grim indeed, as the historian Barbara Tuchman described in *A Distant Mirror*:

> A physical chill settled on the fourteenth century at its very start, initiating miseries to come. The Baltic Sea froze over twice, in 1303 and 1306–7; years followed of unseasonable cold, storms, and rains, and a rise in the level of the Caspian Sea. Contemporaries could not know it was the onset of what has since been recognized as the Little Ice Age . . . Nor were they yet aware that, owing to the climatic change, communication with Greenland was gradually being lost, that the Norse settlements there were being extinguished, that cultivation of grain was disappearing from Iceland and being severely reduced in Scandinavia.

By 1318, the harvest was so bad that in Ireland bodies were dug up from graves and eaten, and in Silesia executed criminals became food. The Black Death that appeared in the 1330s probably began in China after repeated flooding of the Yellow River culminating in 1332 with the estimated loss of 7 million lives. (Rats, fleeing the waters, may have carried the disease.) And later, during the worst of the Little Ice Age – the 1690s – when temperatures may have fallen 1.5 degrees C (2.7°F) below average, repeated failures of crops and cod fisheries in Scotland drove 100,000 Scots to settle in Ulster (Northern Ireland). A century later, the crop failures of the 1780s played a major role in precipitating the French Revolution.

Now, for the model predictions. In his *Global Warming*, published in 1989, Schneider painted a possible scenario for the 'greenhouse century'. He visualized a significant rise in sea level in New York City and fall in lake level in Chicago; the stagnation of river traffic on the Mississippi; the bayous of Louisiana continuing to disappear; the inhabitants of Dallas and Phoenix, Arizona, experiencing repeated searing temperatures; smoke from wildfires filling the skies near Denver and San Francisco; and drought in the Sierra Nevada and Rockies desiccating the lawns and swimming pools of Los Angeles. 'Will northern Canada and Siberia become the new breadbaskets with shiploads of their grain plying ice-free waters of the now-frozen North?' Will devastating floods in Indonesia, India, Pakistan and Bangladesh become yet more frequent, threatening the security of these developing nations? 'Will trade in coal reduce to a trickle and the deserts of the world become energy parks covered with solar collectors?'

These are all reasoned possibilities – not doomsday scenarios – based on existing levels of greenhouse gas emissions fed into present models. Sea level rise is probably the most striking, though not the most significant of forecast impacts. Water expands when heated, just as mercury rises up the walls of a glass thermometer tube; it is fairly simple to calculate how much the ocean will rise from thermal expansion alone. The observed average rise this century has been about 4 inches (10 cm), that is 0.04 inches (1 mm) per year. The IPCC, as we know, expects a rise of 0.25 inches (6.5 mm) per year during the next century. (It does not as yet accept the counteracting effect mentioned in Chapter 8, a negative feedback: that an increase in the polar ice cap due to increased warmth and precipitation might lead to a *decrease* in sea level.)

So no one now seriously proposes that the Statue of Liberty is going to drown, as the wilder scenarios once suggested. But many coastlines may be at serious risk. After all, about one-third of humanity lives within 40 miles of a coastline. Of the 27 countries most at risk, the most vulnerable (in descending order) are Bangladesh, Egypt, Thailand, China, Denmark, the US (Louisiana), and Indonesia. Preliminary calculations suggest that 300 million people could become 'environmental refugees' within 40 years from now: a migration 40 times the size of that at the end of the Second World War.

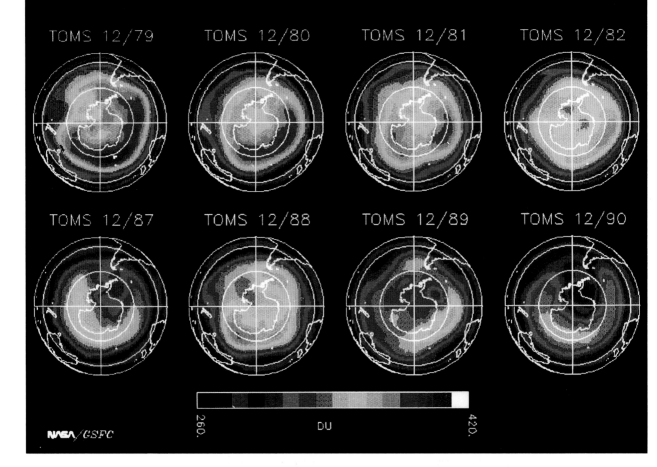

TOMS 12/79   TOMS 12/80   TOMS 12/81   TOMS 12/82

TOMS 12/87   TOMS 12/88   TOMS 12/89   TOMS 12/90

NASA/GSFC   260.   DU   420.

The Antarctic ozone hole.
During the 1980s, there was a steady decline in ozone concentrations above Antarctica, as measured by the Total Ozone Mapping Spectrometer (TOMS) on board the *Nimbus 7* satellite. This can be seen in the disappearance with time of red and yellow patches (indicating higher ozone concentrations) and the appearance of blue and purple patches (indicating lower). The low ozone values in the tropical region (the outer rim of the images) are typical for that region.

Besides this flooding and erosion, storms will have greater impact on coastlines in a warmer world. A US government report noted that for southern US coasts, a 1-metre rise in sea level would enable the size of a storm expected every 15 years to flood many areas that today are flooded only by a '100-year' storm. And what happens if storms increase in frequency and intensity too? Like so much else connected with climate change, we do not really know.

The doubt is probably greatest of all in the area of agriculture. While different models show some consistency in predicting the movement of climatic zones – all agree that the warming will be greatest in the higher latitudes – estimates of change in rainfall patterns vary hugely, depending on the assumptions made by the modellers about the vexed matter of cloud behaviour. There is also remarkably little experimental data on how existing crops respond to changing levels of carbon dioxide, particularly tropical crops such as rice. What data do exist come mostly from glasshouse experiments under controlled conditions – not from on-site experiments in the areas likely to be affected. The atmospheric increase in carbon dioxide may well fertilize a crop and produce a better yield – as predicted half a century ago – other factors being equal. Such fertilization is common practice in growing, say, tomatoes under glass. But what if the temperature and rainfall change too? In one experiment on winter wheat, conducted in Britain, doubled carbon dioxide at unchanged temperature increased the yield by about a quarter. When the temperature was increased, however, the grain became smaller; with an increase of 4.5 degrees C (8°F), the two effects cancelled each other out. According to the economist Martin Parry, perhaps the foremost authority on climate change and agriculture,

> we do not, at present, know whether changes of climate are likely to increase the overall productive potential for global agriculture, or to decrease it. There is therefore currently no adequate basis for predicting likely effects on food production at the regional or world scale. All that is possible at present is informed speculation.

One such informed speculation is that the US Corn Belt may move northwards into Canada – with all that that would imply for international economics and politics. A US report published in mid-1992, while bullish about technology's capacity to cope with change, reckoned that the Dust Bowl of the 1930s could be repeated, either where it happened before or in another region such as the Corn Belt.

The worst sufferers (farmers apart) are likely to be trees. Climatic limits are estimated to shift by 125–185 miles per degree C of warming, or 60 miles per decade under the IPCC Business-as-Usual scenario. A forest can shift at half a mile per year, 5 miles per decade, maximum: fast enough to adapt in earlier periods of climatic change, such as the milder ice ages. Faster than that and it will die – as the acid-rain drenched forests of central Europe and Scandinavia already have. The first signs are expected early next century.

None of the above is a worst-case scenario. All are based on the cautious middle ground of the IPCC estimates. A worst-case scenario is a runaway greenhouse effect. The global temperature might rise as rapidly as it did at the end of the last ice age, 5 degrees C (9°F) within a century, for reasons unknown. Obviously this scenario is highly speculative: we have no reason to anticipate such a rapid rise in temperature. The IPCC report does not even consider it. But it does state that simply to stabilize the concentrations of carbon dioxide at today's level (nearly 360 parts per million) would require a *60 per cent reduction* in emissions from human activities. Not in 2025, not in 2000, but right now.

The history of climate. The precise growth patterns of tree rings can provide useful indications of fluctuations in climate. Here, the researcher's pointer is resting on the narrow ring for AD 543. The specimen is from a vertical roof support post in a pithouse in Broken Flute Cave, Arizona, in the southwest of the United States.

But where is the evidence – irrefutable proof of man-made warming happening right now (as opposed to the observed small increase in global temperature that might be chiefly the result of natural climatic variability) – evidence that might justify taking costly steps, whether revolutionary or only tentative? There is none. Even Lovelock, while strongly advocating cuts in emissions as 'common sense', feels constrained by his training as a scientist to admit the uncertainty:

> When governments ask scientists what will happen as the greenhouse gases rise, and how urgently we should act, it is hard for them to know what to say . . . The affair is very complex. And though their theories tell them it should grow warmer, when they look for confirmation in the temperature record, there seems to be little evidence that the increase of greenhouse gases so far, in the last 200 years, has done anything.

Nevertheless, the vast majority of scientists favour action in the 1990s – the sooner the better. The strong likelihood is, we have entered the greenhouse century already; but we will not know it beyond reasonable doubt for a while yet. The greenhouse 'signal' will take another decade or two to emerge unequivocally from natural climatic 'noise'. ('Natural variability could still mask the effect of man for 30 to 40 years', warned Tom Wigley, Britain's leading authority on world temperature trends, in 1992.) This may be about the same period of time it will take for science as a whole to reorient itself to think globally. The support required will need to be on the scale of the US space programme in its heyday – indeed NASA has already launched its Mission to Planet Earth – but this time it will need to be a totally international effort.

Of the possible areas for investigation, five have been identified as the most critical. They are: the control of the greenhouse gases by the Earth system; the control of radiation by clouds; precipitation and evaporation; ocean transport and storage of heat; and ecosystem processes. Many decade-long programmes are now underway, and the scientific world is bristling with globally correct acronyms. Sponsored by the World Meteorological Organization and the International Council for Scientific Unions, there already exist two umbrella programmes, the World Climate Research Programme (WCRP) and the International Geosphere-Biosphere Programme (IGBP), that between them shelter the Global Energy and Water Cycle Experiment (GEWEX), the World Ocean Circulation Experiment (WOCE), the Joint Global Ocean Flux Study (JGOFS), the International Global Atmospheric Chemistry Programme (IGAC), the Tropical Oceans Global Atmosphere Programme (TOGA), and studies of Biospheric Aspects of the

Hydrological Cycle (BAHC), Global Change and Terrestrial Ecosystems (GCTE) and Past Global Changes (PAGES).

If results are to have a chance of living up to hopes, much of the work will involve persuading all nations to invest in ways to observe and document the fundamental aspects of the climate system, on land, in the oceans and in the atmosphere. Not nearly enough reliable data are available: rainfall figures are especially defective, and may fail to record up to half the actual rainfall; the dearth is worst in tropical regions. And the insufficiency of data is compounded by scientists' need for data to be collected over many years in order to establish trends. How much more compelling the observed evidence for warming over the past century would be if temperatures had been measured regularly and accurately by the same instruments located at numerous stations throughout the world, stations chosen for their suitability and fixed throughout. It was the lack of on-the-spot data that prevented anticipation of the 1987 'hurricane' in Britain. Unless the situation is improved, a British scientist lamented recently, 'we run the risk of going to considerable expense trying to predict what the climate might do, while neglecting to find out what it actually does.'

Of course data alone, however stored and manipulated by the most powerful number crunchers available, will not produce breakthroughs in understanding of climate change. There is also a need for interdisciplinary thinking. The specialization of science has gone too far; and reductionism, unprecedentedly effective though it has been, has reached something of a dead-end (epitomized by the whimsicalities of today's subatomic particle physics).

Where global monitoring began. It was here on the slopes of Mauna Loa in Hawaii in 1958, during International Geophysical Year, that regular monitoring of the Earth's carbon dioxide began – one of the earliest projects of its kind. Today, scientists from almost every discipline are collaborating on studies of Earth systems which should allow them to improve their models of future climatic change.

Deforestation. In Brazil's state of Pará, in the Amazon basin, cattle ranchers and settlers burn the forest for new land. In the 1980s, the deforestation rate almost doubled. We have already lost half of the world's tropical forests; in just another few decades, at the present rate of destruction, there could be no tropical forest left.

For progress with global problems to take place, scientists must compel themselves to look at problems from the top down, as well as from the bottom up; so that the process of rock-weathering by carbon dioxide, say, is viewed as part of the Earth's web of processes controlling carbon dioxide in the atmosphere, oceans and on land – not merely as a chemical reaction between rock and rain water. 'That mainstream science still thinks in separated terms is well illustrated by the acceptance of the title International Geosphere-Biosphere Programme for the principal global scientific programme', says Lovelock. 'As a geophysiologist I cannot accept that the geosphere and the biosphere can properly be investigated as if they are separate and independent.' The geobiochemist Peter Westbroek, who sees both the strengths and the weaknesses of the Gaia hypothesis, agrees. Thinking of his native Holland, he commented in *Life as a Geological Force*: 'Where are the specific physical, chemical, biological and cultural elements in Holland's waters, skies, vegetation, houses, ditches, and dikes?' But as a working scientist he cautioned: 'Today, the integration of geology and biology is fashionable among science managers, but in reality that integration is most difficult to achieve. All we have learned so far is how ignorant we are about the most fundamental aspects of the dynamics of our planet.'

Science, then, so far as it can, has delivered a verdict on the possibility of extensive climatic change within the lifetimes of most people now living on the Earth: probable, but not proven. Now it is up to all of us, to the politicians we elect and to other leaders, to decide what ought to be done. Scientists can devise scenarios but they cannot make them happen. The hard choices have to be made by governments, and, perhaps more likely, by individuals, families and organizations, large and small. What priority should we give to some ill-defined and distant threat over the pressing military, political, economic and social conflicts of the 1990s? Most people would instinctively feel that rising population is a more serious threat than global warming. Obviously the two are linked: more people means more consumption and more production of greenhouse gases. Would it be wiser for the world to spend money on the population problem rather than on cutting emissions? 'What if money spent on improved child-health in poor countries, by blunting the advantages of large families, did more to reduce the potential demand for fossil fuels than the same sum spent on reducing rich countries' use of oil?' asked the editor of *Nature* before the 1992 Earth Summit in Rio de Janeiro.

The failure of that event at the intergovernment level dramatized the failure of scientists to communicate the sense of urgency about combating global warming that most of them feel. 'Most people do not yet accept the fact that this crisis is extremely grave', wrote Al Gore, the leading environmentally-minded US politician, in his *Earth in the Balance*, published in 1992 before his election as vice-president. Most people now know of the ozone hole, but how many are aware that in Queensland, Australia, more than three-quarters of those over the age of 65 now have some form of skin cancer? Children on their way to and from school are required by law to wear large hats and neck scarves as a protection against ultraviolet radiation. There are similar problems in Punta Arenas, the town at the tip of South America that regularly falls inside the boundary of the Antarctic ozone hole. 'What will it do to our children's outlook on life if we have to teach them to be afraid to look up?' Gore asked. Unfortunately, this is not rhetoric.

The existence of the ozone hole is a scientific certainty, that of man-made global warming is not. Not yet. There is still room for scepticism, still a measure of respectability for the view that we need do nothing. A well-known British political commentator, Auberon Waugh, could write (in 1991) that 'nobody in a position to know is in the least bit impressed by all this twaddle about carbon dioxide or global warming' – and be believed. The caution of the IPCC, the existence of a few reputable scientists advising us to wait 10 years or more, and the inherent intractability of long-

以经济建设为

Human beings as a plague? The more of us there are, the faster the increase in greenhouse gases, even if we ride bicycles instead of driving cars. We have to find ways to reduce our rate of increase – before Nature finds solutions for us.

term prediction – not to speak of ill-advised apocalyptic warnings from scientists in the past – all create a climate of doubt.

But instead of being prudent, we may be behaving like the frog in the laboratory experiment. Dropped into a beaker of hot water, it hops straight out. Kept in warm water slowly heated, it swims round and round until it is boiled to death. If we could smell carbon dioxide or methane in the atmosphere – like the artificial odour added to natural gas – instead of looking at them on graphs, the greenhouse effect would shoot straight to the top of the political agenda. It is no good Friends of the Earth sending leaflets warning that 'global warming is increasing *by the hour*': our senses and our immediate environment tell us otherwise. Other issues, such as too many people and too many cars, seem far more pressing. There are no photographs of global warming to make headline news, as there are of earthquake-shattered freeways, rivers of volcanic lava, hurricane-torn cities, oceans of flood water, thousands of people dying from drought and famine, or even (so to speak), the ozone hole. The best we can do is oblique: roaring flames, blackened sky and an oil-soaked desert, as the oil wells of the Gulf 'evaporate into the air' (recall the prescient observation of Svante Arrhenius, writing in 1896 about the burning of coal). Or did you know that hippos' bones have been found beneath London's Trafalgar Square? Hippopotamuses, elephants and lions all flourished where London is now, 125,000 years ago. On IPCC projections, they could do so again by the middle of the next century – maybe sooner.

The 1987 Montreal protocol limiting the production of CFCs is a hopeful sign that our civilization can take difficult decisions. It committed the signatory nations to eliminating CFCs from the developed world by 2000, and from the developing world by 2010. Subsequent agreements with chemical companies mean that CFCs should disappear from the former countries sooner. But the protocol was forced into existence by emergency conditions: the discovery and persistence in the mid-1980s of massive ozone-layer depletion above Antarctica. And it had the active support of a chemical industry hoping to create a new market in CFC-substitutes. So far there are no satisfactory substitutes for the processes that emit carbon dioxide, methane and nitrous oxide – and we are locked into making far more of them than of CFCs.

'For societies apparently committed politically, structurally, psychologically even, to the idea of economic growth and higher levels of consumption, this particular form of pollution [i.e. the rise in greenhouse gases] represents a fundamental challenge', observed Clive Ponting in *A Green History of the World*. The book you are reading now is not principally about history, politics, economics or ecology. Nor is it a manifesto for changing the relationship between Man and Nature. I shall not stun you with statistics of population, gross national product and per capita consumption, Third World debt, land degradation, deforestation, loss of biodiversity, industrial pollution and waste disposal – astonishing and disturbing as these figures often are. Instead let us focus on just two of the many pieces in the extremely complex global warming jigsaw.

The first is deforestation of the rain forests. In the short term, it may benefit both rich and poor in the country concerned, by producing land for ownership, speculation, cultivation, livestock rearing, and timber for export. The developed world too may benefit, from the timber, and maybe from debt repayment and beefburgers. In the longer term, however, everyone – Man and Nature – loses. 'When a forest is cut down and sold, a country appears to grow richer', commented a report published by Oxfam in 1992,

> even though a valuable resource has been lost, food and fuel supplies have been reduced for local people and soil erosion and flooding may have increased. The world as a whole has lost some capacity to regulate climate. In the distorting prism of market economics, the value of a single plank of wood from a felled tree can appear greater than the true value of the forest left intact.

For all these reasons, said the report, deforestation is neither 'socially acceptable, ecologically sustainable, nor economically prudent'.

Closer to home now, and therefore less theoretical, is energy consumption. US citizens form about 5 per cent of the world's population (now well over five thousand million people) but they are responsible for 30 per cent of the world's consumption of energy (in the 1940s, the figure was nearly 50 per cent). The average American uses $3\frac{1}{2}$ times as much energy as he or she did in 1900, twice as much as today's average European and 30 times more than the average Indian. Most of the energy consumed (four-fifths, remember) comes from the burning of fossil fuels: three-quarters of it takes place in the developed world, which has one-quarter to one-third of the world's population. The number of cars in the world has multiplied 7 times in the past 40 years: 88 per cent of these are found in the rich countries. In the US, more than 60 per cent of oil burned goes into vehicles. The average tax on a gallon of gasoline is 25 cents. When the price of diesel fuel jumped less than 20 cents, through no fault of the US government, drivers from all over the US blockaded Washington DC. In the words of the US secretary of energy, speaking after the Gulf war in 1991, the American people 'really do believe the Bill of Rights gave them unleaded regular for $1.06 a gallon, and they better get it or, by God, they'll get the bums out of office.'

'If you're going to be sceptical about climatic change, you can stonewall for a heck of a long time before you have to be convinced', the chemist Charles David Keeling (of carbon dioxide curve fame) remarked a few years ago. 'If there are economic reasons not to believe in solid evidence, you won't. That's why two-thirds of Congress, I would predict, won't agree to do something about the greenhouse effect until we are practically into the doubling, in the middle of the next century.'

The silence from the US on proposals in 1991/92 for a schedule to cut greenhouse gas emissions, shows that many in the West have yet to be convinced of the case for global climatic change. Nor are the leaders of many Third World nations yet ready to curtail their plans for industrial development. China, for instance, intends to double its consumption of coal by 2000, which would make it more than double the present consumption of the United States.

The challenge now is to find ways for a degree of economic growth to occur that will not continue to destroy the quality of life of all of us, including those in the country that is benefiting from the growth. For greenhouse gas emissions are no respecter of national boundaries. For the first time in history human beings face a genuinely global challenge. The 1992 Earth Summit, despite its failure to produce concrete measures, undoubtedly concentrated minds worldwide – not in the vivid manner of the ozone hole, true, but significantly. A protocol to control emissions of carbon dioxide is going to take years longer to agree than the one to control CFCs. But it will come eventually because, as Sir Crispin Tickell has emphasized, the cost of doing nothing is great and becoming greater year by year. The longer the period before emissions start to be controlled, the greater the potential temperature rise – even if other factors may (temporarily?) act to suppress it. There is simply no possibility – leaving aside megalomaniac chemical 'fixes' of the atmosphere – that we can reduce greenhouse gas concentrations once we have increased them.

Awareness of these unpalatable facts has been spreading among millions of people who are not consciously 'green'. And at a time of economic recession worldwide, to consume less energy, in whatever form, makes economic as well as environmental good sense. A Gallup poll taken in both North and South, announced at the Earth Summit, was a notable indicator. 'Not only do [people] place a greater priority on environmental protection than on economic growth,' the pollsters reported, 'they also indicate a willingness to pay for environmental protection.'

Here then is the deeper issue at stake in the debate about how we should react to the scientific consensus on global warming. How are societies in the 21st century to view their relationship with Nature? Does humanity really want to become a greater force than Nature: to grow and grow and manage the Earth, be its boss? Approaching the millennium, we are now practising for the role – willy-nilly – and for all our astounding knowledge of science, we are floundering. Faced by the forces of Nature at their most nakedly powerful, explanation and prediction fail us. We know more about a black hole than we do about the Black Sea, as the science writer Nigel Calder pointedly remarked. Even senior politicians admit it. Al Gore again:

The more deeply I search for the roots of the global environmental crisis, the more I am convinced that it is an outer

The effects of acid rain. Vast stretches of forest in Europe and the United States have been killed by acid rain. Of Sweden's 90,000 lakes, 40,000 are known to be seriously acidified, as are one in five lakes in the US. The photograph shows dying trees in Bavaria, Germany. Acid rain is caused primarily by sulphur dioxide and nitrogen oxides from power stations, and by the same nitrogen oxides from vehicle exhausts. Global warming could become an even greater tree killer early in the next century.

manifestation of an inner crisis that is, for lack of a better word, spiritual. As a politician, I know full well the special hazards of using 'spiritual' to describe a problem like this one. For many, it is like one of those signs that warns a motorist, Steep Slope – Truckers Use Brakes. But what other word describes the collection of values and assumptions that determine our basic understanding of how we fit into the universe?

Western civilization's success in science derives primarily from its capacity to see Nature as detached, objective, independent of Man – what Albert Einstein once called his 'religion'. Reflecting further on his admiration for Kepler's revelation of the planetary laws (which we saw in Chapter 1), Einstein wrote intriguingly:

> It seems that the human mind has first to construct forms, independently, before we can find them in things. Kepler's marvellous achievement is a particularly fine example of the fact that knowledge cannot spring from experience alone but only from a comparison of the inventions of the intellect with the facts of observation.

There is no unity between Man and Nature, Einstein believed; they are intrinsically 'independent', alienated from each other. That view has been vastly influential in the formation of the modern world. An alternative view, distinct from Einstein's and also scientifically fruitful, is to see ourselves as part of Nature: one of tens of millions of species, many of them living now, the majority extinct; superior to all others in intelligence, certainly, but not different in essence, not unique. It is the view that James Lovelock espouses in the Gaia hypothesis:

> The essence of living green, of being a citizen of Gaia, is not a fretful puritanism. If we can think of ourselves as a part of a giant living organism and perhaps even a cause of its indigestion, then we may be guided to live within Gaia in a way that is seemly and healthy. Even thinking this way is an antidote to the fatalism of accepting the Earth as dead with life as just a passenger.

This cannot satisfy me, nor, I suspect, the majority of people. It is no more satisfying than Einstein's vision. Neither view encompasses the phenomenon of consciousness, the irrefutable existence of our unquenchable desire to comprehend Nature: both views are content to assume that life – and out of it consciousness – somehow appeared on a lifeless Earth. I continue to demand: how did the world, including our minds – Gaia if you wish – originate?

We need to make progress in tackling such questions, at the same time as continuing to probe the physical reality of Earth's systems.

We need 'the inventions of the intellect' mentioned by Einstein, as much as 'the facts of observation'. Only by a gradual comparison and synthesis of the two will we establish worthwhile answers to the questions about the forces of Nature that continue to plague us. What really does cause earthquakes? We do not know – but it is more and more apparent that a simple theory, such as friction between moving crustal plates, will not fit the facts. We need to develop new insights that 'embed' mind in Nature (Ilya Prigogine's word), without relegating humans to the level of bacteria or merely a miraculously sophisticated assemblage of chemicals. Conceivably, the threatened global crisis will help to usher in these insights. If it does, I think they will arise from the same source as the wonder, humility and, yes, reverence, that all of us may still feel – including of course the greatest of scientists – when we ponder the ultimate unanswered question: what is life?

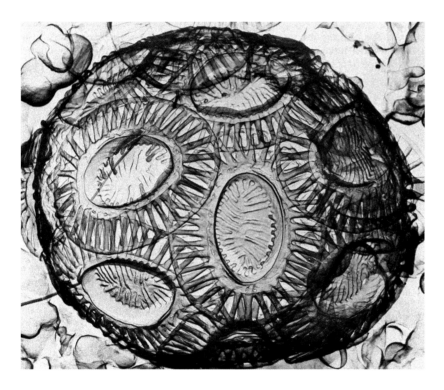

The web of life. This single-celled algae, *Emiliana huxleyii*, sometimes known as Emily, is magnified 1800 times. The shield-like structures on the surface of the cell are composed of calcium carbonate, which goes to form chalk when the cell dies. Blooms of *Emiliana* cover large areas of the ocean. They perform a vital regulatory role by removing carbon dioxide from the air and producing dimethyl sulphide, which acts to nucleate clouds.

MAN AND NATURE:
A CHRONOLOGY

MOST of the entries in the Chronology have been selected because
they are referred to in the text; for reasons of space, many major
natural disasters and numerous milestones in the scientific
understanding of Nature (not to speak of the scientists involved) have
been omitted. Dates in italics refer to man-made events.

PRE-20TH CENTURY

8000–6000 BC	Ice ages end
before 5000 BC	Tropical animals painted on rocks, Sahara desert
c.3500 BC	Irrigation begins, Sumer, southern Iraq
c.1800 BC	First major attempt to control river flooding, Nile Valley, Egypt
1600 BC	Volcanic eruption, Thera, Aegean Sea
c.480–c.425 BC	Herodotus, Greek historian
384–322 BC	Aristotle, Greek philosopher
312 BC	First aqueduct built, Rome
218 BC	Avalanches in Alps kill part of Hannibal's army
AD *23 or 24–79*	Pliny the Elder, Roman natural historian
79	Volcanic eruption, Vesuvius, Italy, destroys Pompeii and Herculaneum (at least 2000 deaths)
61 or 62–113	Pliny the Younger, Roman writer
132	Seismograph invented by Chang Heng
526	Earthquake, Antioch, Turkey (250,000 deaths)
641	Nilometer installed at Roda to measure River Nile
874	Iceland settled by Norsepeople
986	Greenland settled by Norsepeople
1271–92	Marco Polo travels in Far East; describes Gobi Desert
1281	Typhoon, Japan, smashes invading army of Kublai Khan
1290	Earthquake, Chihli, China (100,000 deaths)
1332	Floods, Yellow River, China (up to 7 million deaths); may have led to Black Death, as infected rats flee water
c.1430	'Little Ice Age' begins
1543	Heliocentric theory of universe published by Copernicus
1556	Earthquake, Shansi, China (830,000 deaths; the worst ever earthquake)
1588	Storms around British Isles smash invading Spanish Armada

1592	Thermometer invented by Galileo
1609	Laws of planetary motion published by Kepler
1631	Volcanic eruption, Vesuvius, Italy (more than 4000 deaths)
1643	Barometer invented by Torricelli
1650s	Archbishop Ussher dates Creation to 4004 BC
1669	First attempt to divert lava, Etna, Italy
1686/87	*Principia Mathematica* published by Newton
1735	Circulation of winds explained by Hadley ('Hadley cell')
1737	Earthquake, Calcutta, India (300,000 deaths)
1750	Lightning rod suggested by Franklin
1755	Earthquake, Lisbon, Portugal (70,000 deaths)
1769	Gulf Stream charted by Franklin
1772	*Observations on Mount Vesuvius, Mount Etna and Other Volcanoes* published by Hamilton
1783	First earthquake commission, Calabria, Italy
1811/12	Earthquakes, New Madrid, Missouri, USA
1815	Volcanic eruption, Tambora, Indonesia (90,000 deaths)
1827	Greenhouse effect recognized by Fourier
1830s	Glaciers first studied, in Alps, by Agassiz, who propounds theory of Ice Age
1830–33	*The Principles of Geology* published by Lyell
1831–36	Darwin's voyage on *Beagle*
1835	Circulation of winds formulated by Coriolis
1841	First volcano observatory established, Vesuvius
c.1850	'Little Ice Age' ends
1850	Reliable temperature records begin
1855	Earthquake, Edo (Tokyo), Japan (several thousand deaths)
1857	Earthquake, Fort Tejon, southern California, USA
1859	*Origin of Species* published by Darwin
1862	Age of Earth 20–400 million years

	according to Kelvin
1871	Wildfire, Peshtigo, Wisconsin, USA (at least 1500 deaths)
1872–76	Voyage of oceanographic vessel *Challenger*
1872	Yellowstone National Park founded
1879	Mississippi River Commission established
1883	Volcanic eruption, Krakatoa (Krakatau), Indonesia (36,000 deaths)
1887	Floods, Yellow River, China (900,000–2½ million deaths)
1889	Damburst, Johnstown, Pennsylvania, USA (2209 deaths)
1892/93	Modern seismograph invented by Milne
1896	Tsunami, Sanriku, Japan (more than 22,000 deaths)
1896	Greenhouse effect formulated by Arrhenius
1898	Radioactivity discovered by Becquerel

20TH CENTURY

1902	Stratosphere/stratopause discovered by Teisserenc de Bort
1902	Volcanic eruption, Pelée, Martinique (30,000 deaths)
1906	Earthquake, San Francisco (700 deaths)
1908	Earthquake, Messina, Italy (120,000 deaths)
1909	Mohorovičić (Moho) discontinuity discovered
1912	Iceberg sinks *Titanic* (1513 deaths)
1915	*Entstehung der Kontinente* (translated in 1924 as *The Origin of Continents and Oceans*) published by Wegener
1916	General theory of relativity published by Einstein (verified in 1919)
1921	'Fronts' introduced into meteorology by Bjerknes
1923	Great Kanto earthquake, Tokyo, Japan (140,000–160,000 deaths)
1925	Tornadoes in Midwest, USA (689 deaths)
late 1920s	Age of Earth 3–4 thousand million years according to radioactive dating
1927	Floods, Mississippi, USA (246–500 deaths)
1928	Flood Control Act, USA
1930s	Ozone layer discovered
1930s	Dust Bowl, Midwest, USA
1935	Earthquake magnitude scale devised by Richter
1935	Hoover Dam, Colorado River, USA, completed
1936	First institute for snow and avalanche research established, Davos, Switzerland
late 1930s	Radar invented
1938	New England hurricane, USA (at least 600 deaths)
1943	First flight into hurricane by aircraft

1946	Tsunami, Hilo, Hawaii (159 deaths); leads to establishment of first Pacific-wide tsunami warning system
1946	Electronic digital computers invented
1947	Mid-Atlantic Ridge discovered
1948	Transistor invented
1953	'Double helix' structure of DNA discovered by Watson and Crick
1957–58	International Geophysical Year
1957	*Sputnik 1*, first space satellite, launched by USSR
1958	Atmospheric carbon dioxide records begin
1960	Earthquake, Chile (5700 deaths)
1960	*Tiros 1*, first meteorological satellite, launched by USA
1964	Earthquake, Anchorage, Alaska (131 deaths)
1965	Plate tectonic theory outlined by Tuzo Wilson and others
1966	Flash floods in Florence, Italy, damage works of art
1968	Drought in Sahel (sub-Saharan Africa) begins
1968	Earth first seen from space, by *Apollo 8*
1969	Lightning strikes *Apollo 12* during take-off
1970	Earthquake, Peru (66,000 deaths, 18,000 of which are result of avalanche from Nevado Huascarán)
1970	Cyclone, Bangladesh (300,000 deaths)
1970	Aswan High Dam, Egypt, completed
1972	*Landsat 1*, environmental monitoring satellite, launched by USA
1973	Gaia hypothesis published by Lovelock
1973	Lava cooled by water in volcanic eruption, Iceland
1975	Earthquake, Haicheng, China (300 deaths)
1976	Earthquake, Tangshan, China (more than 240,000 deaths)
1977	United Nations Conference on Desertification, Nairobi, Kenya
1980	Volcanic eruption, St Helens, Washington, USA (57 deaths)
1982–84	Ozone hole above Antarctica identified
1982	Volcanic eruption, El Chichón, Mexico (up to 3500 deaths)
1982/83	El Niño event, Pacific Ocean; causes floods, storms, droughts and wildfires on both sides of Pacific
1983	'Ash Wednesday' fires, Australia (76 deaths)
1984/85	Drought and famine, Ethiopia (1 million deaths)
1985	Volcanic eruption and landslide, Nevado del Ruiz, Colombia (22,000 deaths)
1987	Airborne Antarctic Ozone Experiment

1987	Montreal Protocol to control chlorofluorocarbons (CFCs)
1987	'Great Storm', England and France (17 deaths)
1988	Wildfires, Yellowstone National Park, USA
1988	Earthquake, Armenia (25,000 deaths)
late 1980s	Drought, Australia, California, southern Africa; continues into 1990s
1989	Mission to Planet Earth launched by NASA, USA
1989	Earthquake, Loma Prieta (San Francisco), USA (62 deaths)
1990	United Nations International Decade for Natural Disaster Reduction begins
1990	*Climate Change* published by UN's Intergovernmental Panel on Climate Change (IPCC)
1990	Earthquake, NW Iran (36,000 deaths)
1991	Satellite-based Global Positioning System begins to operate
1991	Oil wells in Kuwait set on fire after Gulf war
1991	Cyclone, Bangladesh (at least 150,000 deaths)
1991	Volcanic eruption, Pinatubo, Philippines (800 deaths)
1991	Floods, central China (2000 deaths)
1991	'Iceman' discovered in glacier, Austrian–Italian border
1992	Volcanic eruption, Etna, Italy (largest on Etna this century)
1992	'Earth Summit', Rio de Janeiro, Brazil
1992	Hurricane Andrew, Florida, USA

SUGGESTIONS FOR FURTHER READING

THE books mentioned below are a brief selection of significant, non-technical writing on the forces of Nature, both generally and individually, published mostly in the last ten years or so. The place of publication and the name of the publisher are omitted to avoid confusing readers in several countries; the date given is the date of first publication, unless otherwise indicated.

General

CALDER, NIGEL: *Spaceship Earth*, 1991.

CARPENTER, CLIVE: *The Changing World of Weather*, 1991.

MAYBURY, ROBERT S. (ed.): *Violent Forces of Nature*, 1986.

National Geographic (monthly).

Nature (UK-based weekly; mainly technical, but with non-technical summaries).

New Scientist (UK-based weekly).

PONTING, CLIVE: *A Green History of the World*, 1991.

Science (US-based weekly; mainly technical, but with non-technical summaries).

Scientific American (monthly): Sept. 1983 (Earth – special issue); Nov. 1983 (eruption of Krakatau); Feb. 1984 (ice ages); Apr. 1984 (tornadoes); July 1984 (undersea volcanoes); Feb. 1985 (earthquake prediction); May 1986 (Darwin as geologist); June 1986 (El Niño); July 1986 (structure of mountains); June 1987 (drought in Africa); June 1988 (ocean circulation); Nov. 1988 (lightning); Jan. 1989 (deep earthquakes); Apr. 1989 (global climatic change); June 1989 (hidden earthquakes); July 1989 (rift volcanism); Aug. 1989 (age of Earth); Sept. 1989 (water supplies); Nov. 1989 (Yellowstone fires); Jan. 1990 (ice ages); Mar. 1990 (mid-plate earthquakes); Apr. 1990 (impact cratering); June 1990 (ocean ridges); Aug. 1990 (global warming); Oct. 1990 (mass extinctions); Jan. 1991 (self-organized criticality); June 1991 (ozone depletion); Apr. 1992 (continental movement); Aug. 1992 (Kilauea volcano); Sept. 1992 (mind and brain – special issue); Oct. 1992 (biodiversity); Feb. 1993 (environmental change and violent conflict).

SMITH, KEITH: *Environmental Hazards: Assessing Risk and Reducing Disaster*, 1992.

Time-Life Books: 'Planet Earth' series: *Arid Lands*, 1984; *Atmosphere*, 1983; *Continents in Collision*, 1983; *Earthquake*, 1982; *Flood*, 1983; *Glacier*, 1982; *Ice Ages*, 1983; *Restless Oceans*, 1983; *Storm*, 1982; *Volcano*, 1982.

WEINER, JONATHAN: *The Next One Hundred Years: Shaping the Fate of Our Living Earth*, 1990.

1 Man and Nature

BOURRIAU, JANINE (ed.): *Understanding Catastrophe*, 1992.

LOVELOCK, JAMES: *The Ages of Gaia: A biography of our living Earth*, 1988.

McKIBBEN, BILL: *The End of Nature*, 1989.

MIDGLEY, MARY: *Science as Salvation: A modern myth and its meaning*, 1992.

PRIGOGINE, ILYA and STENGERS, ISABELLE: *Order Out Of Chaos: Man's New Dialogue with Nature*, 1984.

STEWART, IAN: *Does God Play Dice?: The Mathematics of Chaos*, 1989.

WALDROP, M. MITCHELL: *Complexity: The Emerging Science of the Edge of Order and Chaos*, 1992.

2 Earth, Ocean, Atmosphere and Life

DYSON, FREEMAN: *Origins of Life*, 1985.

GREGORY, K. J. (ed.): *The Guinness Guide to The Restless Earth*, 1991.

LEAKEY, RICHARD and LEWIN, ROGER: *Origins Reconsidered: In Search Of What Makes Us Human*, 1992.

LOVELOCK, JAMES: *Gaia: The practical science of planetary medicine*, 1991.

WEGENER, ALFRED: *The Origin of Continents and Oceans*, 4th revised edn, 1929 (Dover edn, 1966, translated by John Biram).

WESTBROEK, PETER: *Life as a Geological Force: Dynamics of the Earth*, 1991.

WILSON, EDWARD O.: *The Diversity of Life*, 1992.

3 Earthquakes

BOLT, BRUCE A.: *Earthquakes*, 1988.

HADFIELD, PETER: *Sixty Seconds That Will Change The World: The Coming Tokyo Earthquake*, 1991.

OLSON, RICHARD S.: *The Politics of Earthquake Prediction*, 1989.

TAZIEFF, HAROUN: *La Prévision des séimes*, 1989 (*Earthquake Prediction*, 1992).

TRIBUTSCH, HELMUT: *When The Snakes Awake*, 1982.

4 Volcanoes

BLONG, R. J.: *Volcanic Hazards*, 1984.

DECKER, ROBERT W. and BARBARA B.: *Mountains of Fire: The Nature of Volcanoes*, 1991.

FRANCIS, PETER: *Volcanoes*, 1976.

STOMMEL, HENRY and ELIZABETH: *Volcano Weather: The story of 1816, the year without a summer*, 1983.

5 Thunderstorms, Hurricanes, Tornadoes and Lightning

BURROUGHS, W. J.: *Watching the World's Weather*, 1991.

HILL, GEORGE: *Hurricane Force*, 1988.

PIELKE, ROGER A.: *The Hurricane*, 1990.

SIMPSON, ROGER H. and RIEHL, HERBERT: *The Hurricane and its Impact*, 1981.

UMAN, MARTIN: *All About Lightning*, 1986 (originally published as *Understanding Lightning*, 1971).

6 Floods, Dambursts and Tsunamis

CLARKE, ROBIN: *Water: The International Crisis*, 1991.

McPHEE, JOHN: *The Control of Nature*, 1989 (concerns Mississippi, and also landslides in Los Angeles and lava flows in Iceland).

PEARCE, FRED: *The Dammed*, 1992.

PURSEGLOVE, JEREMY: *Taming The Flood: A history and natural history of rivers and wetlands*, 1988.

7 Deserts, Droughts, Wildfires and Desertification

ADAMS, W. M.: *Wasting the rain: Rivers, people and planning in Africa*, 1992.

CROSS, NIGEL AND BARKER, RHIANNON: *At The Desert's Edge: Oral Histories From The Sahel*, 1992.

GOUDIE, A. S.: *The Search for Timbuktu: A view of deserts*, 1986 (booklet).

GRAINGER, ALAN: *The Threatening Desert: Controlling Desertification*, 1990.

REISNER, MARC: *Cadillac Desert: The American West and Its Disappearing Water*, 1986.

TIMBERLAKE, LLOYD: *Africa in Crisis*, 1985 (2nd edn 1988).

8 Avalanches, Glaciers and Ice Ages

HAMBREY, MICHAEL and ALEAN, JÜRG: *Glaciers*, 1992.

HOYLE, FRED: *Ice*, 1981.

LAWS, RICHARD: *Antarctica: The Last Frontier*, 1989.

SHARP, ROBERT P.: *Living Ice: Understanding Glaciers and Glaciation*, 1988.

9 Global Climatic Change

GORE, AL: *Earth In The Balance: Forging A New Common Purpose*, 1992.

Intergovernmental Panel on Climate Change: *Climate Change: The IPCC Scientific Assessment*, 1990, and *Climate Change 1992: The Supplementary Report to The IPCC Scientific Assessment*, 1992 (both reports are mostly technical).

OXFAM (Joan Davidson and Dorothy Myers with Manab Chakraborty): *No Time To Waste: Poverty and the Global Environment*, 1992.

PARRY, MARTIN: *Climate Change and World Agriculture*, 1990.

REVKIN, ANDREW: *Global Warming: Understanding the Forecast*, 1992.

SCHNEIDER, STEPHEN H.: *Global Warming: Are We Entering the Greenhouse Century?*, 1989.

TICKELL, CRISPIN: *Climatic Change and World Affairs*, 1986 (new edn forthcoming).

WYMAN, RICHARD L. (ed.): *Global Climate Change and Life on Earth*, 1991.

SOURCES OF ILLUSTRATIONS

Aerofilms 122; Jürg Alean, Zurich 227, 239 (bottom), 242, 247 (bottom right); Agence France Presse 75, 185; Arizona Bureau of Land Reclamation 211; University of Arizona, Tree Ring Research Laboratory 286; Y. Arthus-Bertrand/Impact 173 (top); Associated Press 126, 131, 157 (bottom)

Bettmann Newsphotos 6, 62 (top); Bildarchiv Preussischer Kulturbesitz, Berlin 21; Bibliothèque Nationale, Paris 97; F. Blickle/Network 288; Howard Bluestein, University of Oklahoma/NCAR 142; J. Roger Bowman, Australian Seismological Centre 58; after British Antarctic Survey 263; Von Bucher/Science Photo Library 59 (top); J. N. Butler, Wayland, Mass. 27

Cambridge University, Collection of Aerial Photographs 156; J. Allan Cash 36–7; Camera Press 202; Canadian Climate Center 276 (middle); University of Colorado/NOAA 98

University of Dundee 122 (bottom)

Earthquake Engineering Research Center, University of California 59 (bottom); EISL, Davos, Switzerland 225 (both), 235 (all)

R. Faidotti/FAO 173, 205 (all); Rhodes Fairbridge 249; FAO/NASA 204; Jack Finch/Science Photo Library 41; Frank Lane Picture Library 207

Nigel Gallop, London 101 (top and middle); Alberto Garcia/Katz Pictures 260–1; Georg Gerster/John Hillelson Agency 196–7, 208, 264; Ben Gibson 87 (both), 154, 268; Jane Gifford, Bath 281; V. Gippenreiter/Colorific 91; Goddard Space Flight Center/NASA 272–3 (all); Greenpeace Communications 259, 293; J. D. Griggs/USGS Hawaii Volcanic Observatory title page, 82 (middle), 102–3

Peter Hadfield 77 (top); R. Hadlan/USGS 90; Professor M. Hambrey, Liverpool 235 (top), 247 (bottom); J.

Hartley/FAO 220 (bottom); University of Hawaii 287; Hawaiian Volcano Observatory/NOAA 82, 83 (all); H. Helbush/NOAA 183; D. Hoadley 143; R. G. Hoblitt/USGS Hawaiian Volcano Observatory 114 (right); R. T. Holcomb/USGS Hawaiian Volcano Observatory 102; Holle Photography/World Meteorological Center, Geneva 117

Innsbruck University 226; INS News Agency, Reading 158; I. Isaacs/FAO 200; Frank Ischinsky, EISL, Davos 234

K. Jackson, US Air Force/NOAA 113, 115; by courtesy of the Japan Meteorological Agency 69 (both), 120, 121

Carol Kallay/Network 267 (top); R. Kubota/Magnum 169

After P.J. Lamb in Smith 1992 (p. 263) 204 (bottom left); C. J. Langer/NOAA 60; F. Lanting/Bruce Coleman 18–19; C. Lenars 178–9; Library of Congress, Washington DC 79, 99, 127, 181; after Lovelock 1991 (p. 109) 280

Kristján Magnússon half-title page; E. W. McCaul/NCAR 135; by permission of W. H. Freeman & Co, from *Earth and Life through Time* by S. M. Stanley 295; Gideon Mendel/Network 201; D. Murawsky, Cambridge, Mass. 45 (all)

By courtesy of NASA 18 (inset), 31, 118, 193, 208 (inset), 215, 256, 257, 260, 284; NASA/Science Photo Library 165; National Center for Atmospheric Research, Boulder, Colorado 139, 142 (both); by courtesy of National Hurricane Center, Coral Gables, Florida 133 (both); by courtesy of National Meteorological Office, Bracknell, Reading 38, 122 (top), 276; by courtesy of National Severe Storms Laboratory, Norman, Oklahoma 135 (bottom); Natural History Museum, London 52; Thomas Nebbia 254; by courtesy of NOAA title page, 60, 82, 83 (all), 90, 102–3, 111, 113–14, 115, 135, 138–9, 183, 267 (top); NOAA/EDIS 182–3

Panos Picture Library 290; David

Parker/Science Photo Library 62, 73; after Pielke 1990 (pp. 7 & 27) 125; Austin Post/USGS Vashon, Washington 243, 247 (top); H.M. the Queen 159

Prof. C. G. Rapley, UCL-MSSL, NERC-JCR and University of Texas 131; Vittoriano Rastelli, Rome 50, 161 (both); after G. Retseck, January 1990, *Scientific American* 253 (below left); C. G. Robins/National Meteorological Office 40; University of Rhode Island School of Oceanography 130; Royal Swedish Academy of Science 271

M. Savonius 44; Omar Sattaur 178; F. A. Schiermeier, Cary NNC 277; Emil Schultess 198; Alain Sebe, Vidauban 196–7; Vittorio Sella, CAI Biella 237, 245; Nanina Shaw-Reade, Eastleach, Glos. 195; after R.B. Simon, 1981, *Earthquake Interpretations: A Manual for Reading Seismograms* 56 (right); after Smith 1992 (p. 262) 204 (top left), (p. 173) 230; Solarfilma, Reykjavik 110; SOS Sahel 220 (top); Edwin Smith 84 (courtesy Olive Smith); Space Media Network, Stockholm 208 (inset); G. Stoughton, Hawaiian Volcano Observatory 82 (middle right)

Marie Tharp, N.Y.C. 22–3; Tokyo University Library 49

UPI/Bettman 62; US Army Corps of Engineers/NOAA 182–3 (top); USIS 172

A. C. Waltham, Nottingham 101 (bottom), 103 (top), 104–5 (all), 106 (bottom), 107 (all), 191 (bottom), 238 (both), 239 (top); Bradford Washburn, Boston Museum of Science 233; H. Weyer 106 (top); Wide World Photos 114 (right); Prof. Earle A. Williams 147; James Wilson/NCAR 142 (inset); University of Wisconsin Space Science and Engineering Center, McIdas 135; Woods Hole Oceanographic Institution 22 (inset)

All diagrams are by Annick Petersen except for pages 55, 63 and 269 (M.L. Design) or where otherwise credited above.

INDEX

COUNTRIES are not indexed individually but grouped into continents, e.g. for United States see North America. (Greenland, Hawaii and Iceland are separately indexed.) Page numbers in *italics* refer to the captions of illustrations. Principal entries are indicated by **bold** numerals.